Varieties of Empathy

Varieties of Empathy

Moral Psychology and Animal Ethics

Elisa Aaltola

London • New York

Published by Rowman & Littlefield International Ltd
Unit A, Whitacre Mews, 26-34 Stannary Street, London SE11 4AB
www.rowmaninternational.com

Rowman & Littlefield International Ltd.is an affiliate of Rowman & Littlefield
4501 Forbes Boulevard, Suite 200, Lanham, Maryland 20706, USA
With additional offices in Boulder, New York, Toronto (Canada), and Plymouth (UK)
www.rowman.com

Copyright © 2018 by Elisa Aaltola

All rights reserved. No part of this book may be reproduced in any form or by any electronic or mechanical means, including information storage and retrieval systems, without written permission from the publisher, except by a reviewer who may quote passages in a review.

British Library Cataloguing in Publication Data

A catalogue record for this book is available from the British Library

ISBN: HB 978-1-7866-0610-5
PB 978-1-7866-0612-9

Library of Congress Cataloging-in-Publication Data

Names: Aaltola, Elisa, 1976- author.
Title: Varieties of empathy: moral psychology and animal ethics / Elisa Aaltola.
Description: Lanham: Rowman & Littlefield International, 2018. |
  Includes bibliographical references and index.
Identifiers: LCCN 2017058208 (print) | LCCN 2017059054 (ebook) |
  ISBN 9781786606112 (electronic) | ISBN 9781786606105 (cloth: alk. paper) |
  ISBN 9781786606129 (pbk: alk. paper)
Subjects: LCSH: Empathy. | Animals (Philosophy) | Animal rights. |
  Animal welfare. | Ethics.
Classification: LCC BF575.E55 (ebook) | LCC BF575.E55 A25 2018 (print) |
  DDC 152.4/1—dc23
LC record available at https://lccn.loc.gov/2017058208

Contents

Acknowledgements		vii
Introduction: From Rationalism to Affective Morality		1
1	Good and Bad Empathy: The Need for Distinctions	17
2	Projective and Simulative Empathy	27
	Definition	27
	Projection and Anthropomorphism	31
	Simulative Animal Narratives	35
	Projective and Simulative Morality?	45
3	Cognitive Empathy	55
	Definition	57
	Moral Agency or Moral Monstrosity?	63
	Anthropathy	69
4	Affective Empathy	81
	Definition	82
	Hapless Empaths and Desubjectification	85
	Affective Moral Agency	93
5	Embodied Empathy	103
	From Atomism to Embodied Engagement	103
	Definition	108
	Somatic Intersubjectivity	113
	Embodied Moral Agency	120

6	Reflective Empathy	129
	Definition	131
	Cultivation and Attentiveness	137
7	Criticisms of Empathy	153
	Biased Empathy, Biased Ethics	155
	Empathy versus Reason	169
	Empathy or Anger?	185
	Compassion Fatigue	194

Conclusion	217
References	223
Index	237
About the Author	245

Acknowledgements

I am thankful for all those scholars who have sought to make evident the role of emotions in our moral behaviour, both in their negative and positive form. Among them, I am particularly grateful for those who have explored the affective nature and moral psychology of our attitudes towards other animals, thereby pushing forward radically new approaches to animal philosophy. One such scholar is Lori Gruen, who reviewed the first draft of this book and whose texts I carefully underlined as a twenty-year-old student, some twenty years ago, drawing exclamation marks in the paper margins. Also, conversations with and the texts of Ralph Acampora have always been gentle and thought provoking. In a more native context, I am indebted to Sami Keto, with whom I have written a Finnish book on empathy (Empatia: myötäelämisen tiede 2017) in which the taxonomy of empathy is discussed, albeit in a different, shorter style and without a focus on the animal issue. My further gratitude goes to the Jenny and Antti Wihuri Foundation, which offered the financial backing for the writing of this book.

On a more personal note, I would like to thank my canine companions for staying close and reminding me of the virtues of love rather than judgement. They will never read these words, but their joy lights up the spaces in which I navigate.

Introduction
From Rationalism to Affective Morality

In Western traditions, rationality has tended to be the chosen method of moral philosophy. It is via detached, neutral and logical analyses that one can discover how we ought to value and act: in order to construct or discover values and norms, one must detach from the lived reality, look at it from afar and – governed by the rules of logics – establish the content of morality. At the root of this ethos stand many classic figures, perhaps most famously Immanuel Kant in his *Groundwork of the Metaphysics of Morals*. For Kant, the way towards morality is the use of autonomous reason. Emotions, such as sympathy, even if at times seen as virtuous, are inevitably irrelevant.

Yet rationalism has its dangers. It may facilitate us to ignore the lived experiences of others and replace the subjectivity and individual worth of those others with utilitarian calculations (Husserl 1970), ultimately enabling forms of systematic, even institutionalized violence. A common claim is that the Holocaust, together with its calculative, mechanic and bureaucratic efficiency, is the product of modernity. Here specialization, rationalization and moral indifference become the rule, and as a result the subjectivity of the victims is lost – "What is being done to someone just becomes 'what is being done'" (Cohen 2002, 90). Dissociation and numbing are also an integral part of the late-modern culture, which increasingly resorts to moral apathy when faced with difficult questions concerning the subjectivity and treatment of others (ibid.). In other words, subjugation of and violence towards others become possible when morality is hidden under detached, rationalizing calculations, and this ethos of moral numbness is very much present also in the contemporary culture. Simply put, if "rationality" is taken to mean optimization, the subjectivity of others – if it serves a goal one wants to achieve – is quickly lost and replaced with faceless, utilizable categories. Something is missing from the equation, and this something is, arguably, our emotive, experiential side.

This book addresses the role of emotions, and particularly empathy, in directing our morality and moral agency. The claim will be that given emotions and forms of empathy rescue us from detachment, numbness and the objectification of others and enable the sort of moral agency resistant to subjugation and violence. Although reason has a distinct part to play in morality, it alone does not suffice, and next to it various categories of emotions and empathy are required – it will be argued that the core of moral agency is found from emotive, empathic attunement, without which others cannot be perceived and experienced as subjects of value.

The book takes part in the revival of sentimentalism, which has been taking place across academic disciplines in recent years ("sentimentalism" is here referred to without its contemporary, negative connotations). Whereas rationalism defends the notion that moral agency rests on the use of reason, sentimentalism maintains that the roots of such agency are to be found in emotions. One of the latter's most notable defenders, David Hume, argued in the eighteenth century that emotions enable us to conceive something as "good" and "bad" and form the foundation of virtues. For Hume, knowledge does not stem primarily from a priori, rational thinking, with its internally built logic and detachment, but from sensed impressions concerning the world and ourselves – it is founded on our capacity to experience rather than on detachment. Morality is born from emotive responses towards experiences such as suffering and happiness: it is these responses that offer us a sense of value and disvalue. Thus, in his *Treatise on Human Nature*, Hume proclaimed that "morality, therefore, is more properly felt than judg'd of" (*Treatise* 3.1.2.). Before him, Baruch Spinoza, although otherwise rationalistic in his philosophy, posited in his *Ethics* that the emotion of joy allows us to witness goodness, whereas melancholy will lead to notions of moral wrongness. Hence, again, it is emotions which reveal or point towards moral values. Sentimentalism has not held only a marginal role in Western cultural history. The age of humanitarianism celebrated emotions such as compassion as the core ingredient of humanity: to be a human being in the proper sense of the term, one had to have given emotive responses towards the suffering of others (Turner 1980). Emotions surfaced as the necessary criterion for our very personhood – instead of Kantian autonomy and reason, the quintessential, defining factor of humanity was the capacity to feel for others.

Perhaps the most damning verdict on rationalism came from Arthur Schopenhauer, who, drawing from Eastern philosophy, was exceedingly sceptical of prioritizing rational analysis in ethics and particularly attacked Kant for overaccentuating reason. Schopenhauer did not aim for politeness: "I allude to the daily hackney compilers, who, with the ready confidence born of stupidity, imagine that they have given a foundation to Ethics, if they do but appeal to that 'Moral Law' which is alleged to the inherent in our reason" (Schopenhauer 2005, 10). For Schopenhauer, the type of sheer rationality advocated by Kant was nothing but "shells without kernels" due to its disconnection from the empirical realm (ibid., 21): "The structure floats in the air, like a web of the subtlest conceptions devoid of all contents; it is based on nothing, and can therefore support nothing, and move nothing . . . [it is] a performance which yields results that no man would ever turn to in the stern stress and battle of life, and which, in face of the storm of our passions, would be about as serviceable as a syringe in a great fire" (ibid., 32). According to Schopenhauer, the empirical rather than the purely rational dictates ethics, as the basis of morality is found from human nature and, more specifically, emotions.[1] He has a rather blunt and succinct way of showing why emotion rather than reason holds primacy: if someone were to tear of another person's jaw as a trophy, leaving her in agony, we would not ponder on rational moral reasons for why this is wrong but would instead be shocked by the perpetrator's lack of compassion. Indeed, Schopenhauer (ibid., 108) argues that in this and many other instances, talk of rational moral principles would be nothing short of comical.

With the ongoing revival, these suggestions have found new support in fields as diverse as neurosciences, psychology and philosophy, as studies, according to which moral judgements are primarily emotion based and only rest on deliberate, reasoned analyses in a limited number of cases, are becoming more commonplace. The "linguistic turn", which claimed human mindedness, including morality, to stem from propositional language and reason and which dominated much of the twentieth century,[2] has been, to some extent, replaced by the "affective turn", with affects and, more specifically, emotions re-emerging as the key constituent of the human grasp of reality. This exultant comeback applies particularly to the moral realm. The Humean claim that morality is rested on, and takes flight from, emotive responses is gaining ever-growing popularity (Prinz 2006; McGreer 2008; Crary 2009).

For many, Hume stands as the still-relevant forefather of sentimentalism, positioned as a figure who can offer a credible alternative to the Kantian desire for detached rationality. For instance, Patricia Churchland, one of the most famous contemporary advocates of sentimentalism, refers to Hume and posits that "Kant's conviction that detachment from emotions is essential in characterizing moral obligation is strikingly at odds with what we know about our biological nature" (Churchland 2011, 175). Victoria McGreer similarly rests on Hume: "I claim in a broadly Humean way that we human beings are moral beings . . . because of our affective natures" (McGreer 2008, 247). Whereas Kantians too easily assume there to be a neutral dimension to existence, within which one can think in purely logical terms, the Humeans insist on the biological rootedness of human beings and moral agency: we are coloured by our sensory, emotive realms, and they not only affect but in many ways constitute morality.

One of the pivotal and earliest contemporary advocates of sentimentalism was Martha Nussbaum, who has consistently brought forward the role of emotion in moral decision making. One of her central claims has been that without emotion, one cannot talk of "moral understanding" – to say without any emotive dimension that the murder of X was wrong implies that one does not truly understand the moral dimension of what one is saying. Moreover, following the influential work of Anthony Damasio, Nussbaum (1990, 2001) argues that one simply cannot categorically separate reason and emotion and that thereby emphasizing only the former is foundationally misguided. Therefore, we ought to approach emotion and reason as co-constitutive and interrelated rather than depict reason as something wholly detached – we also should note that emotions are necessary for moral understanding. Ultimately, Nussbaum ties the relevance of emotions back to our biological, sensing, feeling constitution and the sort of fragility it implies. She suggests that "emotions should be understood as 'geological upheavals of thought': as judgments in which people acknowledge the great importance, for their own flourishing, of things that they do not fully control – and acknowledge thereby their neediness before the world and its events" (Nussbaum 2001, 90). Hence, emotions intertwine with our fragility and sentience – we are not robotic, almost omnipotent reasoning machines but living, vulnerable, embodied and sensing creatures who via emotions recognize their own intrinsic dependency on others and their surroundings. Emotions are the vessel to noting vulnerability in ourselves and others and to perceiving value in those things, which enable us to live fuller, more meaningful and flourishing, less damaged lives, and it is this which acts as the main cause for their moral relevance.

Further advocates of sentimentalism include Jesse Prinz, who highlights how evidence suggests that moral judgements tend to be emotive in nature. Prinz founds his claim on several reasons. First, emotions co-occur with moral judgements (for instance, we have negative feelings towards moral wrongs) and offer the latter their phenomenal feel.[3] It is because of this that moral judgements often seem "obvious" – emotions appear as self-evident, and morality entwined with emotions strikes as equally obvious: "Emotionally grounded moral judgments have a kind of perception-like immediacy that does not seem to require further support" (Prinz 2006, 37). Second, emotions impact moral judgement: our emotions often determine the content of moral judgements, as negative emotions spark negative appraisal and positive emotions lead to positive evaluations (following suit, people often hold on to their moral judgements motivated by emotions, even when there are no rational reasons to back them). In this vein, Prinz argues that "to believe that something is morally wrong (right) is to have a sentiment of disapprobation (approbation) towards it" (ibid., 33). Third, emotions are necessary for moral development, as they educate us into the realm of values – it is by learning appropriate emotional responses that we adopt moralities. Fourth, emotions motivate moral action and are the cause of us going from "this is wrong" to "I want to stop this" so quickly (ibid.). Therefore, emotions accompany and offer the "feel" of moral values and norms; they can spark the constitution of those values and norms; they are necessary for us to learn the contents of morality; and they motivate moral action. On these grounds, Prinz makes a bold claim, suggesting that emotions are what morality is founded on: "Emotions are both necessary and sufficient for moral judgment" (ibid., 32).[4]

In this way, "we project our experiences onto the world" (Prinz 2006, 35) and by doing so find morality. Emotions render the world morally meaningful to us: they colour it with normative hues.[5] Prinz recognizes that reason also does play a part. However, its role is limited to offering us factual knowledge and analyses, which go on to determine whether a given action belongs to the sort of a category towards which it is appropriate to have a specific emotive response – so in the case of anger, we are to analyse if feeling anger in situation X is warranted (Prinz 2006). Hence, reason can render emotions more consistent and coherent and give them direction, but this remains a formal dimension – the actual content of morality stems from emotions themselves. This places much of Western moral theory under question due to the dominating status it has given to reason, and one may even doubt if many of the key concepts and principles celebrated by moral theories match with ordinary emotively charged normative notions. Following this line of thinking, Prinz suggests that there is a gap between theory and praxis, as principles such as "the categorical imperative" may find little emotive support and fail to make sense on an empirical, moral psychological level. As a result, moral theory anchored solely or primarily on reason has veered too far from the origin of moral judgement, values and norms: "There is no analytic tie between ordinary moral concepts and the descriptive concepts that designate the properties implicated in the moral theories of Mill, Kant, and other normative ethicists" (Prinz 2006, 40).

Philosophical sentimentalism finds support from other sciences, such as psychology and social psychology. Just as Hume argued most of our decision making to be based on something sensuous and often automated rather than on aware, abstract reasoning, contemporary sciences are demonstrating that human beings are much less rational than previously considered. Hume stated that "the experimental reasoning itself, which we possess in coming with beasts, and on which the whole of life depends, is nothing but a species of instinct and mechanical power, that acts in us unknown to ourselves; and in its chief operations, is not directed by any such relations or comparisons of ideas, as are the proper objects of our intellectual faculties" (Hume 2007, 78), and his claims are being empirically verified. Simply stated, we are experiencing, sensing creatures who learn to follow our experiences, senses and emotions to a point of being "automated" rather than intellectual, and it is this claim which is offered support by recent findings.

Representing these fields, Jonathan Haidt, a social psychologist who has become one of the most prominent advocates of sentimentalism, maintains that morality consists predominantly of automated responses and particularly emotive and stereotyping factors. For instance, instantly upon seeing a representative of a given social group, we may hold a given moral judgement grounded in both existing cultural stereotypes and the sort of emotions that support and offer impetus for them. Haidt's "social intuitionist model" thereby posits that moral judgements are based on moral intuitions, which are characterized as "the sudden appearance in consciousness, or at the fringe of consciousness, of an evaluative feeing (like–dislike, good–bad) about a character or actions of a person, without any conscious awareness of having gone through steps of search, weighing evidence, or inferring a conclusion" (Haidt and Björklund 2008, 188). In this model, moral reasoning is merely post hoc, even a type of an epiphenomenon, as people seek to offer justification for their responses when faced with internal conflicts (one judgement goes against another) or external conflicts (one tries to convince another of one's own judgement). Indeed, people often hang on to their intuitions, even when they cannot offer rational justification for them,[6] and change happens primarily via the social sphere, which affects our automated responses by altering our stereotypic notions or sparking specific types of emotion. Intuitions (stereotypes, emotions) largely determine our values and norms, despite reasoned analyses, and thus Haidt boldly claims that reason is used superficially, while the real work is done by other factors: "Moral reasoning is often like the press secretary for secretive administration – constantly generating the most persuasive arguments it can muster for policies whose true origins and goals are unknown" (Haidt 2007, 1000).[7]

Therefore, the suggestion is that intuitions, formed of cultural stereotypes and emotions, are the building material of moral judgements, whereas reason is only used in times of conflict. For Haidt, it is particularly emotions which guide judgement and which ought to be prioritized if we are to understand the roots of moral agency. Therefore, emotions make us moral – instead of reason, they are the necessary constituent of moral ability. Haidt makes a daring claim: "Emotions are in fact in charge of the temple of morality" (Haidt 2003b, 854). Hence, sentimentalism speaks of the immediacy of moral decision making. It tells us that rationality is often an epiphenomenon when it comes to morality – something that can occur but the occurrence of which is not always evident nor even necessary. Morality is grounded more on immediately and usually effortlessly experienced intuition and related emotions than on reasoned deliberation.[8] Following suit, it is increasingly common for neuroscientists and social psychologists to conclude that "emotion is a significant driving force in moral judgment" (Greene and Haidt 2002, 522).

It is ultimately the gap between theory and practice, between abstract reason and lived, felt moral decision making that sentimentalism seeks to abolish, as its aim is to anchor questions of value on de facto moral psychology. Rather than assuming that morality is only about theoretical postulations, it brings forward the emotive constituents behind moral agency, broadening our conception of what it is to think, feel and act in a normative fashion. Now, if moral numbness and desubjectification of others results partly from the overaccentuation of reason, it may also result from overestimating the power of moral theorizing. Indeed, perhaps contemporary societies struggle with moral apathy partly because moral theory has become so far removed from the actualities of everyday moral judgement – perhaps it fails to convince and spark interest on a larger scale precisely because it fails to tap into the processes that define our moral agency and are more resonant with emotion than with cumbersome, reasoned extrapolations. In short, if moral judgements are largely rested on emotions or other forms of intuition, references to theory may fail to convince and may appear practically irrelevant, somehow unconnected from the concerns of most, and ultimately many become quite ineffective, restricted to university lecture halls and carefully edited scholarly volumes rather than manifested more broadly in lived, societal reality.

Perhaps, then, if we are to snap out of moral numbness or indecision, sparked by the overaccentuation of reason and theory, the relevance of emotions should be brought under scrutiny. The state of moral indifference may result both from ignoring the emotive level, and blocking off some of its impact, or – more likely – from following erroneous, misleading, inappropriate and confused emotions without being aware of doing so, while using reason as a justification for the ensuing acts. Thus, racism may be fuelled by emotions such as contempt, greed, disgust and fear without the subject noting the emotions' influence, while various seemingly rational arguments, related to, for instance, immigration policy, are used as a superficial justification. In both instances, the danger remains the same: when the emotive level influencing moral agency is ignored, we may become detached, calculative, apathetic and even violent creatures, incapable of noting and respecting the subjectivity of others. In such a state, people will paradoxically claim to be logical and reasonable and yet (because logics and reason are not their actual motivation) reluctant to pay heed to the sort of principles offered by moral theory, which advocate equality, justice and respect. On the upturn, if the role of emotions in moral agency is made explicit, explored and accepted, nothing less than heightened moral awareness and emotive, other-regarding attentiveness may result. In short, if emotions and other intuitions are the de facto basis of moral agency, it is by highlighting their relevance and investigating them more carefully that inertia, detachment and de-evaluation of others may become less likely.

The key question in sentimentalism should not, however, be which emotions descriptively guide our actions – the emphasis ought not to be on simply mapping out the most influential and common emotions and stating that they form our moral agency. Such a stance would be faulty of the naturalistic fallacy, which equates "what is" with "what ought to be": even if one's morality is factually motivated by egoism, fear and fury, this does not mean that it *ought* to rest on such factors. Instead, focus must be on the prescriptive level: which emotions should we follow were we to do justice to what the meaning and ethos of "morality" comprise? Which emotions should we cultivate in order to enhance our moral ability? What has been largely missing is an exploration into sentimentalism that would dive further into its challenges, questioning precisely what forms of emotions have relevance and why. Much effort has been put into bringing emotions to the surface of moral psychology, but considerably less time has been spent on tackling the ambiguities and difficulties of sentimentalism related to its choice of emotions.

It is this prescriptive question that will be the objective of this book. The aim is to explore whether, and which type of, empathy is linked to moral agency and (following suit) whether it is a specific form(s) of empathy which ought to be cultivated so as to expand and strengthen our moral ability. Empathy has been endorsed and celebrated as a pivotal moral emotion (Hoffman 2001; Slote 2007) already from an evolutionary viewpoint. It helps one to maintain social relations and understand the behaviour of oneself and others (Jackson, Meltzoff and Decety 2005) and is particularly evident when it comes to witnessing adversity, pain and suffering – that is, harm – in others. It opens the door to understanding the harms of others, which, again, may serve a crucial evolutionary function through constituting a tool of learning (so that one may avoid them in the future) and through enabling care and concern for and ultimately bonds with others (Minio-Paluello et al. 2009). The reason why empathy is morally significant stems not only from its potential ability to communicate the harms of others to us but also from its more general capacity to signal to us the viewpoints and motivations of others and to invite us to be affected by them. As already noted by Hume, empathy (or what he called "sympathy") allows one to pay notice not only to the mental contents of oneself but also to those of others, and this paves the way for moral concern, the sudden realization that as a subject of value, one is not alone in this world. This renders empathy into a rather outstanding capacity (Hume 2007).

Yet what is often ignored or downplayed is that empathy comes in many, at times mutually contradictory and highly distinct, forms. The book at hand dives into these forms and distinctions and seeks to map out which of them aid the process of becoming less detached and desubjectifying, and more morally inclusive and capable, in regard to others.

In order to investigate the potential links between different varieties of empathy and moral agency, it is important to specify what we mean by the latter. "Moral agency" will here be taken to include at least four criteria. First, it involves recognition of the harms of other beings or entities (like the environment): rather than more generic conventions like law, it revolves around the impact our actions have on others or our surroundings.[9] Second, it includes the capacity to form, understand and follow judgements. Third, it rests on other-directedness, wherein focus is placed primarily and also on other beings and entities rather than primarily on the self (although of course also the self is warranted attention). Other-directedness refers to aiming our intentions primarily towards other beings: for instance, one's judgements or emotions are motivated by the other instead of being grounded primarily on one's own needs. To witness another creature in pain and to let her pain be the target of one's attention and affect one's thinking, emoting and acting is to be other-directed; to divert attention back to one's own needs – for instance, by shielding oneself from discomfort by offering reasons that explain away the pain – is to be self-directed.

Fourth, moral agency requires openness towards heterogeneity and difference so that the "otherness" or other beings and entities is noted and the "self" is not placed as the model or prototype for what is considered valuable. Heterogenic openness refers to the ability to notice not only shared features but also dissimilarities and specificities, and thereby it rests on being exposed to the subjectivity of another in all its peculiarity, opacity and uniqueness. Instead of aiming our intention only towards the familiar in others, we ought to strive towards grasping and noting also that which is odd, inimitable, even alien, confounding and impervious. In mapping out which types of empathy, if any, should guide moral agency, attention needs to be placed on how well they fulfil these criteria. Since all of them can support and entwine with forming moral judgements and recognizing harms, the focus of this book will be on the last two criteria: Do varieties of empathy facilitate other-directedness, and do they enable us to become open to the difference and heterogeneity of others?

Before continuing, a recent paradigm shift in the study of emotions should be noted. It has been suggested that the classical view of emotions, according to which emotions are innate and universal, naturally taking the same form in each individual, is mistaken. According to scholars such as the neuropsychologist Lisa Feldman Barrett, emotions are in fact actively made rather than innate, as they serve as ways of conceptualizing reality. In short, we create emotions on the grounds of past experience and social learning and use them to categorize phenomena (Barrett 2017). Following this new line of study, emotions are concepts affected by how our social settings create meaning: we learn "appropriate" emotive responses from our environment and again use them to explain our own affects, bodily states and outside stimuli.

This is relevant from the perspective of this book due to three things. First, emotions also act as tools of conceptualizing moral issues, and socially produced beliefs, stereotypes and other categorizations bear an effect on these moral emotions as well. This suggests that the moral impact of emotions is entwined with culture and politics and that empathy can both influence, for instance, cultural stereotypes and be influenced by them. Following suit, this book takes as one of its starting points the premise that in humans, emotions do not take place in a social vacuum and that empathy also directs and is directed by socially formed beliefs, including moral and political outlooks.

Second, the new take on emotions forms a potential challenge to empathy since it suggests that emotions cannot be universally "read" or understood. However, another starting premise of the book is that as vulnerable creatures with needs, limited skills and demanding environments, combined with shared affective capacities, such as the ability to feel distress and pleasure, we often learn to conceptualize emotions in a broadly comparable manner, with or without language, which again spurs empathy. Thus, despite our evident differences, we share the same goals of thriving, many of the same limitations and often similar environmental pressures, which ensure that there is enough synchronicity for empathy. We all are, irrespective of the species, creatures of biology, making sense of reality on account of our ability to hurt, relish and need, and this ensures (some) understanding between individuals.

Third, the new stance on emotions points out that empathy is also a concept, as we construct empathic responses in order to actively make sense of and categorize the mental states of others. It is not a method of accessing objective truths but instead an interpretation based on our life histories, physiologies and contexts. Hence, when it is claimed in this book that we can "identify", "read", "know" or "access" experiences or emotions in others, this should not be taken to imply that empathy is a gateway to objective truths. Indeed, philosophically there are no such gateways to be found anywhere – even reason is founded on conceptualizations rather than on a neutral access to reality. Still, using such words is meaningful, for empathy appears to us as a form of knowing or identifying: in folk terminology – that is, our everyday use of language – it makes sense to speak of empathy as a form of knowledge. Moreover, as will be argued in this book, even if empathy does not reveal things as they objectively are, one can with good grounds draw distinctions between more and less reliable empathies.

This book does not concentrate only on the relation between empathy and moral agency on a general level but does so also and primarily via a particular perspective, as emphasis is on moral agency in regard to non-human animals.

What enables us to be moral not only towards human subjects but also towards non-human beings? In many ways, other animals form the testing zone for moral ability, particularly because of the fourth criterion for moral agency – the capacity to see value also in those who are clearly different and distinct from oneself. Much of Western moral theory has concentrated solely on human beings, assuming that it is species similarity, and thereby a type of collective homogeneity, which acts as the criterion for moral considerability as an individual. This has limited our capacity also to note value in difference and the radical pluralities of quality, which again has curtailed our moral agency. The book will explore in depth what a sentimental take on moral psychology shows us about both the factualities of contemporary, empathic moral attitudes towards other animals (how empathy is predominantly practiced in relation to non-human beings and with what moral consequences) and the potentialities of those attitudes (how both empathy and moral agency could be moulded and extended in regard to how other animals are valued and treated).

Concern for more-than-human animals has, in history, at times entwined with the accentuation of emotion, the most obvious case in point being aforementioned humanitarianism and its links to both sentimentalism and the birth of the contemporary animal advocacy movement (Kean 1998). When humanitarians claimed that emotions, and particularly compassion, formed the determining factor of humanity, it was the vivisector who stood as the epitome of a corrupted human being, and it was claimed that if his desire for utilitarian, detached rationality, ignorant of the suffering of other animals, was to become more widely embraced by the society, the process could warp and distort the whole of humanity (Turner 1980). Emotions were to be extended also towards other animals: if emotion was the defining feature of a moral human being, one was to greet the world with compassion, regardless of the skin colour, sex or species of other beings. In philosophy, Schopenhauer was one figure who gave flight to this emergence of both affective humanity and affective animal ethics, as he maintained that compassion was to be practiced also towards other animals and as he argued that "he, who appears to be without compassion, is called inhuman; so 'humanity' is often used as its synonyme. . . . Compassion for animals is intimately connected with goodness of character, and it may be confidently asserted that he who is cruel to living creatures, cannot be a good man" (Schopenhauer 2005, 89, 114).

The entwinement between sentimentalism and animal advocacy was momentarily lost in the 1970s, as Peter Singer – followed by other formidable figures – wanted to distance the latter from the former, fearing that if concern for non-human animals was reduced to emotive responses, it would lack credibility in the eyes of a rationalistically orientated philosophy (Singer 1975; Regan 1983). His aim was to demonstrate that moral concern towards other animals can be wholly divorced from emotions and gain its basis in the presumed neutrality of reason.[10] This meant that the first and most popular wave of animal ethics, witnessed by the contemporary era, was rooted in not only analytic philosophy but, more specifically, rationalist moral psychology.

It is not difficult to see why Singer and others decided to favour reason. By the twentieth century, "sentimentalism" had become a term shrouded in a heavy, unforgiving layer of negative connotations. In Western analytic philosophy, emotions had become empty conveyers of ambivalent responses towards the external world that had little or nothing to do with "truth" – a suggestion that was robbing emotion-based morality of credibility. To suggest that squirrels and rats are morally significant beings due to our compassionate responses towards them was, thereby, a move that threatened to reinvoke the stereotypical image constructed of animal advocacy: that of emotive, naive, ill-informed and ultimately non-credible human beings with Disney-fied, anthropomorphic, emotional and thus misled notions of animals directing their moral horizons. There were two options: either to demonstrate that moral concern for non-human animals can be grounded in reason and thereby does not lack moral credibility or to demonstrate that emotions do not lack credibility. Singer and many others chose the first option, and arguably the success of their philosophy, together with the incredibly fast rise of animal welfare and liberation advocacy, pro-animal societal attitudes, vegetarianism and veganism in the West, revolves around this decision; cultures soaked in celebration of rationality had to witness that reasoned judgements were in favour of ceasing the instrumentalization of other animals.

Yet some chose the latter option, which led to a second wave of animal ethics. Soon after Singer's first defences of reason, Mary Midgley sought to illuminate the significance of emotion, suggesting that reason and emotion are entwined and that moral concern for other animals must recognize the relevance of the latter. For her, emotion and reason cannot be categorically differentiated from one another: they are like shape and form, forever locked into each other in a strikingly apparent way in morality, wherein emotions serve the role of perception and motivation, while reason offers methods for analytic structuring. It was precisely emotion, and more particularly empathy, that laid the way for the moral significance of non-human animals: as similarly conscious creatures, we could empathize with their standpoint and orientate ourselves emotionally towards their experiences, thus creating a stronghold for emotive fellowship and recognition of value (Midgley 1983). Later, Martha Nussbaum also proceeded to use her variant of sentimentalism to defend the moral value of non-human animals: "We should not deny that the sympathetic imagination can cross the species barrier – if we press ourselves, if we require of our imaginations something more than common routine" (Nussbaum 2001, 125).

The strongest proponents of sentimentalism in animal philosophy have come from ecofeminism and "care theory". Supported by Carol Gilligan's (1993) famous studies, which posit that boys are taught to think of morality in terms of rigid, abstract notions, reason and punishment, whereas girls are pushed towards contextuality, emotion and forgiveness, and offered another resting branch by Genevieve Lloyd (1993), according to whom Western philosophy's tendency to centralize reason has been integrally linked to the centralization of the masculine identity, the feminist scholars have sought to render plain how obsession with reason is entwined with gender divisions.

According to the now-popular notion of "intersectionality", Western morality tends to rest on exclusions based on hierarchical dichotomies. Within this "logic of domination", the world is characterized by presumed binaries such as man–woman, human–animal, culture–nature and reason–emotion, and these binaries again are seen to incorporate hierarchies, wherein the first counterpart is dominant and more valuable in comparison to the second. The binaries are interlinked, and the first counterparts are seen to merge in the same broad category, and the second counterparts form their own, less valuable category. As a result, masculinity, humanity, culture and reason are interlocked, as are femininity, animality, nature and emotion – moreover, the latter are seen to be less significant and subservient in relation to the former.[11] According to intersectional thinking, the sidelining of emotions is, thereby, entangled with the sidelining of women, and both again are entwined with sidelining non-human animals. The task that emerges is to bring forth all of these subjugated categories and to erode hierarchical, dualistic thinking: in practice, if one wants to defend the moral significance of animals, one needs to also bring forth emotions and pay heed to gender politics. (For examples of feminist defences of emotion or the "feminist care tradition", see Donovan 2007; Gruen 2007.)

Here, emotions are to be vitalized as a valid and necessary constituent of moral agency, for when animal philosophy fails to pay them heed, it is in danger of falling back to the logic of domination. Josephine Donovan has argued that "like many feminists I contend that the dominant strain in contemporary ethics reflects a male bias toward rationality, defined as the construction of abstract universals that elide not just the personal, the contextual, and the emotional, but also the political components of an ethical issue" (Donovan 2007, 174) before setting the case for approaching more-than-human animals via emotions. Perhaps most notably, the feminist philosopher Lori Gruen (2015) advocates "entangled empathy" as a way to approach other animals and construe animal ethics.

Next to Midgley, Nussbaum and the feminist care tradition scholars, further frameworks also have been used to point towards a new animal ethic, inclusive of acknowledging the role of emotions. Cora Diamond (2004) has rested her animal philosophy not only on Wittgenstein but also on the notion of invoking "fellow-feelings" towards non-human animals, and Ralph Acampora (2006) has explored continental and post-structural theories in order to support "corporal compassion".

From these different accounts, two deserve particular mention because of their relevance from the viewpoint of this book. Gruen's "entangled empathy" refers to an attentive perception of the experiences of another, inclusive of a sense of relationship with and responsibility towards her. It takes its starting point from the way in which we are already in various relationships with other animals and comes with a feel of moral regard to the needs and viewpoints of those animals. In entangled empathy, various factors – such as attentiveness, emotional engagement, moral awareness and recognition of the relations with and the well-being of the other – combine, leading to a morally charged and multilayered umbrella notion of empathy (Gruen 2015). Acampora's "corporal compassion", on the other hand, rests on embodiment and highlights how the shared bodily existence of all animals (and indeed all living beings), rather than mental abilities, forms the backdrop for animal ethics. Simply stated, as somatic beings we can grasp others who are similarly living through their embodiment (Acampora 2006).

Both of these insightful accounts have illuminated inter-species empathy and its links to ethics in novel, unique ways, and in some respects this book is indebted to them. Gruen's account has certain similarities with the sort of metalevel attentiveness emphasized in the chapter concentrating on "reflective empathy", and Acampora's definition comes close to what here is called "embodied empathy". Yet both concentrate on one interpretation of empathy, while many others are left unexplored, and this book takes a more pluralistic approach by mapping out different alternatives and pointing out their potentialities and limitations.

Moreover, what has been missing in these and many other emotive approaches to animal ethics is a more careful analysis of the moral psychological role played by emotions and a detailed investigation into precisely which emotions ought to guide moral agency. What has mainly been argued is that emotions are "good" and that particularly empathy and compassion should be awarded attention – emotions and empathy have often been embraced rather generically as an all-good, all-positive method of relating to others. What is lacking is noting that "emotions" can also be damaging to moral agency and that there are highly distinct varieties of emotions, including varieties of empathy, which can have both beneficial and detrimental consequences for our capacity to take other animals morally into account. This book seeks to address these issues by exploring the different aspects, benefits, problems and challenges of linking empathy with moral agency and by specifying, in the context of animal ethics, the morally relevant and at times radical differences between varieties of empathy. The hope is to make evident which types of empathy we tend to follow, which of them have moral significance and which of them should we further cultivate in order to become more morally skilful in our dealings with other animals.

By investigating empathy's various forms and consequences and its multiple roles in animal ethics, this book also aims to shed light on empathy's broader relevance to our moral psychology. As argued above, the case of non-human animals provides a fertile testing zone for moral agency and thereby an arena for critically evaluating the building blocks of human morality. It is only when we note those creatures towards whom most moral numbness and indifference is directed, who are largely desubjectified and instrumentalized and whose treatment is primarily governed by utilitarian, rational calculations, that we may learn the current limitations of our moral agency and adopt ways to expand our notion of what it means to feel, think and act "morally".

NOTES

1. Schopenhauer tied the overemphasis of reason to the moral dismissal of other animals. For him, the Kantian approach is "odious and revolting", as within it animals are "merely 'things', simply *means* to ends of any sort; and so they are good for vivisection, for deer-stalking, bull-fights, horse-races, etc., and they may be whipped to death as they struggle along with heavy quarry carts. Shame on such morality. . . . This is a morality which knows and values only the precious species that gave it birth; whose characteristics – *reason* – it makes the condition under which a being may be an object of moral regard" (Schopenhauer 2005, 48). Rationalist, Kantian ethics seeks to separate humans from other animals on account of the presumption that only the latter use reason, and hence those who abide by it have "tried to reveal the existence of a vast chasm, an immeasurable gulf between animals and men, in order to represent them, in the teeth of opposing testimony, as existences essentially different" (ibid., 111). Schopenhauer notes that language is prejudiced against non-human animals, as words such as *it* are used to describe them, thus rendering them into "inanimate objects" (ibid., 112). It is this objectification that leads to the immoral treatment of animals: "The corollary that non-human living creatures are to be regarded merely as things, is at the root of the rough and altogether reckless treatment of them which obtains in the West" (ibid., 115).

2. It also should be noted that those who advocate the primacy of language may support the role of emotions. For instance, Alice Crary (2009) combines emphasis on language with the accentuation of emotions.

3. According to Prinz (2006), a person who knew all about the implications of killing (for instance, that it goes against utility or the categorical imperative) but had no emotion would not truly understand its wrongness – moreover, if a person exhibited strong negative emotions towards killing without being able to stipulate any clear justifications, she would nonetheless understand the wrongness of the act.

4. Prinz makes a distinction into "sentiments", which refer to an emotive attitude, and "emotions", which are individual instances of sentiments. Both constitute

morality: "Moral judgments express sentiments, and sentiments refer to the property of causing certain reactions in us. The reactions in question are emotions, which I regard as feeling patterned bodily changes" (Prinz 2006, 34).

5. This does not mean that we are continually in an emotionally heightened state when making moral decisions. For sentimentalists, moral judgements are "hot" but nonetheless not dependent on a constant flair of emotion: "We make judgments that express sentiments, even when those sentiments are not at the present time manifesting themselves as occurrent emotions" (Prinz 2006, 38). Moreover, sentimentalism does not lead to subjectivism, within which values are wholly relative to each individual's personal emotions. Instead, moral judgements have truth value, which is dependent upon "sentimental policies" to feel negatively or positively about given things – truth value stems from whether or not we are correct in feeling, say, anger in a given context. In short, misplaced emotions may lead to erroneous judgements, and attention needs to be placed on the suitability of our emotions (ibid.).

6. We are often fully sure of our moralities and hold on to our values for years, decades, even lifetimes, without ever questioning their validity and without ever approaching them via the tools of reasoning.

7. Haidt concludes that it is this level of immediate responding which ought to be prioritized and which ultimately also stands as a reliable ground for decision making: "We should look for the roots of human intelligence, rationality and virtue in what the mind does best: perception, intuition, and other mental operations that are quick, effortless, and generally quite accurate" (Haidt 2001, 822).

8. The claim is that "Moral reasoning matters, but it matters primarily in social contexts in which people try to influence each other and reach consensus with friends and allies" (Greene and Haidt 2002, 517).

9. Recognition of harm does not always turn into avoidance of harm, and the latter depends largely on the third criterion of moral agency (other-directedness). It also should be noted that, of course, harms suffered by the self are relevant; however, "morality" in the proper sense of the term begins only when we also turn our attention to what dwells exterior to the "self".

10. Singer has been subjected to some poignant, yet at times perhaps overly dichotomic and generalizing, criticism over his decision. For instance, Cathryn Bailey has asserted that emphasis on reason coincides and sustains the dualism between reasoning human beings and supposedly unreasoning other animals. She posits that arguments supportive of rationalism go on to support anthropocentrism and that rationalist animal ethics serves mainly to bolster the primacy of reason at the expense of emotion (Bailey 2007, 345). Now, rationalism has helped to construct a presumed species divide, but it would be simplistic to suggest that all rationalist discourse maintains boundaries. Like emotion, reason also forms an integral part of human existence, and critiquing it as a villainous outcast serves only to strengthen the false, categorical dualism between the two.

11. As pointed out by Lori Gruen (2007), there are also important differences between the oppressed counterparts, and ignoring these can in itself lead to dubious politics.

Chapter 1

Good and Bad Empathy

The Need for Distinctions

Although the role of empathy has been largely ignored in Western moral theory, there have been recent exceptions, as some have viewed it as a key component of moral agency and even as the latter's sufficient and necessary foundation. Following suit, empathy has even been endorsed as the capacity which renders us into moral creatures (Slote 2007; Hoffman 2001; Aaltola 2014c). Empathy's merit lies in the way in which it enables mind reading and understanding of others and opens a view into the emotions, intentions, motivations and experiences of other beings. This has the potential to evoke moral concern in us, as suddenly it is not only our own internal worlds that we care for but also those of others – hence, via empathy we may begin to see value in the subjective contents of others and are stirred into action on their behalf. On these lines, it has been suggested that "experiences of empathy may reveal to us conditions in the world that we then desire to change", for it "enables us to see others' emotions as reason giving. . . . Empathy is what allows us to see another's distress as a reason to act" (Hourdequin 2012, 410, 414). This capacity to note relevance in the internal worlds of others is the most pivotal feature of morality, for via it we become capable of grasping the moral dimensions of "harm" and are enticed towards other-directedness and heterogenic acceptance of difference. The claim is that individuals who cannot note the interests of others and see them as reason giving are not full moral agents, and since empathy forms the pathway to such noting, it emerges as the hallmark of moral ability (ibid.).

Therefore, empathy has potentially much to offer, for it may entwine with key features of moral agency and push towards perhaps the most astounding dimension of mental existence: the capacity to care for, and act on behalf of, others. Because of this, it holds the promise of combatting the type of moral desubjectification, inertia and failure depicted in the introduction. It can illuminate what it is like to be another, and as such can render those others into subjects worthy of moral attunement and vitality rather than apathy.[1]

There is considerable empirical evidence to support this optimistic stance on empathy. First, studies demonstrate that empathy forms a significant element in the development of social concern and helping behaviours (Slote 2007; Soenens et al. 2007). Empathy can be a deeply pro-social ability and has been celebrated as a capacity that enables fluent social interaction. Indeed, it has been called the "defining feature of human interpersonal interaction" (Minio-Paluello et al. 2009, 55) due to the way in which it enables us to understand and relate to others. As an example of this social potency, high empathy is linked to moral outrage and restorative action, aimed at both locating moral errors and preventing them in the future and in so doing igniting both moral consideration for others, and active, prosocial behaviour (Davis 1996). Indeed, those with higher empathy levels show a significantly higher eagerness to help (Batson et al. 2002). Hence, the claim is that "empathy must be considered a prime candidate for being a universal motive base for prosocial moral behaviour when humans observe others in distress" (Hoffman 2001, 274). Simply put, empathy makes us care about the harms and distress suffered by others and pushes us to act on behalf of those others. Empathy also inhibits aggression, further ensuring socially and morally productive forms of action (Kaukiainen, Björkqvist and Lagerspetz 1999; Ali, Sousa Amorim and Chamorro-Premuzic 2009).

Empathy's connectedness to prosocial behaviour is evident when considering its role in evolution. As the renowned primatologist Frans de Waal suggests, empathy serves a clear evolutionary function as it helps both the empathizer and those around her: "Empathy allows one to quickly and automatically relate to the emotional states of others, which is essential for the regulation of social interactions, coordinated activity, and cooperation toward shared goals" (de Waal 2008, 282); "Being in sync is often a matter of life or death" (ibid., 288). The claim is nothing less than that empathy forms an inherent part of our constitution and survival, and this is again related to the way in which it facilitates prosocial behaviours, including co-operation and altruism: the manner in which empathy enables us to take others into account also facilitates our own flourishing.[2] On these lines, empathy has even been placed as the solver of global problems and collective dangers faced by human beings, ranging from climate change to conflicts. The prosocial evaluation it enables could, according to this reading, ease our way towards a more peaceful, thriving future (Rifkin 2010).

Secondly, empathy has surfaced as an important factor from the viewpoint of norm constitution (Haidt 2003b; Blair and Blair 2009; Deigh 2011). It is particularly in the context of harm that empathy emerges as a vital tool for norm comprehension, for noting that another being is undergoing negative affect appears to gain a moral dimension only via an empathetic response (Hoffman 1990, 2001). Therefore, via empathy we may not only manifest concern and prosocial behaviour but also exhibit the ability to categorize and witness events as normatively charged, "good" or "bad". Here, particularly, matters related to harm are pertinent, as empathy assists in noting and morally responding to them. However, it can open us to also further moral notions, less obviously revolved around harm. For instance, it has been argued that empathy motivates one to perceive and also follow norms related to justice via offering the empathizer an emotive reward (it allows us to feel with the positive feelings of others; Deigh 2011). Hence, we may want justice to happen because we want to see others thrive.

Interestingly, Martin Hoffman claims that even John Rawls's famous "original position", a hypothetical scenario in which norms concerning justice are decided by taking into account all other individuals as if oneself could be any one of them, requires empathy – quite simply, we cannot identify with the other individuals without empathy. Here, empathy renders rationality into "hot cognition" with an "affective charge" that prevents relevant principles from remaining abstract (Hoffman 1990, 168). We not only theoretically, on a neutral level, ponder the rules of an ideal, just society, but we feel something towards and with the contents and consequences of our thoughts. In other words, empathy can act as a type of bridge between theory and practice, between abstraction and our lived experience, which was called for in the introduction. It enables us to perceive and constitute norms and to *feel* their moral relevance.

Therefore, research indicates that empathy is significant both for the development of prosocial behaviours (Thompson and Hoffman 1980; Cummins, Piek and Dyck 2007; Roberts and Strayer 2008) and the formation of moral judgements (Eisenberg-Berg and Mussen 1978; Kalliopuska 1983; Blair 1995; Blair and Blair 2009). Following suit, high empathy leads to not only higher levels of empathic, helping action but also internalization of moral values (Roe 1980; Dadds et al. 2009). With empathic ability, we begin to act on behalf of others and constitute norms and values with reference to their status and treatment – or at the very least, empathy holds the promise of having a pivotal role in such prosocial, promoral processes. (For a more critical review on moral development, sympathetic concern and empathy, see Spinrad and Eisenberg 2014.)

More than this, empathy may be necessary for one's sense of self. It has been suggested that empathy is crucial for the formation of self-identity as it facilitates introspection (Decety and Moriguchi 2007). The logic is this: via accessing the mental contents of others, we become more capable of reflecting on those of our own. This bridge between empathy and self-constitution was already noted by phenomenologists, as both Edmund Husserl (1989) and Edith Stein (1989) posited that we begin to know ourselves only after we grasp that others, too, have their viewpoints, their specific perspectives, onto a shared world. Here, empathizing with how others perceive us plays no small part, as we can learn to see ourselves from their viewpoint and thus gain new dimensions into our self-perception. Therefore, acknowledging and understanding the unique-mindedness of others enables us to comprehend more succinctly our own specificity and uniqueness, the content of what it is to be a particular "I", and it allows us to see ourselves from novel perspectives and angles, also capable of questioning and even shattering our own, inward patterns of self-perception, which again enhances the development of a mature self-identity. Those with limited or non-existent empathy would have a weak, confused or distorted sense of self (something manifested in personality disorders, such as narcissism, which are low on both self-understanding and empathy – a topic we shall return to later). Importantly, a mature sense of self is also the birthplace of mature moral agency – without grasping the "self" in the full sense of the term, "agency" will always remain indefinite and unruly simply because it remains unanchored to something reflective, self-perceptive and relatively fixed. This adds further support for the claim that it is, indeed, empathy which forms the core of moral agency, for not only does it enable prosocial action and moral concern, it also stabilizes such action and concern on the permanence of an aware, reflective "self".[3]

As seen, empathy is the emotion perhaps most frequently brought forward in animal philosophy. It has been celebrated by feminist philosophy, as the feminist care tradition has incorporated its relevance into the non-human context (Gruen 2015), and it has been discussed both in analytic (Aaltola 2013a) and continental animal philosophy (Acampora 2006). Perhaps the first and most notable contemporary animal philosopher to discuss empathy was Mary Midgley (1983), according to whom empathy forms a focal aspect of our capacity to note moral value in the non-human world as well.

It is little wonder that empathy has been endorsed. If it sparks prosocial, promoral behaviour in the intrahuman setting, it most probably does so in relation to other animals: via empathy, we may be evoked to care for the well-being of moose and hawks to the extent that we want to assist them and extend various moral norms to concern them as well (see Furnham, McManus and Scott 2003; Sprinkle 2008; Kielland et al. 2010). Moreover, empathy may allow humans to question and evaluate their own moral character, their moral "selves", from the wider standpoint of how they relate to and treat non-human animals, which again will enhance the reflectiveness and maturity of their moral agency (indeed, perhaps we are also quite inward and immature in our self-understanding as long as we keep blocking off the possibility of acknowledging non-human-mindedness).

There are also further reasons. If we understand it to refer to "feeling with" the emotions or experiences of others, empathy functions as an antidote to scepticism, which forms one of the supporting pillars of anthropocentric attitudes. According to scepticism, we cannot "know" the minds of other animals, let alone comprehend their experiences, and due to this inability, neither can we give them serious moral regard (how can one offer moral concern for the mindedness of a pig if one cannot with any certainty know that mindedness?). Empathy provides a simple answer to this refusal to note mindedness and inherent value in the non-human realm, for here "knowing" the minds of others is not a matter of bullet-proof, theoretical, abstracted certainty but rather a matter of affectively engaging with others so that their inner lives begin to manifest. We do not infer the minds of others, we note them on account of our shared, emotive, experiential ability (an issue touched upon by philosophers such as Ludwig Wittgenstein, Edith Stein and Maurice Merleau-Ponty and revisited later in this book). The difference between the two is stark. Empathy is affective and fluctuates with the emotions and experiences of others; scepticism is rational and disengages from the emotions and experiences it seeks to grasp. Thereby, empathy is epistemologically bound to its subject, capable of accessing and moving with the mindedness of others, and due to this it offers a promising, more reliable and lucid alternative to scepticism.

Indeed, contemporary literature on psychology is, to an increasing extent, suggesting that this sense of emotive boundedness is required for comprehending the subjectivity and moral worth of others – empathy is essential if other beings are to be noted as "subjects" rather than "objects". Hence, one of the most noted psychologists working on empathy, Simon Baron-Cohen, claims that "when you treat someone as an object, your empathy has been turned off" (Baron-Cohen 2011, 7) and suggests that those incapable of perceiving subjectivity in other beings suffer from "empathy corrosion" (ibid). Arguably, the sceptical attitude inherent in anthropocentrism is entwined precisely with empathy corrosion, a mode that perceives others primarily as objects rather than subjects, and thus the moral numbness towards and desubjectification of non-human animals evident in contemporary cultures may result from abandoning empathy. This would mean that the type of mechanomorphia towards non-human animals that depicts them as something akin to biological machineries (Crist 1999) which can be reduced to instrumentalized objects and commodities without moral scruples is rested on not only scepticism but also the lack of its much more warranted and epistemologically grounded alternative – empathy.

Therefore, there are good reasons to highlight empathy in the non-human context, for doing so may help to combat both scepticism and desubjectification of other animals (the very cornerstones of anthropocentrism). Yet, perhaps empathy has been unduly romanticized. As will be suggested, it can lead to projections which ignore the difference and distinctiveness of others, and it can even be used as a method of manipulation and control (as it comes to the latter issue, empathy gains a wide variety of different bases, manifestations and meanings within different cultural settings, some of which are highly calculating and controlling – see Groark 2008; Robbins and Rumsey 2008; Hollan 2011; Hollan and Throop 2011; Throop 2011; von Poser 2011). Both of these matters apply also in empathy directed to other animals. In regard to the risk of projection, it has been stated that "the urge to identify with and so to anthropomorphize another's experience, like the urge to empathize with it, has been even more recently criticized as a form of narcissistic projection that erases boundaries of difference" (Weil 2012, 45). Here, the human gaze will only note those beings who can be made to resemble the imagery of humanity, and in so doing the rest of the animal world is either ignored or emptied out of particularity. As a consequence, the animal becomes a form void of content, a furry or feathery Disneyfied simulation born from mirroring the human self onto the non-human world. In regard to the risk of manipulation and coercion, this "species narcissism" is extended beyond projection towards concrete scenes of habitual violence, wherein empathy is used to gain information on other animals in order to utilize them more efficiently and fluently. Thereby, next to acting as a catalyst for noting non-human subjectivity and value, empathy also holds the treacherous potential for erasing them from our awareness.

We are left, then, at a junction between empathy as the pathway towards recognizing the morally significant individuality of pigs and pikes and empathy as a nullification of any such recognition. To add two more questions that may diminish the enthralling prospects of empathy: Is it possible to "know" non-human-mindedness without human bias? And is it possible to empathize with the ills and sufferings of all non-human creatures around the globe without succumbing to mental fatigue? That is, can one empathize with an animal in any other than a biased sense, and can one empathize with many animals, the sufferings of trillions, without becoming despondent and ultimately empathically incapable and numb?

These questions add to the melancholic prospect that despite its potential to mark others as morally valuable subjects and to thereby combat moral detachment and apathy, empathy may also increase objectification and moral indifference – in animal ethics as well. In order to examine this issue further, we need to know what we mean by "empathy" and what its different varieties are.

Terms such as "empathy", "sympathy", "fellow-feeling" and "compassion" have been repeatedly used when seeking to illustrate why other animals deserve more serious moral attention – yet the meaning of these terms, and their moral bearing, have been largely left without further notice. They are taken as self-evident, even when they are, in fact, difficult, nuanced, intricate terms that hold the potential to not only open up but also close off horizons of moral consideration. Particularly, "empathy" is often mentioned without further exploration into its nature, which forms a major obstacle in establishing its links to moral agency.

Empathy stands as a multifaceted and highly ambiguous notion. On a simplistic level, it is often viewed via two perspectives. According to what is called the "theory theory" account, empathy is rested on the theory of mind – we empathize, because we master the concept of a "mind" and can thereby consciously infer and acknowledge the mental contents of others by filing them under the appropriate lingual categories ("sadness", "joy", etc.). According to this interpretation, empathy consists of our ability to observe the behaviour of another from afar and to conclude what she is feeling – we are as laboratory scientists, harnessed with theoretical concepts such as "a mind" and "cognition" which allow us to examine our test subjects. Within the "simulation-theory", on the other hand, empathy concerns the ability to project and simulate the mental contents of others, as we are to project ourselves into their position and simulate what we might experience if placed under their skin. The empathizer is no longer a detached scientist reliant on reason but someone seeking to imitate and dive into the mentation of another on a more imaginative, felt level. (On this distinction, see Stueber 2006.)

Yet these accounts are overly broad, leaving many aspects of empathy beyond their scope and failing to illustrate what, precisely, empathy is formed of. More detailed definitions are required; however, they are surprisingly rare in the current literature. Almost as frequently as empathy is mentioned, it is left without further clarification. To add to this problem, even when definitions are offered, they tend to be overly specific and lead to a pluralistic fragmentation of empathy, with many competing, highly specialized interpretations all seeking to offer the "correct choice". Therefore, either definitions are too broad or too fine-tuned and specialized. As it comes to the latter issue, within social psychology alone, at least ten different, mutually conflicting definitions have been brought forward (Decety and Ickes 2009). Making the situation evermore confusing, empathy is not only defined in many different ways, many of the definitions themselves are pluralistic and thereby formed of a variety of different capacities. For instance, de Waal maintains that empathy is "the capacity to (a) be affected by and share the emotional states of another, (b) assess the reasons for the other's state, and (c) identify with the other, adopting his or her perspective" (de Waal 2008, 281). Jean Decety and Philip Jackson (2006), social psychologists famous for their work on empathy, argue empathy to comprise three rather different elements: affective responses towards others, cognitive orientation towards the viewpoint of others and emotion regulation.

How, then, to define empathy without being overly generic or (conversely) overly specific? Moreover, which, if not all, of the many definitions offered stand as most relevant to moral agency and as the most fruitful ground for animal philosophy? These are vital questions, for different forms of empathy have strikingly different moral outcomes – some pave the way towards moral concern, whereas some invite bias, manipulation, exhaustion and even violence. This is pertinent also to animal philosophy, for although it has been eager to presume that empathy feeds positive moral outcomes and pushes one to pay normative heed to the hens and pikes of this world, it must be also noted that while some varieties spur moral recognition and awareness of value in the animal world, empathy can also, depending on its definition, feed moral disregard and even crude, egoistic manipulation and control of others.

Choosing how to define empathy, and which of its many varieties one ought to cultivate in moral affairs, must be anchored in the criteria of moral agency, set in the introduction. Morally relevant types of empathy need to enable perception of harm and the formation of moral judgements; they also need to facilitate other-directedness and heterogenic openness towards difference. As mentioned above, since most varieties do support the recognition of harms and formation of judgements, the last two stand as the focus. In regard to animal philosophy, they are particularly significant. It is not difficult to perceive the anthropocentric culture as deeply enmeshed within self-directedness, formed from collectively produced narratives and doxa (social opinion) that sustain the belief in the unquestioned primacy of humanity. The subjectivity of other animals is continuously overlooked with the aid of cultural dogma that tell us it is, for instance, "natural" and "necessary" that animals are utilized or that other animals lack advanced mindedness (Loughnan, Bastian and Haslam 2014; Piazza and Loughnan 2016). The animals themselves often remain unnoted, their experiences hidden from human intention, while intention is turned towards how the human self may best benefit from the non-human world. Moral concern for animals as inherently valuable subjects requires breaking away from this tradition and directing attention and intention towards the specificity and needs of the animals themselves. Heterogenic openness, on the other hand, means that we are to resist anthropomorphia, the urge to see dogs as furry kids and pigs as Babes, and to note that there is much in other animals that surpasses the limits of human understanding. Similarities are limited and offer only a partial stepping stone for understanding what it is like to be a non-human animal, and moral agency in animal ethics must also acknowledge distinctness, uniqueness and opacity.

In what follows, six different definitions of empathy will be mapped out, and their relevance to moral agency will be evaluated from the perspective of how well they support other-directedness and openness to diversity (see also Aaltola 2014c). Perhaps the most famous philosophers to dwell on its meaning are David Hume with *Treatise on Human Nature* (1740/1969), Adam Smith with *Theory of Moral Sentiments* (1759/2009), Arthur Schopenhauer with *The Basis of Morality* (1840/2005), Max Scheler with *Nature of Sympathy* (1921/1979) and Edith Stein with *On the Problem of Empathy* (1921/1989). Quite strikingly, these classics remain highly relevant to contemporary research and offer the perfect platform for distinguishing between six varieties of empathy.

Before continuing, it should be noted that many of the classic texts on empathy use the term "sympathy". Indeed, "empathy" is a relatively recent term, stemming from early twentieth-century German aesthetic philosophy, whereas "sympathy" has far older roots, dating back to antiquity (Cole 2001; Nilsson 2003). Often what has been called "sympathy" is, in fact, "empathy" in contemporary terms, and therefore the notion of empathy has lingered in philosophy throughout centuries, frequently disguised under the category of "sympathy". But is there a difference between the two? Sympathy and empathy are quite separate mental states. Whereas sympathy refers to "feeling for" (we feel, for example, pity or sadness for another's suffering), empathy is often defined as "feeling with" (we do not pity the other but instead share her suffering), while compassion can be positioned as one of empathy's subcategories, akin to affective empathy. However, since empathy can also include non-affective dimensions, it is here defined, in the broadest possible terms, as "feeling with or identifying the mental states of another".

NOTES

1. It is on such grounds that Nel Noddings, speaking from the perspective of ethics of care, has suggested that empathy sparks morality into existence and thereby acts as a shield against factors which may erode moral consideration: "There is considerable evidence that a mature empathy – one that can reach into and feel with others, even those whose physical and moral conditions are very different from our own – may be our best protection against complete demoralization" (cited in Verducci 1998).

2. Other animals also can feel empathy. As de Waal has pointed out, empathy is "a phylogenetically ancient capacity" (de Waal 2008, 292) which takes different forms and which we share with many non-human creatures. De Waal argues that empathy in its broadest definition refers to "emotional sensitivity to others" (ibid., 282), which as a definition builds a continuum between species, as chimps, pigs or rats also can emotionally tune to the needs of their conspecifics. The type of immediate emotional connectedness empathy involves has evolved much before the birth of *Homo sapiens* and can be found in (at least) avian and mammalian worlds. Indeed, emotional responses to the emotions of other individuals are, according to de Waal,

common among non-humans: rats and pigeons display distress when they observe distress in others and alter their behaviour so as not to cause pain, and many animals (such as apes, birds, dolphins, whales, elephants, dogs and cats) demonstrate efforts to comfort and console others. Moreover, common behaviours such as co-operation and food sharing are telling of empathy (ibid.). The existence of non-human empathy is something highlighted by philosophers such David Hume (1969), for whom it was evident that many other animals can undergo and express empathic capacities.

3. This is not to say that one cannot have any sense of self without empathy – indeed, there are many groups of both human and non-human animals who do have some sense of self despite of their lack of empathy. The claim merely is that mature or "full" selfhood, consisting of the capacity for self-reflection and self-perception, requires empathy.

Chapter 2

Projective and Simulative Empathy

Adam Smith, one of the eighteenth-century forefathers of liberalism and free-market politics, was also a thinker willing to devote an entire book to empathy (or "sympathy," as he called it). Although it was his friend David Hume who pushed him towards sentimentalism and explorations on empathy, Smith developed a notably different definition in comparison to Hume's – the latter being the topic of the next chapter. For Smith, empathy was projection, and this notion still lingers strongly in contemporary culture.

DEFINITION

According to Smith, empathy stems from our ability to place ourselves into the situation of another and thereby to imagine what she must be feeling. In short, we are to project ourselves into the position of the other being and envision how we ourselves would feel were we her. This is perhaps still the most common idea of empathy, as children are taught to imagine the experiences of others and as adults may similarly be urged to put themselves in the place of another. "How would you feel?" we are asked, and this is thought to both explicate and cultivate empathy.

Smith was highly optimistic and embracive of this take on empathy, not least because he assumed it to be the only viable option. He posited that "as we have no immediate experience of what other men feel, we can form no idea of the manner in which they are affected, but by conceiving what we ourselves should feel in the like situation" (A. Smith 2009, 13) and thereby suggested that we cannot know anything of the emotions of others unless we project ourselves into their position. Projection is the only means of accessing the experiential states of others – it is the only tool, the only productive method, we have. When projecting, we are to think of what it would be like to the other person, to be in her setting and even to exist in her body, and this again Smith thought would enable us to feel something akin to what the other person is undergoing. Smith explained, "By the imagination we place ourselves in his situation, we conceive ourselves enduring all the same torments, we enter as it were into his body, and become in some measure the same person with him, and thence form some idea of his sensations, and even feel something which, though weaker in degree, is not altogether unlike them" (ibid., 14). He went so far as to suggest that via projection we may even become the other being: "I consider what I should suffer if I was really you, and I not only change circumstances with you, but I change persons and characters" (ibid., 355).

Projection, then, involves in-her-shoes thinking, the placement of oneself into the position of the other, to an extent that we adopt the mental states of the other being and even simulate her very person – that is, become another. We do not infer what the other is feeling, nor do we instantaneously resonate with her (these would constitute "cognitive" and "affective" empathy, to be explored in the next chapters) – instead, we use projective imagination to access her mental states. When encountering a homeless person, I am not to infer from her body language what she is undergoing nor immediately "flow" with her emotions, but instead I am to position myself in her place and envision what it must be like to be her.

Now, it is important to note that such projection can take two different forms – we can project ourselves into the situation of another, and thereby imagine what we *ourselves* would feel in her place, or we can try, via projection, to simulate what the *other person* is undergoing by imaginatively exchanging personas with her. In the first instance, the self is put in the position of the other, as we think of what it would be like for us to be middle class, homeless or in prison, and in the second instance, the self is swapped for the other individual, as we imagine being a specific homeless person or a prisoner. The former asks, "How would I feel?" and the latter asks, "How does the other feel?". The first of these options is self-directed, for the self – even though transported to a different context – remains the focus of attention, while the latter option is other-directed and thereby concentrates our attention on what the other being, not "ourselves as another", is experiencing. For clarity's sake, here self-directed projection will be called "projective empathy", and other-directed projection will be referred to as "simulative empathy".

This distinction can be found also in Smith's account, as he, on the one hand, proposes that we concentrate on how we ourselves would feel in the place of another but on the other, suggests that we become the other. Yet it is the former of these definitions that gains the main emphasis in Smith's thinking, and the latter may only have been introduced in order to combat obvious egoism (Rick 2007). Therefore, although Smith does – as noted above – talk of emulating the other to the extent of becoming her, the real emphasis is on simply projecting the self into her position, thereby replacing her. In Smith's projective empathy, primacy is on transporting ourselves into the contexts of others and taking their place, which means that it is epistemologically self-directed: the self is the centre of attention, despite the transference involved. Indeed, Smith also held a deeply pessimistic view on epistemological other-directedness, for according to him our senses "never did, and never can, carry us beyond our own person, and it is by the imagination only that we can form any conception of what are his sensations. . . . It is the impressions of our own senses only, not those of his, which our imaginations copy" (A. Smith 2009, 13). Therefore, in projection our imagination is limited to pay heed to our own experiences – what it would be like for *me* to be in a cancer ward or composing symphonies – while the other being remains inaccessible. Paradoxically, therefore, this form of empathy does not enable empathy with the other but only with the self in the situation of another – although, on the surface, it promises something quite different.[1]

Projective and simulative empathy are also discussed in contemporary literature. The so-called simulation theorists suggest that empathy is based on simulating either the situation or the experiences of another through the use of imagination, with the central feature once again being the question "How would I feel were I in her position?" (see Gordon 1995; Goldman 2009; Stueber 2006). Here, *simulation* is used to designate the act of imaginative projection. One way it is described is the following: "Empathy is a process or procedure by which a person centrally imagines the narrative (the thoughts, feelings and emotions) of another person" (Goldie 2000, 195; see also Coplan 2011b). As seen from the quote, in simulation theory, self-directedness is not a necessity, for one can seek to imagine how the other feels without detouring via the self. Some simulation theorists, such as Karsten Stueber (2006), highlight that one is to take into account the context, beliefs and motivations of the other, which suggests simulative rather than projective empathy. However, this distinction, albeit a crucial one and something we will come back to, is not always drawn, and simulation theory can entwine with advocacy of projective empathy (indeed, Stueber 2006, 165, also states that "we have to be able to understand that we would have acted or drawn certain inferences for the same reasons if we were in their situation", thereby suggesting projection). Besides simulation theorists, projection is often also brought forward by those who see it as forming one aspect of a plural take on empathy, within which empathy consists of various different elements.

Studies show that in education projection can be an efficient tool of evoking understanding concerning the perspectives of other individuals and also of furthering other forms of empathy – therefore, as a pedagogical method, and particularly when used in an other-directed, simulative fashion, it can be beneficial (see, for instance, Shapiro, Morrison and Boker 2004; on the neuroscientific background, see Lamm, Batson and Decety 2007).[2] However, projective empathy also involves serious risks. They stem from the paradox faced by Smith: we may begin to only pay attention to ourselves and in effect fail to empathize with the other. "Empathy" as a generic term refers to feeling with or identifying the emotions of others, and self-directed projection simply does not accomplish this task – in effect, strictly speaking, it may fail to be empathy to begin with. The relevant risk here does not only concern such an inability to fit the generic definition of empathy, for there are also more potent, practical hazards involved.

The first such danger is that self-directed projection disguised as empathy fails to spur awareness of the other being and can wholly push her aside. Here, a white feminist may project herself onto women all around the globe and speak on their behalf while (often unwittingly) ignoring that women and their political statuses and personal narratives differ radically. She is well intentioned in seeking to project herself into the position of, say, an African woman, but in so doing she may sideline the challenges and experiences of that woman and replace them with her own presumptions (indeed, the anthropologist Clifford Geertz was critical of empathy in the field of understanding other ethnic backgrounds, for the empathizer all too readily projects her own culturally coloured mental contents onto the minds of culturally different others; see Hollan and Throop 2011). The second, related danger is that when projection is introduced as empathy, what we take to be empathizing with another may in actuality be nothing but evaluating her via our own limited, biased, even prejudiced self-directed standards. When a wealthy person with a stable upbringing walks past a homeless individual with a broken past and uses projection, she may quickly conclude that were she to be that individual, she would force herself to better her situation, find work, find housing and make something of herself – she would fail to understand the challenges of the other precisely because she would estimate them from the viewpoint of her own privileged background void of relevant experiences. Therefore, projective empathy easily both ignores the target of empathy and fails to provide us with methods of understanding her.

This does not mean that projective empathy is always doomed. When it entwines with simulative empathy, its outcomes can be quite positive. That is, when we seek to learn how to simulate the position of another and use projective empathy as the first stepping stone, the latter can advance our ability to comprehend others. Crucially here, projective empathy in time turns into simulative empathy and thereby aims towards other-directedness. However, on its own, stuck in self-absorption, projective empathy can hinder rather than enable empathic development.

PROJECTION AND ANTHROPOMORPHISM

Projection and simulation are not uncommon in human dealings with other animals, even if – like all forms of empathy – their scope and frequency are often limited. They are used in efforts to educate children to pay heed to animals, as questions such as "How would you feel if someone did that to you?" are used to spark awareness, concern and the sort of critical self-evaluation required for moral cultivation. They are also used in animal advocacy aimed at adults, with one example being simulative devices depicting a virtual first-person view into industrial farming, shot from the perspective of an animal and aimed at enabling people to imagine what it is like to be, say, a cow facing slaughter. As seen above, there are good reasons for such efforts. Indeed, we do not always need to be pushed and pedagogically coaxed towards projective and simulative empathy, for many arguably feel them quite spontaneously for non-human animals, at least intermittently and in given settings. When we see footage of a pig in an intensive farm, it is not difficult to start envisioning what it must be like and to recoil precisely because of such imaginative simulation.

Although projection can be productive in both facilitating acknowledgement of the mental states of the pig or the sheep and in spurring other varieties of empathy into action, there are also dangers to it, for it can lead us into ignoring the animal in herself. When a human projects herself into the position of a non-human animal, no matter how well intended her effort, she may end up sidelining the experiences of the very subject she is seeking to understand. The obvious danger here is anthropomorphism, wherein human emotions, capacities, wants, intentions and other relevant mental phenomena are mistakenly pushed onto non-human creatures. In projectively and self-directedly empathizing with other animals, humans will begin to perceive mental contents that actually originate from themselves, and in the extreme, pigs and mice will become little humans, void of their own distinct animality.

Disney stands as the prime example of such projection, and although Disneyfied (see Baker 1993) animal imagery may have had a beneficial influence on other, more other-directed forms of empathy towards animals and perhaps may have helped, in some cases (think of Bambi), to raise concern over how those animals are treated, the risk is that simultaneously animals become empty physical forms on whom to paint human characteristics and whose very non-human uniqueness is ignored. As a consequence of such extreme projective empathy and anthropomorphism, animals easily become caricatures which fail to do any justice to what it is to be a pig or a mouse – the very being with whom one is meant to be empathizing is lost under layers of self-serving fantasia. (It is little wonder, then, that anthropomorphic projections can be used to promote the use of the very animals they are meant to be empathizing with and representing: in a rather macabre fashion, McDonald's offers figurines of Bambi and Babe, which come with its children's menu.)[3]

Projective anthropomorphism need not always gain such extreme, fantastical forms. It may come out in the well-meaning and tangible desire to relate to one's canine companions as "little furry children", who are treated as if their mental contents and capacities were those of humans. As pointed out by Lori Gruen (2015), it is all too easy to project human interests and ideologies onto other animals by assuming false similarities and announcing what is best for them while remaining oblivious to their uniqueness and to what is in their own interests. Here, one dresses up a dog in human clothes, "spoils" her with human activities like incessant hugging that she actually may, depending on the individual, not enjoy but merely tolerate, and grooms her appearance as if she were an odd combination of a toddler and vanity (rather than a creature who would probably love nothing more than to be out there running on muddy fields). It may also come out in loving if misled notions, according to which non-human animals in general have the same needs and characteristics as humans – a notion that can lead to wholly ill-conceived expectations for, say, farmed animals to truly feel and behave like humans in pig bodies and spark disappointment when this is not the case. One cherishes animals as Bambies and Babes and gets angry and disappointed when they don't act accordingly. It may also take more negative forms, such as when a person punishes her dog for presumed human vices or moral transgressions or wishes vengeance on pigeons, bears, wolves or foxes for the same reason (for instance, when they break human-made rules over where they are "allowed" to roam). The danger with even cuddly anthropomorphic projections is that they succumb to these negative consequences, and thereby "love" can quickly be replaced with hostility. These projections presume humanity where none exists and punish those who by default will always fail humanity's standards.

Now, "anthropomorphism" is often a politically loaded term, as it is used indiscriminately in order to depict any similarities between humans and other animals as false, factually mistaken and non-existent, and the motive thereby is to strengthen species dichotomies. As such, it is one of the most widespread and potent methods of downplaying animal mentation and subjectivity, and references to it should always be met with a critical eye. Acknowledging similarities is not necessarily anthropomorphism, and when empathizing with other animals and perceiving likeness across species, we may be realistic rather than presumptive, for there are no clear, rigid barriers between "human" and, say, "pig". Many non-human animals share a vast amount of mental capacities and traits with humans, to an astoundingly greater extent than is usually recognized. Pigs, chickens and salmons are cognitively capable creatures, and it is not "anthropomorphic" to acknowledge this: if anything, the much more acute and widespread problem is mechanomorphism, the depiction of other animals as biological machineries (see Crist 1999). However, despite its political underpinnings, anthropomorphism can also be a real phenomenon and oddly supports rather than contests species dichotomies. It comes into the picture when realism is overtaken by projection and similarities are imagined, not actual – here, the human stands as the reference point of inquiry, while the animal becomes an empty canvas. It is then that the aforementioned risks of projective empathy become evident.

Such risks entwine with the downgrading of non-human mentation. For a long time, the mental capacities of non-human creatures have been underestimated because the human mind has been positioned as the reference point: we have judged the behaviour of cows and chickens on account of how we ourselves manifest mental abilities, and since their manifestations are often utterly different (chicken intelligence does not come out in human-like behaviour), the possibility of non-human-mindedness has even been denied altogether. Therefore, for primates to be considered intelligent, the expectation has been that they must master propositional language typical to human beings, and for birds to be considered self-aware, they must be able to recognize themselves in the mirror just as humans do. Arguably, this has been grounded in a type of collective, self-directed projection, wherein efforts to understand the non-human world have stemmed from transporting and positioning human criteria onto that world. Instead of asking, "How would the pig manifest cognitive ability, taking her physiological, evolutionary and environmental context into account?" the peculiar thinking has been, "If I were a pig or a baboon of intelligence, how would I, as a human, manifest it?"

Similarly, as the middle-class person projecting herself onto a homeless individual will produce unfair standards and expectations, humans have held on to a rather dictatorial tendency to demand the wrong type of things from other animals in order for them to be considered mentally capable. When following projective empathy in relation to non-humans, we easily become the white, Western feminist unable to understand or speak for women from less privileged life settings or the anthropologist projecting her own culture onto different peoples, incapable of comprehending their distinctiveness and exceptionality. Here, a type of "anthropomorphic" or "humanizing gaze" nullifies and ignores animal specificity, with at times violent implications.

Therefore, self-directed projective empathy can lead to surprising, quite un-empathic consequences, as dogs or cows are evaluated on a mistaken, inappropriate human scale, and as even "cute", anthropomorphic caricatures can, despite their seeming lovability, support boundaries and mechanomorphism. In the midst of such confusion, it is the other animals who end up being mistreated and unfairly judged. Instead of anchoring projective empathy on self-directedness, the solution is to aim for other-directedness. This means that rather than following Smith's account, it is worthwhile to map out and take up simulative empathy. It is, at times, beneficial to wonder what it would be like for a human to live as another animal, but only with the aim of developing this into directly imagining what it is to be that other animal.

Whereas self-directed projection moves the self onto the other and thereby remains potentially oblivious to the specificities of that other, other-directed simulation begins from those very specificities. Instead of asking what it would be like to be in the place of the other, it asks what it is like to be another. One way to achieve this is to imagine what it is like to inhabit the other's mental and physical attributes: what it is like to have her cognitive capacities, desires, traits and senses and what it is like to exist in her particular body. In relation to other animals, we are to imagine what could it be like to have wings or hoofs; to have the senses and mental traits of an owl, coyote or horse; to figure out one's surroundings via smells and touches; to run on four feet in constellations, wherein one constantly knows the positions of other herd members; to stay as a solitary animal, capable of navigating in air through the densest of forests in solemn darkness; or to hunt in a pack. We are to ask what must it be like for a being with a particular evolutionary history and the sort of particular body-mind that history has shaped. What must it be like to have the unique capacities of lizards and whales or, in general, to fly, swim, run, want, intend, feel, think and sense as a non-human creature?

Another method of simulative empathy is to address the context of the other – her background, personal history, surroundings, daily challenges, treatment, political status and so forth (Stueber 2006). In order to understand the emotive contents of non-human animals, care needs to be taken to consider the settings which have shaped them and in which they currently live – what must it be like to be born into a factory farm, prevented from using one's species-specific inclinations, and what must it be like to roam out in nature, taking care of one's young, searching for food, seeking to survive, contentedly and freely addressing and following one's needs? Contexts are a doorway towards simulating another, as it is via contexts that the broader ramifications, origins and causes of the other's emotions can be understood – through these contexts, we gain a fuller image of the internal movements of others. Indeed, rather than the other being, it is her context that gains attention, as Smith explains: "Sympathy, therefore, does not arise so much from the view of the passion, as from that of the situation which excites it" (A. Smith 2009, 16). It is something like this that Iris Murdoch appears to be addressing when she claims that "contexts are relevant to our ability to move towards 'seeing more', toward 'seeing what he sees'" (Murdoch 1971, 31), and the same applies in relation to non-human creatures. Without paying attention to their backgrounds and surroundings, projection easily becomes self-focused rather than capable of manifesting what it may be like to exist as a baboon or a giraffe.

Therefore, simulation gains flight from both contextual information and imagination. We need the former in order to map out others' life settings and simulate what it may be like to exist as them, but we also need the latter in order to take the leap away from the fixation on the self and into sketching otherness.

SIMULATIVE ANIMAL NARRATIVES

In the light of the above, an antidote to anthropomorphism is found from diving into what it may be like to inhabit the body-mind and context of another animal. One way to further illuminate simulative empathy comes from Shaun Gallagher. Although his stance on empathy highlights embodiment rather than projection, and indeed is quite antagonistic towards simulation theory in general, it offers one standpoint towards simulative empathy as defined here. According to Gallagher, narratives are a central feature of empathy, for via them we begin to perceive what it must be like to be another. Narratives stand at the core of empathy: they depict other beings as creatures with their own subjectivity, their own lives, histories and desires, aims and tendencies. As such, those others become real – their actions and emotions are no longer abstracted from history and present context, and they come to be seen as creatures with their own pasts and futures and thereby their own reasons for feeling and experiencing in particular ways. As Gallagher posits, "I am open to the experience and the life of the other, in their context, as I can understand it, not in terms of my own narrow experience, but in terms that can be drawn from a diversity of narratives that inform my understanding" (Gallagher 2012, 17). Hence, narratives offer a tool for contextualizing others, and – although Gallagher does not speak of simulation – of imagining the perspective of another. As such, it is one guide towards simulative empathy. Narratives provide a way out from self-directedness, for they allow us to begin to imagine the histories and stories of others rather than transporting our own explanations and causes to their position. The middle-class person will not imagine what she, as an individual with a steady and well-fed background, would undergo in the place of the homeless individual but rather begins to merge herself into that individual's own narratives, opening the gate for other-directedness.

When it comes to non-human animals, narratives are an excellent way to achieve other-directed empathy. By mapping out their histories, settings, capabilities, traits and other pertinent factors and shaping them into narratives that enable one to constitute simulative takes into the perspective of a specific animal, we can learn to address the animal rather than "the non-human animal humanized". Instead of thinking how we would behave and feel were we chimps or dolphins, with narratives we explore what it could be like for a particular chimp or dolphin to exist. The task should, thereby, be the construction of "animal stories", which aim to manifest things from the non-human outlook. Such stories can originate from our individual imagination, or they can branch from scientific accounts and cultural mediations, thus varying from, for instance, ethological studies into non-human-mindedness to photographic reports that follow the day of a wild elephant or a captive rat.

These narratives are not meant to convey how an animal would narrativize her own account, and indeed it must be remembered that using narratives as a method of understanding is probably quite anthropogenic (or, at least, the narratives of other animals gain a rather different formula) due to the centrality we give to propositional language. Instead, the aim is to translate the animal standpoint into something more easily comprehended by humans. Here, narratives decipher and interpret the continuity of non-human experiences and their causes, the felt sense of the animal "I", the ongoing feel of what it is to be a particular pig, combined with her memories of the past and how she makes sense of her own condition and surroundings, into a form more readily grasped by storytelling humans.

But is it not difficult to narrativize non-human lives without also humanizing them? After all, most animals cannot lingually tell their own account, and deciphering non-human experience into human narratives runs the inevitable risk of losing the non-human in the process of translation. These are real but not necessarily pressing dangers. First, we often use narratives in relation to those humans whose own, individually told stories we never hear. In both the human and non-human context, we use information from non-personal sources in order to produce the narrative – whether this source be science, media or, for instance, anecdotes. The task is to construct a story centred on the other rather than on one's own wish to see the other in a given light, and here drawing information from various venues, in as a comprehensive a manner as possible, holds primacy. From snippets of such information, a holistic account, capable of conveying at least some aspects of what it is to be another, will begin to emerge without being overly hampered by a humanizing (or, in the case of other humans, for instance, Westernizing) gaze.

Moreover, non-human animals do communicate their own accounts if we just pay attention to their behaviours – that is, they "speak out" their experiences in bodily behaviours – and ideally narratives ceaselessly pay heed to these forms of first-person animal expressiveness (something to be addressed later in reference to "embodied empathy"). Furthermore, although the risk of combining elements of our own subjectivity with narratives concerning others is continuously present, the risk is perhaps to be accepted, for a completely "neutral" access to the personhood of another is an impossibility. No matter what approach we adopt, we are rooted in our own bodies, histories, mental states and concepts, and this will always impact how we make sense of reality. We are not neutral beings, nor could we become ones, and empathy always involves our situated "selves", us as non-neutral, non-abstract subjects with our own histories and contexts. The challenge is to avoid two extremes: colonizing the other with ourselves and losing ourselves into the ideals of complete "neutrality" or simulation. This issue will also be discussed in more detail later, and what suffices here is to note that narratives can, ideally, act as one way to inhabit this middle ground, for via narratives we seek to anchor ourselves to the mindedness of others by actively using our own subjective, imaginative outlook, thereby negotiating and moving between the categories of "I" and "other". (Of course, narratives can also be wildly one-sided, misleading and colonizing, but this is when we ignore their reference point – that is, the other individual and the ways in which she is self-expressing and "speaking out".)

Despite of their risks, narratives therefore hold much potential in permitting us to perceive and feel with the viewpoints of others – including when those others are utterly dissimilar and far removed. As Gallagher (2012) emphasizes, although narratives explain why we find it easier to empathize with those most like us, they also enable us to empathize with beings very different from ourselves. It may be easier to weave a story of a being who is close to oneself, but it is not at all impossible to construe a story of someone dissimilar or distant and, indeed, doing so may bring us closer to understanding her. It is for this reason that narratives are important if simulative empathy is to take place, as well as in relation to the most peculiar and distant of animals. At their best, narratives are a method of translating dissimilarity into something one can more fluently comprehend without replacing it with similarity: they invite understanding difference by using a familiar means, and this logic also can work well in efforts to projectively empathize with the subjectivity of other animals.

Therefore, we need simulative empathy, an imaginative gluing together of the non-human standpoint from various pieces of information, and narratives are one route to sparking such a process of informed imagination. One way to further clarify the role of narratives is through the use of literature. When constructing or telling narratives of other animals, actual stories – stories produced in literature – may be helpful. As highlighted by Martha Nussbaum, our ability to take the perspective of others is often enhanced by both approaching them as if they were characters in a novel and by reading novels. A "poetic" view into others, aided by literature, can thereby evoke an empathetic stance, for it invites us to identify with others and their various motivations and backgrounds (Nussbaum 1990). Arguably, it tends to be precisely simulative empathy which such stories ignite, for one identifies with the characters and thereby places oneself in their position, thus "becoming them". Literary stories are, therefore, one means towards and a manifestation of simulation, wherein we learn the context of the other and seek to understand her from within. This suggestion that literary stories aid empathy has been supported by many (Coplan 2004), and indeed studies have demonstrated that they can significantly improve our empathy skills (Shapiro, Morrison and Boker 2004) and that empathy toward fictional characters can spark empathy and ensuing action towards actual individuals who belong to the same stigmatized group as the character (see Batson et al. 2002). (A related form of cultivating empathy is theatre and acting – see Verducci 2000; Goldstein and Winner 2012 – but one could equally list film and television as potential sources of empathy development.)

As Mary-Catherine Harrison points out, contemporary research backs the conclusion that empathy towards literary characters does enhance our ability to empathize with real individuals – in fact, it is quite efficient in doing so. One example of this efficiency is Charles Dickens, who famously produced "social-problem literature" in order to enhance his readers' knowledge and concern for the plight of the less privileged: "If readers cried for fictional suffering, Dickens and many of his contemporaries believed, then they would try to ameliorate the actual suffering they encountered around them" (Harrison 2008, 262).[4] According to Harrison, the crucial requirement is that readers can categorize the fictional victim as belonging to a social group that they recognize from their own lived reality. This is exactly that Dickens made use of, as his literature is filled with characters who could easily be classified as socially recognizable "types" that one has encountered and has familiarity with (Harrison 2008).[5]

Therefore, fictional stories can invite empathy towards actual individuals as long as the stories bring forth characters with the sort of socially produced backgrounds that one can spot in everyday existence. Now, such fictional stories also may be beneficial in evoking projective and particularly simulative empathies towards non-human animals. First, literature helps us to re-examine our attitudes and invites, as Cora Diamond (2004) has suggested, "fellow-feeling". Second, it can directly contest social presumptions and injustices by bringing forth the subjectivity of those who tend to be socially, culturally or politically silenced, ignored or subjugated and by summoning empathic responses to their plight on a concrete, action-inducing level. Indeed, as Harrison (2008) notes, animal advocacy literature motives also can be depicted as a form of social-problem literature aimed at constituting empathy. Following the Dickensian logic, literature works in inciting socially effective, action-laden and concerned empathy towards non-human others when it invites familiarity with the animals, a form of recognition that individualizes them from the faceless, distant, generic mass of "animality" which animals are often depicted as belonging to. Paradoxically, familiarity requires that anthropomorphism is avoided, for it does not invite recognition. We know that piglets don't speak and that deer don't dance and cry, and hence familiarity that could be applied to lived reality is often missing – or at least, such familiarity is produced only in children and those with unrealistic conceptions of non-human animals. In short, anthropomorphism ultimately distances us from the very animal we are weeping with, for we cannot relate strongly fantastical characters to the animals that we can smell, touch, see or hear and thereby cannot identify the characters in the everyday tangibility of life.

The fictional animals that stir societally effective empathy are ones that we can identify in actual, lived existence: the sort of creatures who are not humanized into a caricature form but rather bring forth their specific forms of animality in ways that enable recognition. The task is to combine such familiarity with stories that simultaneously resist and challenge the sort of anthropocentric stereotypes that tend to nullify non-human subjectivity – hence, familiarity should be entwined with stories capable of extending our grasp of animality away from the stereotypic descriptions of animals (familiar in their own way because they have coloured cultural preconceptions of animals to such an extent that we are used to perceiving them as true depictions). Here, familiarity with tangible, living animals and empathic narratives capable of spurring it contest and even radically challenge the familiarity provided by generic, dualistic and faceless, or conversely caricatured and thereby empty, animal imagery. As such, narrative recognition is not about adhering to the status quo but about bringing forth the realistic subjectivity of those who tend to be marginalized – this was the theme in Dickens's literature and should also be the essence of pro-animal narratives. Hence, social-problem literature (and theatre, film, arts and other related arenas) in the context of non-human animals should, even when based on familiarity, push boundaries and evoke further, fresh understandings of animals capable of broadening our take on what it is to be a non-human.

Therefore, narratives based on both factual information and fictionalized accounts can move imaginative processes into action, leading to other-directed empathy wherein we imagine what it is like to be another *as* another (human or non-human). Arguably, such narratives form one important crux of understanding the inner terrains of others, and their absence is often the reason for failures in empathy: the lives of others are too rarely narrativized, and this adds to the all-too-common absences of empathy and the ignoring of foreign subjectivity. We need more narratives that focus on individual lives, and such narratives are particularly needed in the context of non-human animals, whom we rarely introduced or translated via stories. In short, we need animal stories in literature, film, television and theatre in order to be able to imaginatively simulate different varieties of non-human existence.

However, problems may also emerge when literature is used to entice empathy, and these problems shed light on the further risks of projection. The biggest threat is that literature can edit our empathy so that it is perfectly controlled, politically pleasing and bite-sized to such a degree that the audience is pacified, and empathy becomes entertainment rather than something that would evoke genuine moral concern.

On these lines, Megan Boler has criticized what she calls "passive empathy", found, for instance, in Martha Nussbaum's work. Within such empathy, reading literature is utilized in order for the self to delve into the lives of others, and the presumption is that this form of imaginative penetration suffices for one to form ethically aware understandings of others. Boler suggests that such empathic engagement may be inadequate in sparking moral action, for what we undergo in the grips of literature often rests on simplified, curtailed emotive responses in the midst of which the reader may at any time put the book down and think of something else. In other words, emotions are constantly controlled and kept pleasant, and when this is not the case, the reader can simply leave and forget about the characters she is meant to empathize with. As such, what was meant to invoke empathy can digress into bite-sized snippets that also reduce social issues into something easily digestible and which invite comfortable passivity and even abandonment rather than moral or political concern and action. In sum, Boler (2006) argues that Nussbaum's "poetic justice" approach, within which literature enables empathy and ultimately sparks notions of justice, may not adequately challenge how the reader perceives the world and thereby may fail to produce action. Furthermore, simplified and controlled, our emotions can be moulded so as to include only that which remains familiar, convenient and manageable. The middle-class person soaked in privilege can, as suggested earlier, project onto the literary characters of her choosing only that with which her political belief systems can cope. Indeed, Matthew Schertz (2007) warns that here empathy can be transformed into a method of societal, political control, and the warning appears well placed, as the political landscapes of novels can be interpreted and restricted in ways that support the reader's ideological commitments without ever offering the type of unsettling challenge capable of sparking new modes of comprehending others.

To add yet another element, when rendered as bite-sized, empathy can become something enjoyable: in the grips of literature, we can decide how to empathize, and even in the spheres of simulating the desperation and anguish of the character, the process can surface as a form of tranquil entertainment, for via control the emotions that otherwise hold the potential of destructive unbearableness are rendered manageable, orderly and easily experienced. When enjoying social realism literature, or any literature meant to provoke moral awareness and action, the danger is that the relevant emotions do not get to us with enough uncomfortable vivacity to cause concern. This, again, adds to the potential passivity of literature-produced empathy. Indeed, Susan Sontag has offered a poignant warning against depictions of suffering which transform experience into simulations empty of content and politics and ultimately into forms of enjoyable aesthetic. Analysing depictions of suffering in visual culture, she suggests that they hold the potential to accentuate the already historically potent tendency to render suffering into a curiosity and thereby into a source of amusement that entertains despite its raw content. The viewer wants to see more, to venture into the realms of horror, because this voyeurism remains safe and appeasing from the perspective of apolitical detachment – and in fact, often the replacements of the political, moral dimensions of suffering with pure aesthetics come with politics of their own, as the aestheticized images work to confirm dominating ideologies (Sontag 2004). Again, as a result we only want to witness those emotions, and in those degrees, which remain manageable, confirmative, safe and simplified. Like Boler, Sontag argues that such a pleasurable, edited view of suffering can lead to passivity instead of evoking moral action (ibid.).

Indeed, it has even been suggested that fictional stories may make one pay less attention to actual suffering. This was the concern of William James, who argued that while the rich cry at the sight of fictional characters in theatres, they let their coachmen freeze outside – for him, this superficial empathy, which found solace in imagined suffering while ignoring real suffering, was nothing less than monstrous (Harrison 2008). As noted by Harrison (ibid.), the ensuing "paradox of fiction" is that even though readers may seemingly empathize with literary characters, if their responses do not translate into real-life recognition, they remain disingenuous.

Simplification, pacification and entertainment can, thereby, be antithetical to other-directed empathy, as the other is substituted with politically motivated forms of aesthetics which hide from view the political ramifications of her plight and ultimately replace her with curtailed, biased and comfortable interpretations incapable of bringing forth an appreciation of the unique, politically situated subjectivity of others. In short, suffering caused by given political belief systems is depicted as apolitical and ultimately as a surface, an empty form lacking specificity and depth, from which one can gain enjoyment. Experience becomes stripped bare of its political, historical, localized mechanisms and fails to communicate the rawness of the other's emotions and to challenge how we standardly understand and position her. Moreover, the desirable end goal of empathy – action – is easily missing. What Dickens was striving for, and what Nussbaum perceives as a valuable venue for empathy and moral agency, may, therefore, also have its limitations. These are important criticisms, for they do not concern only fictional narratives but pose a risk to any type of narratives we construct of others. It is dangerously easy to narrativize others in ways that adhere to stereotypic prejudgements and which thereby remain comfortable – both on political and psychological levels. Even when seemingly other-directed, the middle-class witness of poverty can spin stories that depoliticize economic statuses, render it into a personal failing of the poor and thereby reduce empathy into something which conveniently fails to challenge one's own preconceptions and ideologies.

These are vital reminders in the non-human context as well. Empathy provoked by literature, or indeed by any method, such as images or imagination, may work to simplify and aestheticize non-human experience and render it into edited entertainment lacking historical and political dimensions, ignorant of the specific, raw experiences of animals. Narratives on animals may – next to Disnifying non-human emotion – depict that emotion as apolitical and as lacking historical ramifications and thereby may colour the process of empathy itself with pleasurable self-control, easily interlinked with political, anthropocentric orthodoxy. Here, we are invited to feel empathy for the cute, the proximate and the politically non-risky animals – the pandas and the elephants, who remain far enough removed from the lives of Westerners so as to never stir uncomfortable political questions, and the happy cats and dogs who act in humane ways and the depiction of whom does not contest cultural animal imageries. Even suffering that comes close and is political is often represented only in relation to those creatures, the plight of whom does not threaten the anthropocentric social order (shelter dogs), or it is depicted in terms that erase moral and political responsibility (for instance, via reference to "welfare legislations" and the reduction of animal suffering into individual, rare instances rather than something that is habitually and institutionally supported by those very legislations together with ideological suppositions and consumer practices). Therefore, political dimensions are easily removed or interpreted in ways that suit one's preexisting notions and agenda.

Simultaneously, empathy can be bite-sized and as such easily manageable, as one can put away the book or the film depicting animality when it risks becoming uncomfortable and move on to other things. This enables the pleasurableness of empathy, for one controls what kinds of emotions one wishes to empathize with and to what extent. A typical scenario is one in which a person will gladly read and watch happy tails of non-human animals (for instance, cute cat videos) but quickly recoil from scenes of suffering (footage of farmed animals suffering) – particularly, if they are related to her own politics and consumer choices. Empathy is, thereby, edited by the empathizer: she controls what she wishes to absorb. It is this that enables moral and political passivity, for the type of discomfort often required for one to truly grasp the causes and intensities of others' suffering, and to be stirred into questioning one's own culturally loaded beliefs and consumer choices, is missing, and thus anthropocentric notions that easily desubjectify other animals are never fully challenged. James's warning becomes significant here, as one may edit one's empathy to such an extent as not to apply it at all to the real world (this phenomenon all too often takes place when viewers cry over the film *Babe* while eating bacon). Even obvious moral and political problems can be addressed by rendering them bite-sized and removing them from the context of real non-human animals, simultaneously enabling those problems to become pleasurable rather than challenging and action provoking, and it is perhaps precisely this that allows McDonald's and Disney to form such a happy marriage.

Not only can such empathy coincide with strongly anthropocentric attitudes, as the meat eater cries in the face of the torments of dogs while neglecting the possibility of empathizing with the animals she eats, but it can also amplify those attitudes, as the meat eater may, on account of her own tears, demonstrate to herself that she does care, that she is moral in her relation to the non-human animals and that there is no need for a wider change because good people shiver and recoil at the sight of animal pain. Empathy can, thereby, become a ritual or a form of aesthetically orientated play which erases political awareness and the historicity and politics behind animal suffering by focusing narratives on matters which alleviate guilt and direct attention away from wider, real-life problems. This can confirm rather than disturb the anthropocentric order, and in so doing it ensures and validates the safety of one's own stance on animality. The tears risk remaining superficial, aimed at providing us with enjoyable experiences rather than teaching care towards all those others whom our actions may harm. Within such "entertainment empathy", projection moves towards a search for touching, moving texts and images that enable one to bathe pleasurably in sentiment without having to face moral and political realities.

Yet the situation need not be this grim. First of all, we need stories in order to meet non-human creatures – as already suggested, despite their potential risks, stories also hold the potential of being enormously productive. As Sontag posits, we in fact have a duty to listen to such stories and see such images, for it is via them that we can come face-to-face with the realities of suffering others. The argument is not, therefore, that stories ought to be removed but rather that they ought to be rendered political and made into something other than pure enjoyment. According to Sontag (2004), the way to achieve this is to enable criticism and action in the audience by colouring the images of suffering with moral and political dimensions. If suffering or other emotions that we empathize with when reading a book or looking at images or films are clearly attached to their broader moral and political landscapes – their contexts – rendering them "bite-sized" will become much more difficult, as will the act of embracing them with pure hedonism. Furthermore, an important element is demonstrating to the audiences how action is possible. Arguably, the feeling that there is nothing that we can do in order to help others, for the problems are too vast or beyond our control, is often the cause of pacification, and it can be fought by showing how action is always possible and often quite productive. By offering audiences ways in which they may fruitfully take action accordingly with their empathy, passivity and hedonism will become much less likely (this issue will be addressed later in relation to "compassion fatigue").

Moreover, perhaps entertainment value can be further limited and replaced with empathic concern by accentuating the rawness of the experiences of others and thereby preventing their modification into something easy to ignore. In other words, lending the joy and suffering of another a degree of intensity and reality can awake us to the concreteness of other lives and provoke reflection and response rather than diminish the whole process into effortlessly forgettable amusement. Therefore, if depoliticization, entertainment and self-serving, pacifying editing curtail the potentiality of narratives to produce empathy, the challenge is to rectify these problems by producing and offering narratives that situate the lives of others in their political context, offer those lives credible, tangible, realistic agency and introduce ways to take action.

Again, this is also applicable to animal narratives. Many will take a simplifying, apolitical, bite-sized stance towards animal suffering in particular because they feel that nothing can be done, that cows and pigs will be tormented and killed in the billions regardless of anything that people as individuals could do. The scale of animal suffering is enormously vast, so it is little wonder that it is easier to meet it via depoliticizing it, simplifying the issue and enjoying one's "love" and empathy as entertainment rather than as something that would spark moral and political action. Hence, the perceived inability to act may lessen the willingness to pay attention to politics, while the reality of both animals and their experiences is easily dampened by reducing animals into one-dimensional, uninteresting characters lacking the type of multilayered agency and concreteness that kindles concern.

The task is to bring in the moral and political dimensions of human-nonhuman relations, to make them more evident and to simultaneously offer ways in which action is possible (Aaltola 2014b). One example of this are stories of farmed animals which highlight the nuanced, complex and capable subjectivity of the animals and juxtapose it with details of anthropocentric presumptions and the type of actual consequences those presumptions have, manifested in and epitomized by industrial farming units. Bringing forth individual animal experiences while exploring the cultural, political, financial and consumeristic causes which tend to sideline those experiences can open up spaces for the sort of empathic responses and options for action capable of radically confronting the status quo. A similar approach can be used in private, imaginative projection and simulation, whereby we push ourselves to re-examine the political and cultural terrains that affect both animal lives and our own attitudes towards them; here, empathy does not only concern the present emotions of the animal but also takes into account what type of human politics impact them (relevant questions being where the animal comes from, what she is destined to and how she is affected by human choices).

In sum, narratives are also at risk of repeating the sort of problems plagued by self-directed projective empathy, including egoism and lack of genuine regard for the other. These problems are not necessary, however, as long as narratives make the effort to contextualize the emotions of the animals (making evident the historical, cultural or political causes of, for instance, suffering), highlight the solid, raw subjectivity of those animals and offer ways for the audiences to better the situation. This does not mean that stories ought to become "preachy" and thereby potentially quite off-putting, filled with nothing but political fervency and postulations of how to become vegan, but rather that they ought, with as much nuance and subtlety as they wish, to anchor human-non-human relations in their actual, historical settings; depict animals as their own, real creatures; and point towards how a different way of coexisting could be achieved. When these considerations are applied, it is simulative empathy which narratives invite, together with its other-directed benefits. Hence, it is such narratives that can aid simulative empathy and support the effort to envision what it may be like to exist as a pig or a cow.

PROJECTIVE AND SIMULATIVE MORALITY?

But what of the links between projection and moral agency? Do projective or simulative empathy support other-directedness and heterogenic openness? Evidently, only simulative empathy fulfils the first criterion. Indeed, self-directed projection appears quite harmful for moral agency, for it prevents us from properly acknowledging other beings and thereby also allows one to dismiss their needs and interests (such self-directedness may even become hedonism, as in the context of other animals, anthropomorphic animal "loving" easily transforms into something pleasurable while the objects of such "love" may be wholly mistreated – as an example of this, consider animals used for entertainment, including dolphins, whom the audiences claim to "love" but who are severely distressed by captivity). Quite simply, self-directed projection precludes the possibility of acknowledging others as creatures worthy of our serious attention and as such fails to accommodate moral agency, while other-directed simulation quite obviously fairs much better in this test.

Projective empathy fails in regard to openness, too, for instead of difference and specificity, we only see ourselves in the other, thus reducing difference and distinctness into bland sameness, wherein the "self" acts as the prototype of subjectivity and moral worth. In noting specificity and heterogeneity in others, again only other-directed simulative empathy completes the task. By mapping out the contexts and narratives of others, simulative empathy aims to comprehend their unique perspectives and emotions and indeed may succeed in this quite well, since simulating the situations and backgrounds of others offers much space for noting their particularity. Hence, simulation holds the prospect to entice us to identify the dissimilarity and even the peculiarity of others, thereby allocating space for the recognition that other subjects are their own diverse creatures and worthy without being assimilated into the prototypic "self". Therefore, self-directed projection (imagining oneself in the place of another and replacing the other with one's self) can be detrimental to moral agency, while simulative empathy (seeking to imaginatively become the other) may be quite supportive of and beneficial for our moral ability – both in relation to humans and other animals.

As seen, there are also pedagogic merits to simulative empathy, as it can act as a method of educating us towards a more morally embracive attitude towards others. It teaches us to pay attention to others' perspectives and also advances the development of different forms of empathy, particularly affective empathy (Batson et al. 2002). Via simulative empathy we are invited to recognize the myriad variance in how this world can be sensed and perceived – it summons us to pay note to the way in which perspectives differ, and in particular using imagination to access specificity in others is morally fruitful. Therefore, simulative empathy lures us to further the ability to recognize and value difference, which again aids in entering other modes of empathy (imagining the perspective of a pig can spark, for instance, resonation – the key ingredient of affective empathy – with her experiences). In this way, simulative empathy holds both direct and indirect value in enabling us to deepen our empathic and, ultimately, moral capacities. (Again, it must be stressed that such merits are probably short-lived in self-directed projection, for it merely promotes the notion that only similarity with the self has relevance; hence, even when it is a catalyst for resonation, it is our projected self in the other whom we are resonating with. It is essential to keep these two varieties apart, for they have quite different outcomes for our empathic and moral ability.)

Yet there are also difficulties which undermine both projective and simulative empathies' connections to moral agency. Many phenomenologists remain dubious over their starting point (a matter that will be revisited in the chapter on embodied empathy). The claim is that it presumes minds to be separate from one another, as if they existed in their own cells, with clearly and categorically distinguishing borders; hence, they exist atomistically – independently of each other. We are as if entirely internal creatures, locked into the privacy of our minds. The underlying assumption is that there is no direct access between minds and that the only way to understand another is to project oneself into her place or simulate her internal life. It is for this reason that Shaun Gallagher has criticized simulation theory, claiming that it is founded on solipsism, wherein we are encapsulated into our own minds and cannot know another without projection. Because of this starting premise, particularly underlying projection, Gallagher goes so far as to suggest that it "seems too restrictive and indeed seems to cheapen morality" because "I only have to simulate the affect rather than really feel it" (Gallagher 2012, 7; see also Blum 1988). The mistake, according to Gallagher, is to overlook that other minds are continuously merging with ours by impacting our experiences and engaging with us – minds are entangled and constantly expressing themselves to and affecting each other. Minds enmesh; how others feel and think affects my own mindedness and vice versa. Nobody is locked into their private, internal spheres but rather they experience things with and as a result of each other. The claim is that projection and simulation simply rest on a mistaken view of what minds are and as such also offer a crooked, shallow approach to morality.

Hence, it is suggested that projective and simulative empathies by necessity overlook how tangibly others co-constitute our experiences and mindedness and how, for this reason, we do not need to transport ourselves into their position nor simulate them from afar in order to grasp them.[6] The basic error is that of ignoring the interaction and engagement between minds (or more specifically, embodied minds). Gallagher summarizes this ethos, together with the foundational problem of simulation theory, in the following: "Our understanding of others and their situations, and hence the possibility of empathizing with them, is not based on attempts to get into their heads in a mentalising fashion, since we already have access to their embodied actions and the rich, worldly contexts within which they act" (Gallagher 2012, 21). Dan Zahavi has offered similar criticism. Correlating projection with simulation theory, Zahavi argues that on the level of lived experience, it remains wholly superfluous: we do not project ourselves, our own identities, onto others in order to recognize their mental states. He refers to Wittgenstein's question, "Do you look into yourself in order to recognise the fury in his face?" (Wittgenstein 1992, #220), and suggests that this type of projection is only utilized in the context of prediction or control (Zahavi 2008). What stands at the root of projective and simulative empathies is a distinctly odd understanding of mentation, succinctly and famously criticized by phenomenologists, within which the mind and the body remain separated and the former are encapsulated into the latter, as if our bodies did not constantly both affect and express mindedness, and thereby form the arena via which the experiences and thoughts of different individuals can be related to and accessed (ibid.). It is precisely through embodied contact and interaction that we come to know others – no projection or simulation is needed. The moral potency of projection and simulation is significantly amplified by grounding them in embodied engagement rather than atomism: via such grounding, they become less superficial and more proficient at other-directedness and noting of heterogeneity.

Ultimately, the issue of what it is to be a "self", and to know other "selves", stands at the root of projective and simulative empathies. Within atomism, the "self" exists as a division between the body and the mind, and between oneself and others, and makes empathy at worst a process of assimilation, whereby the authenticity, difference, uniqueness and primordiality of others remain elusive, and at best a dive into the other that rests more on imagination than actual, emotional correspondence. Simulative empathy can invite other-directedness and heterogenic openness, particularly when aimed towards the other being via contexts and narratives, and here lies its educative promise and moral potential; yet something more may be needed for a deeper comprehension of others. This is because despite of its good intentions, simulative empathy reaffirms the notion that an abyss lies between ourselves and others, and hence efforts to project and simulate are ultimately like throwing ropes from one prison tower into another: the rope can create connections, but nonetheless the prisoners remain separated in their states of isolation.

When seeking to grasp what it is like to be a mink or a raven projectively, one will, thereby, risk repeating the atomistic presumption that highlights solipsism. In relation to non-human animals, such atomism and solipsism are perhaps more obvious than anywhere else, for they are supported by anthropocentric beliefs according to which human minds exist separately from those of other animals, following a clear, uncrossable border between the two which gives birth to the sceptical question that has haunted Western thinking for centuries: How could we ever know anything certain about the minds of other animals? Quite dangerously, projective and simulative empathies can thereby reaffirm anthropocentric doubt over non-human minds. Since imagination rests on the atomistic presumption of distance and impenetrability, its very starting point easily nullifies its efforts, and hence the human eager to empathize with a fox may continually be frustrated over whether she actually knows anything or whether it is all her own fantasy.[7]

The element missing is engagement with the animal so that her mindedness can communicate with and impact our own mindedness, thereby rendering her emotions more readily accessible for humans to understand. In projective and simulative empathies, interaction is not a necessity, nor is the bodily presence of another, and it is this that may greatly limit the scope of those empathies, as well as their links to moral agency. Without the presence of the pig or the hen, in all her peculiarity, we easily remain stuck in our own emotions, harnessed only with our own mentation – regardless of how much we seek to see beyond. What is required, thereby, is engagement with others wherein our bodies communicate our minds to them and vice versa and wherein mental states impact and entwine with each other, thus enabling access, understanding and moral recognition.

This does not mean that we ought to have direct, embodied contact with all those we empathize with. What suffices is that we have some of such contact with other animals, which we can then use as a platform on the basis of which to approach those we never encounter. Having actual, physical engagements with one pig can help to broaden our conception of animality so that we can more fruitfully seek to comprehend those pigs or cows we are and remain unfamiliar with. Nor does this mean that simulative empathy is always a faulty option and something to be avoided. It can be vastly beneficial, as long as it is rooted in interaction between minds rather than atomistic solipsism. The aim should be to let ourselves and our minds become open to the influences of the other and to build understanding of that other on such openness so that simulative efforts also feed from it. We cannot physically encounter all the pigs of this world, and simulation aided by narratives and contexts is a good tool to envision those we do not know, but it ought to be anchored in notions of engagement rather than isolation. Hence, Gallagher and others go too far in suggesting that simulation is always to be shunned – it isn't, as long as it is informed by previous exposures to the embodied mindedness of others.

Bringing such an element into human-non-human relations could help to broaden our conception of what an animal "self" is. Anthropocentrism has heavily accentuated the belief that the "human self" consists primarily of a mind, anchored in, yet dualistically separated from, a much less significant body, and the belief that the "animal self" is nothing but a body or its instinctive responses, inaccessible to humans and projective empathy – albeit often unwittingly – risks repeating and reaffirming this presumption. Challenging atomism could thereby also help us to challenge anthropocentrism, as the dualistic divide between "human minds" and "animal bodies" would be eradicated. Reinforcing the notion that minds and bodies, us and others, entwine and impact each other would enable the "human self" to notice that she, too, is an animal existing in an animal body capable of communicating with and understanding other animals and that the non-human animal is equally a being with a mind capable of impacting our own mentation. Relocating projection away from divides and basing it on direct, embodied exchanges between us and others could combat the very foundation of anthropocentric presumptions.

In letting ourselves become impacted by and engaged with other animals, we are embarking on something quite radical, for arguably anthropocentric dualisms have led to a situation where, due to assuming that doing so is impossible, we refuse to enter into states of direct access and appreciation. Many will walk past pigs and remain mentally closed off from any possibility of paying attention to or being affected by their experiential states, and many will hold on to scepticism for the same reason. The act of eradicating atomistic presumptions, entangled with anthropocentrism, can thereby open wholly new possibilities for knowing animal mentation.

Caution should be used when it comes to the foundation of simulative empathy, but not all hope is lost. When basing that simulation on experiences of actual, open and mutually impacting encounters with other animals, it can be quite productive. This, however, requires that simulative empathy learns from embodied empathy – alone it struggles.

Before continuing, one more danger, which also points towards the need of embodied encounters and which has already been alluded to, warrants more attention. There is another atomism-related hurdle posed in the way of particularly self-directed projective empathy and its normative status: egoism. The self is transported into the position of the other creature, extended to cover her and take her place. If we cannot leave our state of isolation, if we truly are imprisoned in the solitude of our own minds and if others will thus forever remain inaccessible mysteries, the only option left is to expand the scope of that isolation so as to include others within it; shouting out from our prison tower, we hear our own echoes, not the replies of others. The incomprehensible is substituted with the comprehensible, the unfamiliar with the familiar and the other with the self.[8] Such a process amounts to egoism because it warrants the self with authorship over others and in so doing eradicates the latter's independence, leaving them at the mercy of the powers of the self.

Max Scheler, a philosopher whom we shall return to in the chapter on embodied empathy, was acutely critical of projective empathy from this standpoint. He claimed that projective empathy makes its most fateful blunder in ignoring the other self and replacing her with the empathizer: "'How would it be if this had happened to me?' Whatever the place such a comparison may occupy in life, it certainly has nothing to do with genuine fellow-feeling. . . . True fellow-feeling betrays itself in the very fact that it includes the existence and character of the other person as an individual" (Scheler 2009, 39). We are not to compare the other to ourselves, for this fails to do justice to the uniqueness of the other and suffocates her inside the perimeters of the self: "Wherever fellow-feeling has a direct reference to the other person, as such, or to the individual uniqueness of his sorrow or joy . . . it follows that 'comparison' must already be ruled out as insufficient for an understanding of the situation" (ibid., 40). Consequently, projective empathy is egoistic; within it, we feel with our own emotions, not those of others: "Our attitude would indeed appear, phenomenologically speaking, to be directed merely upon our own sorrow or joy, and therefore be an egoistic one" (ibid., 40). Here, empathy becomes "a self-regarding emotional reaction" (ibid., 40) which egoistically focuses on oneself and wholly leaves the other outside of the equation.

This egoism flashes continually in human-non-human relations. It exists not only in anthropomorphism but also in mislead accusations of anthropomorphism – that is, egoism is evident both in falsely depicting pigs as humans and in claiming that all recognition of mentation in pigs is anthropomorphic. The latter is a common affair, as it is often sceptically argued that since we cannot know for sure what it is like to be a pig, any positive assertions concerning pigs' mental abilities are anthropomorphic. Hence, the sceptic may staunchly assert that all recognition of animal mentation is founded upon the expansion of the human self, the naive broadening of one's own mental ability to engulf and explain the behaviour of other animals. Therefore, the denial of non-human mentation also repeats the egoistic logic: here, the other is not assimilated into the self but rather her whole existence is denied on account that she is external to the latter. In both instances, the self is seen as the definer and dictator of others.

The most worrisome aspect of such egoism is the incapacity to notice and feel awe at specificity and difference. Non-human animals are not recognized in their partial unfathomability, peculiarity and particularity – instead, they are replaced with the dullness of that which is familiar to the human mind. What could have astounding colour, depth and variance – the utterly heterogenic animal world with is unique, inimitable capacities and ways of perceiving and relating – is lost. Recognition of similarities is vital, and one ought never to insist on full difference or abysses between species, for this again presumes the anthropocentric notion that humans must be wholly, categorically different from other animals. However, recognition of difference is equally vital, for without it we sink into anthropocentrism from the opposing end – that of presuming that it is only via sameness that animals can be understood and valued and of thereby feeding an egoistic orientation towards the world. Here, moral agency struggles because other animals are not acknowledged or respected as the type of beings they are in themselves, whose harms, subjectivity or uniqueness matters, but rather as empty extensions of human interest.

Thus, in transferring ourselves into the position of another, thereby replacing her, we ultimately ignore her unique subjecthood. In this process, opacity and specificity are lost, and a form of narcissistic anthropomorphism may suddenly emerge as the human contemplates how she would feel in the position of a cow or a whale without recognition that such contemplation makes no sense, for others are not us. Here, we only see mirror images and echoes of ourselves in the world – from thinking that we can only know ourselves, we move to assuming that others are like ourselves. What a cow or a whale senses and experiences is buried under human imagination and assimilated into the human ego. Such projection serves to affirm the type of human bias that takes note of only that which is humanlike and restates that only the human viewpoint stands as viable and legitimate. This standpoint fails to achieve immediacy with others, for there is no "with", and acts as a frail foundation for interaction with those others, for there are no "others". On the level of practice, results of such narcissistic projection can be grotesque and familiar from above. Foxes in fur farms or pigs in crates may appear as mentally dull or (even worse) happy animals, for we may not see in them the type of behaviour we ourselves would undergo in captivity. Animals who do not behave like humans will, then, frustrate self-directed projective empathy, and since difference is not offered adequate space, one may smugly declare that all is well within the anthropocentric regime. As such, projective empathy may even feed contempt and hierarchies; the disappointment of not seeing little people in foxes and sheep will serve to justify their substandard treatment.

Simulative empathy is more promising in this regard. We ought to try and imagine what it would be like to be a chicken or a jaguar. Yet an important question remains: On what grounds can imagination be used? Are these abstract questions, to be pondered in one's living room or on the pages of fiction books, or questions that require contact with the animal world? Again, it is embodied interaction with other animals that emerges as something which can significantly deepen understanding and help to eradicate atomism. The processes of simulation require pre-exposure of the embodied sort in order to function fully and to recognize that we are not creatures secluded from the mentation of other animals. Without this, it gives us an imagery of non-human animals constructed by humans, our way of perceiving animality, and un-co-authored by the uniqueness and difference of what it is to be a cat or a rat. Simulation may spark something, cause upheavals, moments of clarity and the ensuing need to reorient towards others with concern and openness; yet it alone will not suffice. On its own, simulation remains a light beaming in the right direction without embodied forms against which to reflect. Interaction with other animals can, thereby, offer more substance to simulative empathy, remove atomism from its background and enable us to perceive difference and particularity in other animals – most importantly, it helps to remove egoism by reminding us that these truly are their own, unique beings, not "little, furry people". Therefore, again, simulation benefits from embodied empathy and the type of intersubjectivity it inspires – the subject of the fourth chapter. Before exploring embodied empathy, two other entirely different and equally salient forms of empathy warrant focus.

NOTES

1. The emphasis on context lays the ground for further definitions of empathy. For instance, "conditional sympathy" refers to basing empathy entirely on the

context while trying to assess how a generic "we" would experience it (Rick 2007).

2. According to Jonathan Haidt (2003a), moral education aimed at strengthening positive moral emotions may well be more effective than the standard route of offering reasoned arguments.

3. Arguably, this type of extreme projection often ultimately functions to legitimize the sidelining of animal-mindedness. When we witness Disneyfied animals speaking and dancing, we know that it is not really the animal who does so but a humanized version of the animal – empty animal forms on to which human mentation is projected help to reaffirm the boundary between species by reminding us of its existence. Paradoxically, humanized pigs legitimize dualism, for in their obvious anthropomorphism, they point towards the "real" differences under fictional similarities. Indeed, they may become a type of comic parody, wherein humour and cuteness are based on combining two apparently opposite categories. Humans acting as non-human animals and vice versa spark lightheartedness, for the audience is supposed to know that in reality these are two very different and contradictory categories. The function that such parody serves is to stabilize the borders between species categories and keep them distinct. (On this notion of parody, see Bergson 2005.) Therefore, self-directed projection may not only ignore the animal by replacing her with human mentation, but it may also help to strengthen the presupposed divide between humans and other animals. Of course, at times (and, indeed, perhaps often) anthropomorphic animals may also invite concern, but if such concern is based on mistaken projection, it cannot have long-lasting, productive consequences (i.e., when one learns that sheep are not little people in sheep bodies, one may suddenly decide not to be concerned over their futures).

4. Dickens did harbour worries concerning the possibility that his readers may not enact their concern and thereby would refrain from alleviating the plight that they witnessed, and indeed he was keenly aware of the risks of sentimentalism, which included the perturbing possibility that readers would merely weep instead of acting. However, these reservations were not robust enough to deter him from the belief that representations of emotion could spark politically, morally aware forms of empathy in his readers (Harrison 2008).

5. The aim was inviting pathos or feeling, which again would ultimately lead to real and realistic emotions towards real people: in this sense, sentimentality was a method of achieving realism in our social relations (Harrison 2008). One could argue that in order to be effective, pathos needs to be of a certain variety: not of the kind that becomes purely pleasurable but of the variety that also disturbs. Here, the reader does not gain comfort from happy endings, but rather the story leaves open the need to care and the need to act; such pathos would not offer closure but would rather push the audience towards seeking that closure via their own actions in the social world.

6. This type of criticism spawns not only from phenomenology but also for "enactivism", a theory of mind which stipulates that mindedness spurs into being, both in form and content, from interrelations with others and the surrounding world.

7. Perhaps it is precisely atomism which paves the way for anthropomorphism, as familiarity is projected onto those who are also marked by evident difference simply

because it is presumed that difference cannot be accessed or known, for non-human minds remain enclosed into their own worlds and are entirely excluded from human imagination.

8. Such egoism is also argued to follow literature as an educational tool for empathy. Megan Boler posits that in the context of literature, empathy can be inherently selfish, for one fears that what happens to another could happen to oneself: "'I know what I am feeling because I fear that it could happen to me'. The agent of empathy, then, is in fear for oneself" (Boler 2006, 260). Here, empathy eradicates the other by erasing her difference and assimilating her into oneself, and thus the empathizer's claim to "know" the other can emerge as a patronizing act. This, for Boler, constitutes the "psychosis of our time" (ibid.). As Schertz summarizes, "I do not really ever learn to know the other at all, but can only imagine myself as other. In the end we are left with a self-aggrandizing subject who acts out of fear. It follows that actions are only initiated for the preservation of the self" (Schertz 2007, 188). Yet the critique is too strong, for there are different, more allowing and less egoistic ways of empathizing with characters, in line with simulative empathy.

Chapter 3

Cognitive Empathy

David Hume stands as the key figure behind the sort of modern moral theory that is willing to take psychology and particularly emotions into account. As already pointed out, for Hume morality was not primarily a matter of rational inference and logical analysis but rather found origins in emotive responding – it is our sentiments towards ourselves, others and the world that go on to construct the foundations of morality. Thereby, whereas Immanuel Kant suggested that a person soaked in sympathy but incapable of using reason was not a full moral agent[1], while a person stripped of sympathy while being wholly rational was, for Hume, things are rather different.[2] Morality stems from emotions or "sentiments", and – importantly – is none the worse for being so construed. The most basic building blocks are found from our emotive responses towards pain and joy – responses which make us disvalue and value the sources of these experiences. Starting from such responses, we go on to build other emotions and complex moral belief systems, inclusive of various virtues.

Among the different emotions, Hume paid particular emphasis to empathy (or what he called "sympathy" but in a fashion akin to current usages of "empathy"). For him, empathy played a pivotal role in morality because it allows one to note not only one's own emotions but also those of others. Without empathy, our emotive responses would lead to values limited to ourselves, whereas via empathy we instantaneously can also perceive value in relation to others. Simply stated, this is because empathy allows us to flow with and grasp the experiences and emotions of others: we no longer have emotive responses only towards our own pain but also towards that of others. On these grounds, Hume went on to define empathy (sympathy) as the most astonishing quality in us (and in many other animals, as he was careful to point out): "No quality of human nature is more remarkable, both in itself and in its consequences, than that propensity we have to sympathize with others, and to receive by communication their inclinations and sentiments, however different from, or even contrary to, our own" (Hume 1969, 367).

This sentence reflects what is often ignored in both moral theory span around reason and everyday rationalistic moral discourse: without the capacity to feel with others, to instantaneously share their experiences, we would exist as the lonely atoms of the previous chapter, forever incapable of grasping others on an experiential level and also left alone in morality. Empathy is not just one emotion next to many but the key to entering the emotions of others, the threshold of facing others as morally worthy "subjects", and as such it stands as an astounding feature of the human (and often non-human) mind. The sentence also reflects what is frequently sidelined in contemporary moral discourse: that we can feel empathy towards and also perceive value in those who are utterly different from us. The era of anthropocentrism is founded on in-group thinking, according to which it is only those like "us" who can be the appropriate targets of empathy, and Hume defies this stubborn exclusiveness by rendering it abundantly clear that empathy is much more expandable.

For Hume, empathy is shaped by first observing *impressions* (bodily behaviours such as a painful grimace) in others, then constructing *ideas* ("She is in pain.") concerning those behaviours and finally letting the ideas become impressions felt in oneself. In short, we perceive bodily behaviours, develop an idea of what experiences or emotions are causing them and then feel the experiences or emotions within ourselves (Hume 1969, 367–68). Hume summarizes: "'Tis indeed evident, that when we sympathise with the passions and sentiments of others, these movements appear at first in our mind as mere ideas, and are conceiv'd to belong to another person, as we conceive any other matter of fact. 'Tis also evident, that the ideas of the affections of others are converted into the very impressions they represent" (Hume 1969, 370). Thereby, observations of others are transformed into emotions, rendered into tangible states in oneself. Here, particularly, one feature emerges as significant: resonation. Empathy is ultimately resonation with the experiences and emotions of others – that is, we undergo similar impressions with others and feel sadness or excitement with them. Thus, Hume suggests that minds are "mirrors to one another, not only because they reflect each other's emotions, but also because those rays of passions, sentiments and opinions may be often reverberated" (Hume 1969, 414). Like a wave hitting a reef can make that reef flow in its sync, we begin to flow in sync with the emotions of others. This is perhaps the most astonishing part of empathy: the capacity to become primordially, experientially open to the experiences of others.

Therefore, empathy is born from (1) perceptively and conceptually noting impressions in others and (2) resonating with those impressions and their underlying emotions. But can such a state be considered an accurate source of knowledge concerning others? Hume was adamant that empathy is a valid way of understanding others. According to him, empathy offers us accurate representations of the emotive states of others simply because we undergo the very same state as they do, with the only difference being that its intensity is lower than that of the original. When we empathize with others, our feeling can have "such a degree of force and vivacity, as to become the very passion itself, and produce an equal emotion, as any original affection" (Hume 1969, 367). It is not an interpretation of the suffering or joy of others that we feel in our own bodies but rather the same suffering, the same joy that moved the other in front of us, and this in Hume's opinion renders empathy into a highly accurate way of knowing the emotions of other beings. Hence, Hume believed strongly in the accuracy of empathy (a matter that will be discussed in more detail later).

Interestingly, Hume's stance on empathy fits smoothly with two contemporary definitions. First, the notion of noting emotions in others by reading their impressions or behaviours and forming an idea on the grounds of this reading matches what in contemporary literature is called "cognitive empathy". Second, letting the emotions of others become impressions or behaviours in oneself – that is, resonating with them – follows the formula of what is now called "affective" or "emotive empathy". (It should be noted that for Hume, the formation of an idea and the following state of reverberation went together, and therefore he would not have separated these two states; however, making a distinction between them opens the door for contemporary discussion on empathy.)

This chapter focuses on the first of these – cognitive empathy – and affective empathy will be discussed in the next chapter.

DEFINITION

Cognitive empathy refers to either inferring or instantly perceiving emotive states in others. Here, we note facial expressions, behaviours, tones of voice, ways of touching and form a representation concerning the emotions that trigger them. With instant perception, a fraction of a second can be enough for one to note, say, fear in another creature – here, empathy is something akin to "translation", within which perception deciphers or interprets the mental states of others into a form we ourselves can cognitively understand (Blair 2005, 702; Book, Quinsey and Langford 2007), as we "read" behaviours in others and almost immediately come up with a category for the emotion we take them to be undergoing. One glance at, or sound from, another can be enough for us to instantly conceptualize their emotion as love or disgust. With inference, the process is more laborious and less immediate. We look for evidence, roam for different clues in the behaviours of another and go through different hypotheses in order to conclude whether the other individual is in a state of anger, fear or something else – this form of cognitive empathy requires at times lengthy thought processing based on not only the evidence right in front of us but also our prior knowledge of the individual in question. Inferential cognitive empathy, thereby, "involves setting aside one's own current perspective, attributing a mental state (or 'attitude') to the other person, and then inferring the likely content of their mental state, given the experience of that person" (Baron-Cohen and Wheelwright 2004, 164).[3] We are to step back, concentrate on noting the other and rationally conclude what she is undergoing. In both perception and inference, the context will have a strong impact on how we interpret the other (see Barrett 2017).

Crucially, cognitive empathy in itself is an emotively cool, relatively neutral state, even if it can evoke other, more emotionally engaged types of empathy. It allows one to note pain, anxiety or suffering without much affective movement in oneself. Thereby, cognitive empathy relies more on "theory of mind" than emotions (Blair 2008); it is a truly cognitive, reason-based state, centred on comprehension rather than affect and related to knowledge claims concerning the mind of another rather than emotive flowing with her. We do not feel what others feel but only note, from a detached perspective, what they feel. As such, it comes close to the "theory-theory" approach to empathy, mentioned in the introduction. Whereas projective and simulative empathies are "simulation-theory", cognitive empathy gains impetus from approaching others via a rationalizing distance, where we interpret and explain their behaviours on account of theories (be they culturally stereotypic explanations or our own hypotheses built on prior observation) concerning mindedness. If simulation often draws from the first-person perspective ("If I were her, I would feel sorrow."), cognitive empathy is founded on the third-person perspective ("Because she shivers, she must be excited.") that one seeks to construct from observation and inference.

Here, two things need bearing in mind. First, as will become evident, cognitive empathy does not necessarily lead to accurate readings of others, and a critic could complain that it is not "observation" but rather "interpretation". As pointed out in the introduction, how we perceive reality is our own construction, and this also applies to cognitive empathy. Hence, the choice of words such as "observation" should not be taken as a declaration of objective truths. Second, it too is influenced by the affective level. It gives us an impression of neutrality and aims towards a lesser use of emotion but is nonetheless embedded in our constructive, interpretative, affective constitution – its neutrality is not complete.

Despite of its relative detachment, cognitive empathy fulfils an important role in our understanding of others, for efforts towards emotional non-involvement can be needed for a holistic take on another's mindedness. Indeed, despite of their many merits, emotions can, in given conditions, muddle one's capacity to comprehend the mental states of other subjects. To take the example of affection, it can invite us to note the other being in her uniqueness but also runs the risk of leading to misconceptions, as an affectious gaze may cloud many of those characteristics and emotions of the other that do not, for instance, match our interpretation, and thereby (as all those who have fallen literally "madly" in love can recall) it renders us prone to perceiving only what we wish to perceive. Similarly, hate would offer a rather skewed account of its subject, accentuating flaws and negative emotions while ignoring the nuanced or positive in the other. Cognitive empathy facilitates a more neutral form of understanding and can stir us to also notice those elements which affection or hate would wish to hide – it also pushes us to question whether our emotively laden interpretations are correct and hence enables critical explorations into the mind of the other. Such an outlook allows a step back from the sort of emotively coloured beliefs concerning others that we tend to follow and can be required for us to know what the other is like in herself rather than what she appears to be in our own emotional horizons. Cognitive empathy brings reason clearly into the equation and, interestingly, matches it with empathic capacities; as such, it serves the role many rationalists, such as Plato, saw reason to carry: it can enable one to govern emotive interpretations in our effort to understand. Although emotion is pivotal (as the soon-to-be-mentioned downsides of cognitive empathy manifest), the value of more neutral, reasoned comprehension should not be underestimated.

Therefore, the detachment cognitive empathy invites may at times even be necessary for one's knowledge of others. Varying from immediate perception of emotions (for instance, from their expressions) to more time-consuming inference ("Why did she look at me like that?"), cognitive empathy is required for one to know others in ways that rest on observation from afar and can thereby facilitate more precise and succinct ways of knowing – in given contexts. This is important for two reasons: first, because it can lead to a more truthful depiction of the other, and thereby do better justice to her, and second because it can keep us from being misled by the other. In relation to doing justice to the other, the intentions and aims of others, their prior experiences, life narratives and specific viewpoints at times open up only when we withdraw to some extent from our own emotions, which tie us to our personal needs and perspective – in other words, highly emotive readings can also be highly self-directed, revolving more around what we feel than the mental states of the other being. This is something often ignored in research highly embracive of emotions, as the image frequently is that emotions are always enabling and orientated towards the other. If we are to avoid the stereotypic negative view on emotions as factors that only hinder understanding, we should be equally dubious of an overly optimistic, uncritical celebration of emotions, for they can be exceedingly self-orientated and thereby biased. The task is to channel emotions in ways that facilitate realistic other-directedness, and cognitive empathy can be one such vehicle.

In regard to the second reason, following only emotive ways of relating to others risks rendering us quite hapless, for we might become incapable of reading their true intentions and mental states. Adam J. Smith (a contemporary author, with the classic Adam Smith as a namesake) argues that from the viewpoint of evolutionary functionality, cognitive empathy is pivotal precisely for the latter reason. It enables the type of social awareness that is required to note deception and manipulation undertaken by others – in other words, its inherent detachment ensues the all-important metalevel from which to scrutinize whether our emotive responses to and readings of others are accurate or whether we are being misled (A. J. Smith 2006). More broadly, cognitive empathy allows us to dive more vividly below the surface, into the underlying causes and qualities of emotions.

Cognitive empathy is often used in human encounters with other animals. Hunters can perceive the emotive states of the elks and deer they are chasing, and farmers use their detached observations of the fear, curiosity or pain of goats and geese in order to coax them to desired ways of behaving. Yet the context of cognitive empathy need not always be that of utilizing other animals. It is also required when we wish to neutrally observe what our canine or feline companions are undergoing, and it offers a tool which scientists wishing to understand animal cognition and behaviour can use in order to build a reflected take on non-human minds. In short, cognitive empathy offers a way of knowing other animals, and this knowledge can be used in a myriad of ways – for exploitation as well as for sympathetic observation. Both instant perception (say, of the vocalizations of pigs) and prolonged inference (say, a scientist perplexing over a given behaviour in dogs) are frequently used in our dealings with other animals as we form ideas of their bodily behaviours and make conclusions over how they must be feeling. The whole process – although it can lead to emotive involvement – in itself is relatively non-emotive, as the human is affectively disengaged with the fear or the vibrant happiness of the pig or the dog.

Also in relation to non-human animals, cognitive empathy and its detachment may be important simply because acknowledging the other animal in her uniqueness may require, depending on the context, some distance from personal emotions. Even someone with intense affection for her non-human companion can become misled by that affection to such a degree that she no longer notes the specific needs of the animal. She may, for instance, wilfully ignore signs of unhappiness, discomfort or illness because her love prevents her from accepting manifestations of anything that are threatening to that love. Those with anger, contempt or resentment towards non-humans are particularly prone to such emotive distortions, as the farmer may interpret the behaviour of pigs refusing to move due to intense fear as something malevolent and "cocky" and thereby altogether fail to understand the animals' mental workings. Again, the danger is that humans become too involved with and enclosed to their own emotions – positive or negative – in order to truly note what the animal is undergoing, and such self-directedness can even spark grotesque misinterpretations (such as when wolves are depicted as conniving, destructive aggressors by those who disproportionately fear and hate them). Cognitive empathy helps us to step back from self-directed emotiveness and to note the animal and her mental states in a richer, more nuanced light. It may also direct us to grasp what other animals are hiding or what is veiled under or coded into their behaviour. For instance, prey animals can hide vulnerability and fear under seemingly confusing behaviours, and it takes a trained observer to see behind the surface. More commonly, animal emotions are "concealed" into radically different mannerisms than those we are used to in other humans, and their curiosity, envy, excitement or love can gain quite distinct outward appearances which are difficult to decipher. Again, cognitive empathy can offer the much-required method for understanding.

Hence, cognitive empathy is helpful. Without it, one would not grasp animality as fully as is possible, for cognitive empathy enables the reaching towards the intentions and beliefs, histories and contexts that underlie the experiences of hedgehogs and foxes. It is a way of moving beneath the exterior; its aim towards neutrality rather than emotive involvement enables the sort of a critical standpoint from which to evaluate the accuracy of our own interpretations. Being able to partly detach from the felt immediacy of things lends the perspective that is at times required to know why and ultimately what another animal feels – whether what appears as joy is actually an effort to please or whether apparent anger is in fact fear. With emotive attunement alone, the complexities of non-human mentation would be, in some settings and to some extent, lost, as only that which is readily felt, egoistically or not, within interaction would surface as relevant. All this points towards one of the pivotal roles of cognitive empathy: manifesting the type of depth and complexity in others that emotional involvement alone at times struggles to kindle. In short, we are often more than can be detected in instant interaction, and here cognitive empathy may serve a fruitful function in shedding light onto the less obviously present emotions and motivations guiding us and other animals. Inference has its place in appreciating animality, particularly when those we aim to appreciate are quite dissimilar and their mental states therefore are more challenging to notice.

Yet detachment may become overt and, instead of furthering knowledge of the pig or the hen, hinder or even prevent such knowledge. As argued in the introduction, reason and emotive ability are entwined with and in need of the support of each other. Relying too readily on emotions can lead to biased, distorted perceptions, but this is also the case with seeking to rely solely on reason. Efforts towards sheer detachment, aloofness and rational calculus will fail, in their emotional hollowness, to grasp the content of the emotions in others and will be inclined instead to search for logical reasons under the behaviour of other subjects – reasons which rarely apply simply because we are not logical creatures. Instead of acknowledging that another is behaving out of emotion, the disengaged observer may begin a cynical quest for mapping out underlying rational motives that explain emotion away. What was done out of love may be described as an act done out of self-gain – indeed, natural sciences have been quite eager with explanations such as these. For instance, evolutionary sciences may depict all human affection, hate and love as nothing but meaningless movements in the game of "selfish genes" (the underlying presumed causes), and non-human emotions are explained away by reference to mechanical, self-preserving "instincts". Overt detachment, the striving towards complete emotional involvement, sparks inept, misguided and mechanical depictions of mindedness.

In the context of other animals, this is evident when detachment entwines with scepticism. Within the already mentioned sceptical tradition, we are to doubt the existence of other minds and their contents until we are offered certain proof – until then, the underlying causes are presumed to be purely mechanical in nature. This is an issue that has plagued the understanding of other animals for centuries, particularly in Western cultures, as reliance on inference and the constant demand for evidence has led to dogmatic assumptions, according to which non-human creatures do not have minds until adequate, scientific evidence is found – assumptions which have played no small part in the anthropocentric insistence that animals are objects of use rather than subjects of moral value.

Cognitive empathy as perception can invite immediate belief in the mindedness of the other, but cognitive empathy as inference can alienate us from that other and her emotions to such an extent that we begin to doubt all aspects of her subjectivity. When an ethologist perceives mental states in pigs, she will probably note the animals' subjectivity at least to some degree, but when she begins to infer if behaviour X really signifies the capacity to have emotions, she may become quite disconnected from such subjectivity and instead immerse herself in the forever doubtful, cynical attitude which presumes that other animals are instinctual automata until proven otherwise. The sceptic simply cannot note non-human emotions in their vividness and richness because she is so withdrawn from her own affective zones, and this spurs the mission for some mechanized and therefore logical cause for those behaviours of cats and rats that actually root from emotion. The consequences of emotive withdrawal can, therefore, be quite dangerous, as they may do nothing less than nullify the emotions and thereby the subjectivity of others. Scepticism faces severe problems, for its outlook of doubt often skews our capacity to fully understand others – if we doubt that another being has a mind, we may lose ourselves into the infinite regress of questioning. As a result, we become incapable of perceiving such a mind and thereby incapable of noting the other's value as a subject (for discussion and further literature, see Aaltola 2013b). These problems also interlink with and haunt cognitive empathy when it aims to be completely severed from affective realms.

MORAL AGENCY OR MORAL MONSTROSITY?

But what are the links between cognitive empathy and morality? Could cognitive empathy provide the basis for moral agency? Can neutral perception and inference offer us the way towards morality and animal ethics? Here, attention needs to be placed again on how well cognitive empathy enables the key factors of moral agency, particularly other-directedness and openness towards difference.

There is some promise of other-directedness and recognition of diversity in cognitive empathy – at least on the surface. After all, it does require one to pay note to the other and to acknowledge even the most perplexing forms of difference: its focus is primarily on the other being, and in order to be precise at reading her, concentration on her differences is required. When we use cognitive empathy to approach a cow, we will, thereby, pay attention to her, trying to map out what her mental states are, thus becoming other-directed, and if we are any good at cognitive empathy, we will also keep in mind that she is a bovine creature, with her specific, distinct behaviours and ways of being. Indeed, cognitive empathy is taking place in most of us, in most of our dealings with other creatures; in this sense, it is often inescapable and can add to our moral understanding of other subjects.

Yet there is also a darker side to cognitive empathy, which weakens its links to moral agency and which stems from the problems already mentioned – excessive disconnection from emotion. As Adam J. Smith points out, those with high cognitive empathy and little emotional attunement live according to a Machiavellian rule. Lack of emotive engagement with others can have drastic consequences from the standpoint of morality. Lives become consumed by competition, hierarchies, incapacity to form lasting bonds and ultimately aggression – such individuals also become masters of deceit, manipulation and control, the smooth operators easily managing their way up the ranks of the social world, masking their will to power under superficial social skills, charismatic charm and pretence (A. J. Smith 2006). The epitome of the disconnected cognitive empathizer is nothing less than a Nietzschean individual, dizzy under the spell of competitive, hierarchical, manipulative and egoistic desires for control over others. Therefore, when detachment becomes inordinate, when the emotional level is subsided, the consequences can be morally catastrophic – full detachment enables lack of concern, the capacity to look at others without affect, and when such drastic emotional disconnectedness combines with mind reading, it facilitates manipulation, deception and a search for power.

The reason why withdrawal from emotional part-taking can lead to such blatant, power-orientated egoism can be found in Hume's suggestion: only reverberation or resonance with the emotive landscapes of others draws us away from focusing solely on our own self-directed needs and emotions. Up until then, we remain cocooned into a rather primitive, self-serving existence, where others are evaluated on account of how we may benefit from them – the consequential worldview is that of one against the rest and inevitably feeds the urge to instrumentalize, compete with and manipulate others. In short, with nothing but cognitive empathy to guide our way to knowing others – when detachment from emotions in how we understand others is excessive – we risk becoming psychopathic.

The case of psychopathy offers a fruitful venue to explore the limitations of the connections between cognitive empathy and moral agency. Psychopathy is characterized by high or typical levels of cognitive empathy and very low levels of affective empathy, as psychopaths are excellent observers of the mental states of other individuals while simultaneously exhibiting an inability to feel with those others (Mullins-Nelson et al. 2006; Wai and Tiliopoulos 2012). In fact, defects in affective empathy are the most underlying sign of psychopathy; those with psychopathic tendencies have clear difficulties with emotional attunement and particularly with caring whether they have hurt others, while their cognitive perspective-taking capacities are intact (Jones et al. 2010). Individuals with psychopathy comprehend the experiences of others, but do not manifest involvement, concern or care, and thereby "individuals with psychopathic traits may actually lack feeling for the individual in distress while knowing that the person is distressed" (Book, Quinsey and Langford 2007, 541). Following suit, studies show that psychopaths have no defects in evaluating or cognitively inferring the mental states of others and thus that they have a theory of mind – however, their key trait is that they do not resonate with what they witness, nor do they react with concern to the distress their victims undergo (ibid.). Psychopaths can perceive, quickly and efficiently, the fear and pain, distress and anxiety in others but will not resonate with those states; they are the cool readers of others and lack emotional involvement (Book, Quinsey and Langford 2007; Blair 2008; Ali et al. 2009).

Indeed, psychopaths rejoice in the opposite of affective empathy and can take part in what is called "callous empathy", which refers to the "lack of feeling for others while exhibiting definite understanding of their mental states by using the information to their own ends" (Book, Quinsey and Langford 2007, 531) and which not only facilitates gross instrumentalization of others for one's benefit but can also intertwine with sadism, a state of enjoying the suffering of others. Other pivotal traits of psychopathy include egoism, manipulation, control, deception, irresponsibility, intelligence, impulsiveness, hedonism, lack of guilt, lack of fear, high risk-taking, and difficulties in grasping the value of other individuals to be anything other than instrumental (Mullins-Nelson et al. 2006; Kiehl 2006; Book, Quinsey and Langford 2007; Blair and Blair 2009).[4]

Therefore, the psychopath's worldview is egoistic, for lack of resonation disables her from broadening it towards other-directedness. As a result, others are instruments to be used, and cognitive empathy is utilized as a technique of rendering that use as smooth as possible, as the psychopath will gather information on others in order to deceive and govern them. Cognitive empathy, when unaccompanied by emotive reverberation, becomes a tool of manipulation, a method in the service of ego-driven ends: in order to know how to twist and bend as successfully as possible, one needs to know equably, without slithers of emotion, what one is twisting and bending. Were affective empathy to take place, one could not twist and bend, for one would not want to: one would reverberate with the emotive state of others and begin to see value in them, thereby perceiving egoism and the manipulative will to power as moral catastrophes. Therefore, it is the absence of the emotive level which stands as crucial – to repeat, psychopathy is detachment gone too far. As Frans de Waal points out, "Without emotional engagement induced by state-matching, perspective-taking would be a cold phenomenon that could just as easily lead to torture as to helping" (de Waal 2008, 287), and these words apply well to the psychopath. Overly detached recognition of the mental states of others enables one to utilize that knowledge for one's own advantage without further moral scruples. This has obvious implications when considering the moral relevance of cognitive empathy: albeit it can be a practically useful form of empathy, it alone, unaided by emotional participation, will not advance our moral ability. Indeed, if anything, when taken alone it appears worryingly destructive from the viewpoint of moral agency.

This gulf between "extreme" cognitive empathy and moral agency is heightened by the fact that a further distinct feature of psychopaths is their inability to grasp the meaning of "morality", as for them "morality" and "convention" are identical terms, with the former being reducible to the latter.[5] To offer a simple example, from this perspective harming others is wrong because it is illegal – the moral dimension is left unattained, and explaining that dimension to a psychopath amounts to an effort similar to explaining to a colour-blind person what the colour blue looks like. Some simply cannot intuit or fathom the meaning of "morality" (again, most probably because such fathoming would require resonation and emotional involvement). Such an inability renders psychopaths not only potentially immoral but also amoral; they are creatures who lack full moral agency, for they do not comprehend what the substance of morality is (Mullins-Nelson et al. 2006; Book, Quinsey and Langford 2007). In her project of self-fulfilment, the psychopath will not be connected to others via bonds of responsibility, and she will, as pointed out above, lack the capacity to understand the intrinsic moral value of others. The element of moral awareness is missing. As such, cognitive empathy cannot be a key to moral agency. Even if it can, when accompanied by other emotions, enhance our understanding of others, cognitive empathy alone does not suffice. It is particularly cognitive empathy's inability to spark other-directedness which constitutes the main worry, as in extreme cognitive empathy the self stands as the focus of orientation. Cognitive empathy can feed openness towards diversity, for via observation and inference we can learn about the creatures most dissimilar to us, and (as will be argued) it can, for this reason, aid other modes of empathy; however, the self-directedness of its excessively disconnected variety forms a definitive obstacle for its relevance to moral agency.

Hence, even if cognitive empathy is an important part of human mentation in its ability to step beyond the immediate and render obvious the potential complexities, even deceitfulness, behind the emotions of others, on its own it stands as a poor ground for moral agency. It can foster openness towards heterogeneity, for it can strengthen one's ability to acknowledge the more intricate and otherwise hidden aspects of others – those relating to their specific life narratives, histories, intentions, contexts and so forth. Yet cognitive empathy will need to be accompanied by an affective component for it to participate in other-directedness; alone it will not suffice for moral agency.

As pointed out above, like projective empathy, cognitive empathy can also feed an atomistic orientation towards others, which stipulates that we are ultimately detached from others and thereby unable to know them with any amount of certainty. The smile of another can be a facade hiding her will to swallow us under her power – nothing can be fully trusted; doubt is the appropriate way of approaching others, for behind the immediately accessible lies a terrain of potential deceit, misreading and complication. Therefore, precisely in its ability to reveal deceit and thereby reveal hidden complexities in others, cognitive empathy builds barriers between beings, formed of epistemic distrust: inference can become suspicious, frustrated, confused, even paranoid, as we feel forever doubtful whether we genuinely have grasped the intricacies behind others' emotions or if we were mistaken, misled or simply naively ignorant. It is this type of paranoid solipsism and atomistic imprisonment that also may go on to spark scepticism, the doubt over our capacity to know the mental states of others to begin with. Such paranoid scepticism, again, can be quite destructive from the viewpoint of one's ability for other-directedness and moral regard, as the other remains a potential enemy – she is perceived with suspicion and even hostility rather than via affinity.

One manifestation of such epistemic distrust comes from the close kin of psychopathy – the narcissistic personality disorder. While psychopathy is primarily characterized by power orientation, the primary definer of narcissism is the wish to be respected and adored. The narcissist displays a grandiose sense of self; the incentive of her life project is to be noted as a spectacular being. Her self has two layers: that of the "false self" (defined by capacity, charm and potency, and the one she believes is her genuine mode of being) and the truer, more authentic self (defined by imperfection, vulnerability and insecurity, and the one she feels deep shame for and therefore tends to escape and deflect from). The narcissistic mode of relating to the world is, then, characterized by the need to maintain and keep up the false self, perceived as worthy of admiration, while toning down and obsessively hiding the more realistic, incapable, vulnerable self (see Cain, Pincus and Ansell 2008; Maxwell et al. 2011).

Since the narcissist is continually immersed in the project of manipulating an image of the false self for others, and thereby gaining admiration and rewards from those others, she will also be quite tangibly aware of the difference between the immediate and that which lies beyond – an awareness that may feed paranoia in relation to other beings as she fears they might see through her facades. The narcissist will harbour all-consuming doubt over whether others truly value her or if they display genuine emotions; she will live in the mode of continual suspicion over the complexities behind the emotions and motivations of others, made particularly painful by the fact that her sense of self-worth is dependent on their approval. Hence, the world of the narcissist includes paranoia, as she is disconnected from the realm of others, forever doubting them, and indeed from the realm of the self. Again, in narcissism it is precisely cognitive empathy that is emphasized at the expense of emotive attunement; like the psychopath, while the narcissist may be quite capable of cognitive empathy, she is lacking in affective empathy (see Twenge and Campbell 2003; Cain Pincus and Ansell 2008; Ritter and Dziobek 2011). Paranoia may partly originate from an incapacity to emotively engage with others: relying solely on disconnected observation and analysis will quickly escalate into distrust over what others are truly thinking or feeling.

Therefore, in both psychopathy and narcissism, cognitive empathy, detached from emotion, will offer an existence of not only domination but also paranoia. This adds to the way in which cognitive empathy, taken on its own, is a potential counterforce for moral agency. Aided solely by this form of empathy, not only do we become capable of power-orientated manipulation of and control over others, we may also become incapable of viewing them with the sort of basic trust, recognition and affinity required for other-directedness and ultimately for moral regard. When sceptical and paranoid over the mental states of others, we quite simply cannot become fully acknowledging of those others, their traits and their needs, which again eliminates the capacity to fully note their subjectivity and its moral worth.

Narcissism also points towards the links between egoism and cognitive empathy. The heightened sense of self-value, characteristic of narcissism, tends to lead to both a contemptuous and a needy attitude towards the world, as any notions of failure in oneself are covered by projecting faults onto others while requesting admiration from them. The narcissist will hold such unrealistic notions of self-perfection that she will both hold others in contempt and search for affirmation in order to sustain her self-image. It is such efforts of maintaining a sense of superiority that lead to hostility and even aggression as one punishes others for imperfections in oneself and ceaselessly seeks to render those others as subservient admirers against whose lowlier status perceived self-perfection can be restated and reaffirmed (see Twenge and Campbell 2003; Cain, Pincus and Ansell 2008; Maxwell et al. 2011). Again, it is arguably the detachment provided by resting one's understanding primarily on cognitive empathy rather than on affective resonance which enables one to revolve around the ego in such an extensive manner – the atomism and solipsism which detachment supports create a very lonely, isolated view of reality and almost by necessity focus one's attention on the self. Egoism forms an extreme mode of self-directedness, wherein one estimates everything primarily from the viewpoint of how it benefits one's own aims, and thereby the connection between it and cognitive empathy in narcissism strengthens the claim, according to which cognitive empathy alone will not suffice for the sort of other-directedness required by moral agency.

Therefore, psychopathy threatens moral agency by disabling one from fathoming the meaning of morality and by leading to a manipulative, instrumentalizing view of others, and narcissism adds to these dangers a general distrust and thereby dis-acknowledgement of others, together with blatant egoism. Both are characterized by cognitive empathy unsupported by emotional involvement, which suggests that cognitive empathy on its own is a poor support for moral agency. With cognitive empathy acting as the sole guide, emotive attunement and states such as intersubjectivity, wherein there is movement and exposure between the inner, lived realities of oneself and others, are replaced with detachment and doubt, which again feed efforts of manipulation, control and even aggression. When connection is lost, all one has left is the effort to place oneself in control of others and position one's atomistic cell above them (Aaltola 2014a).[6] (Yet individuals with these personality traits may simultaneously have a wholly different perspective on themselves: they can perceive themselves to be quite capable of emotional resonance and thereby quite affectively empathic. Interestingly, one hypothesis is that it is this illusion that defines the relevant moral inabilities: "Arrogant, overly disdainful, critical, or aggressive reactions toward others' feelings, or, in more severe forms, attempts to con, manipulate, or emotionally exploit others, could be due to an overestimation of emotional empathy with an actual lack of ability" – Ritter and Dziobek 2011, 245. Hence, perhaps it is when we think of ourselves as moral and affectively involved while being motivated by wholly other considerations that moral agency is particularly threatened.)

ANTHROPATHY

These are all important reminders in animal ethics and may help to illuminate the moral psychopathology of anthropocentric attitudes. Psychopathy and narcissism point towards four dangers in particular which are related to the overaccentuation of cognitive empathy: (1) self-directedness and grandiose egoism, (2) paranoia/scepticism over the minds of others, (3) power over/manipulation of others, and (4) disregard for moral considerations. These also are, to a worrying degree, evident in anthropocentric beliefs and ways of relating to other animals. As such, anthropocentrism may carry elements of a type of collective narcissism and psychopathy in its manner of making sense of animality – elements which will here be called "anthropathy"[7] and which rest on relying excessively on cognitive empathy at the expense of emotional involvement and affinity. (As will be explicated later, this is not to suggest that individuals with anthropocentric beliefs are psychopathic but rather that these beliefs in themselves are plagued by rarely noted psychopathologies.)

Self-directedness and grandiose egoism are evident in the animal context, as the non-human realm is often perceived primarily via its use-value to human beings and as humans are depicted as the most advanced species on earth, who have the right to utilize the rest of the animal world due to this advancement. Indeed, such self-directedness also impacts the other three dimensions of anthropathy and perhaps forms the latter's core.

Self-directedness is manifest in the manner in which anthropocentric beliefs categorize other creatures on the basis of their utility to human beings: pigs are not their specific, sensing, cognitive, experiential subjects but "farm animals" meant for food production, and even companion animals may be defined by their purpose of use (indeed, Western cultures have historically tended to map out and categorize non-human animals on the basis of their use-value, see Thomas 1983; Ritvo 1997). The subjectivity of other animals becomes quite easily lost when cognitive empathy is afforded too much primacy – just as the narcissist or the psychopath perceives others primarily via their use-value to herself, the anthropocentric ideology defines fishes and birds on account of how she may benefit from them. It is within such a mindscape that other animals become physical forms largely or wholly empty of subjective content and moral significance. The experiences and moral worth of those animals are routinely and institutionally ignored, as if they lacked relevance, and arrogance grounded in the notion of human supremacy is often evident, echoing in sentences such as "they are only animals". The approach is both self-directed (one's own outlook is taken to be primary) and egoistic (others are manipulated and governed so as to serve the benefit of the self). Indeed, anthropocentrism emerges as a form of blatant egoism, wherein the rest of the world is approached as an arena of resources which one can use and control without boundaries. This is the mindset of collective hedonism, where one species is seen to be justified in reducing others into sheer sources of financial, consumeristic, recreational or culinary gratification and even indulgence.

Egoism does not limit itself to the practical usage of other animals – it has also further psychological and cultural dimensions, for it helps to build and sustain the grandiose image of "humanity". Other animals are used as a reference point against which human identity can be constructed: not only are humans traditionally defined as something more capable, complex or developed than non-human creatures, their self-image as "pinnacles of evolution" may be further maintained via the very usage of other animals. The utilization of other creatures bolsters the notion of human uniqueness, for the rest of the world appears as if it truly exists for the benefit of the human self and as if humans had risen – via their capacity to control and exploit – to the very top of the order of things. Once more, lack of emotive, other-regarding responsiveness, combined with primacy of cognitive empathy, acts as one probable cause for the unfortunate state of things, and in a very straightforward manner erodes moral agency towards other animals, as other-directedness in relation to them surfaces as a relatively rare phenomenon (particularly in regard to those animals who are used the most).

Just as the narcissist concentrates on her self-value and sees others as vehicles which can further enhance her own grandiosity, the anthropocentric ideology exaggerates the presupposed brilliance of humanity and approaches other animals via utilization. At the far end, notions that other animals are deterministically "meant" for human benefit or that they even willingly "sacrifice" themselves to serve humans reveal the narcissistic preoccupations that linger within anthropocentrism, for within such a discourse, humans are both the pinnacle and the centre of their own cosmos, while other animals remain the supplies which both practically and metaphorically feed humans' sense of uniqueness.

In regard to paranoia, overemphasized cognitive empathy risks sparking distrustful scepticism in relation to non-human minds. One is continually doubting what non-humans' true emotions or motives are and even if they have any mindedness at all – when there are no emotive channels of confirming mental states, everything becomes theoretical and thereby potentially false. This form of paranoid scepticism is culturally common, as many remain uncertain about what is taking place even in the minds of their own companion animals and as scientists are seeking to "verify" the sort of mental states in animals that via emotive engagement appear obvious (one example being whether other animals have scientifically established emotions). When relying too much on reasoned observation and inference, and refraining from affective ways of relating, one enters the rather absurd and hollow world of distrusting even that which ought to be evident and becomes obsessed with finding ever more "proofs" and "counter-proofs", dipped in layers of detached analyses that ultimately take us ever further away from understanding non-human mentation. The epitome of this is the scientist who looks at a joyous or fearful dog or cow and asks, "Yes, but does she really have any emotions?"

As with projective empathy, with cognitive empathy scepticism over non-human mindedness is a real, often materialized risk and manifests precisely when the obvious is questioned. It is good to scientifically explore matters we have little knowledge of (say, the communication systems of whales) but ill-warranted to still doubt that which continually presents itself (for instance, the fact that mammals have emotions). As Dan Zahavi posits, the tools of natural sciences are often irrelevant to understanding other minds: "To suggest that the indirect means of verifying claims about black holes or subatomic particles can 'give us a model for verifying hypotheses in the area of the study of human and animal subjectivity' is deeply confused" (Zahavi 2007, 33), and this is an important reminder.

Scepticism may also become something more than mere doubt over the existence of non-human mentation and emerge as a hostile form of paranoia: the minds of crows and squirrels are not only doubted but also viewed with the type of hostility that cognitive empathy unaccompanied by the affective level may feed. Other animals become potentially harmful, a threat, a culprit or an obstacle. Within such a scenario, they are always depicted as potentially dangerous (via their physical force, competition over resources or, say, spread of disease) and as creatures to be firmly distrusted, one example being culturally produced fears of "dangerous dogs", bears, wolves, snakes, rats, foxes, bees, cockroaches and pigeons, to name a few. In the context of such animals, the potential risks are severely overstated, as their aggression or their ability to spread disease are built up to mythical proportions. Here, it is the lack of emotional involvement which causes the problem – when there is no affective resonance with the viewpoints of wolves or pigeons, it is astoundingly easy to enter into socially constructed paranoia that exaggerates their dangerousness.

Within such a mindset, other animals become enemies to be controlled rather than fellow-beings to build affinity with. The perceived threat can also concern identity. "Animality" contains connotations of something ungovernable and antagonistic towards humanity and civility: it represents instinct, bodily functions, sexuality, emotions and other factors deemed oppositional to reasoned order. Its presence is a risk to the Western notion of "human identity", for such identity is built in opposition to all that ferality, which "animality" represents. In order to maintain one's existence as "human", the animal internal and external to us must be governed (Agamben 2003). Once more, lack of emotive attentiveness and overemphasis on cognitive mind-reading supports such paranoid detachment, which may form the very core of "humanity".

Moreover, perhaps it is this state that nourishes the construction of competition and hierarchies between humans and other animals, the sense that both cannot be given full moral attention due to non-human animals' potential risks. If non-humans are deemed as a potential threat to one's existence, they are also easily perceived via the lens of competition, subjugation and exclusion – if wolves are depicted as untrustworthy, violent, hazardous creatures ready to kill children or as metaphors of lost identity in the shape of boundary-crossing werewolves, they may also be depicted via the terminology of conflict and competition, wherein one must choose between who has the right for existence and who does not. Perhaps the notion of power, so central to anthropocentrism, also gains ammunition here. Other animals must be defeated, controlled and rendered into easily digestible commodities, for in a state of competition, use of power is justified, and when the other is rendered utterly passive, she can no longer pose a threat.

The Cartesian dualism between humans and other animals, characterized by one-sided subjugation, then gains a psychopathological motive: the desire to render the world safe by reducing the "others" into controllable objects. Paranoid detachment can have far-reaching consequences, wherein humans emerge as Machiavellian rulers and controllers of the non-human world. Indeed, when the levels of manipulation and control of other animals are fully considered – when we take into account the intensity and prevalence of animal industries and the human impact on wild animals – it is rather difficult to avoid the image of humans as Machiavellian dictators, overly eager to practice power over their non-human kin. Again, it may be the overaccentuation of cognitive empathy at the expense of affective resonation which partly enables such a state of exploitation.

The aforementioned points towards a central aspect of anthropocentrism: power. As creatures whose minds are doubted, who are even deemed as risks to human identity and who are perceived as utilities destined to serve human benefit, animals are also continually controlled. Farmed animals stand as the most obvious, extreme concretization of this power, as they are forced to live in highly controlled environments defined by cages, fences, walls and the absence of respect for their own tendencies and needs and as their bodies are manipulated to become ever more productive (currently, this includes the use of bioengineering; see Twine 2010). Yet power is also evident in relation to companion animals, whose living conditions are often similarly restricted, who have to behave according to human norms and whose bodies are neutered, spayed and microchipped so as to enable a more thorough governance over their behaviours and "risks" (see Palmer 2001).[8] Likewise, wild animals are placed under severe control, as their populations are carefully monitored, manipulated and culled by humans and as human actions often have had – via deforestation, growth of human population, pollution and climate change –a severe impact on even the most remote and secluded of species. Anthropocentrism rests on the notion of human control, power over other species is one of its central themes, and the practical implications of this are both manifold and easily observable. Again, emphasizing only cognitive empathy plays a key role here and indeed enables the successful, often extreme manipulation of other animals: via cognitive empathy alone, we can learn how to operate non-humans most effectively, without the uncomfortable pressings and pullings of emotional responding. Just as cognitive empathy facilitates the psychopath to govern and manipulate her victims efficiently, it allows the anthropocentric society to use power in a smooth, industrialized fashion.

Finally, the disregard of moral consideration towards other animals is often painfully evident. Animal welfare legislations across the globe are notoriously minimal and fail to offer adequate protection for animal well-being, let alone their subjectivity, and even though many profess to care about animals, animal industries and the subjugation and extermination of wild animals are growing with worrying speed. This is the era of both the Anthropocene and industrialized animal agriculture – two extreme manifestations of non-human exploitation – which both rest on the failure to take the moral value of other animals and species seriously into account. Again, it is arguably the primacy of cognitive empathy and the refusal to accompany it with affective resonation which support the gravity of the situation. Non-human creatures are presumed to be lacking in inherent value, or their treatment is not perceived to be a moral issue to begin with: anthropocentric ideology may adopt not only immoral (disregard for the value of pigs and chickens) but also an amoral (disregard for morality) approach to animal issues, wherein reflection on how one ought to treat other animals is absent.

This is the most worrying tenet of anthropathy, for when all emphasis is placed on the self and one's ability to practice control, others are left without moral standing. Moral agency is placed under jeopardy, for other-directedness is replaced with blatant efforts to accentuate the self at the expense of the other. Just as the psychopath will fail to notice the inherent value of her victim, the anthropocentric attitude either avoids animal ethics or scoffs at the notion that other animals are subjects of inherent value or holders of rights. When the topic is non-human animals, ethics all too often simply does not enter the scene – we become amoral creatures committing immoral acts.

The question that emerges then is as follows: Is the societal, collectively adopted and reaffirmed way of treating non-human animals primarily as recourses psychopathic and narcissistic? The answer appears both worrisome and clear. The key elements of psychopathy and narcissism – power, self-directedness, paranoia and disregard for morality – are all present in anthropocentric attitudes towards other animals and pose a major obstacle for moral agency in relation to them. Although the judgement may sound harsh, it is difficult to avoid perceiving anthropocentric attitudes as inclusive of collective, culturally maintained psychopathic and narcissistic dimensions, amounting to anthropathy. Animals are physically and psychologically manipulated to become ever more productive; their ways of being are controlled with often-extreme measures. Human benefit, however trivial, takes continuous priority over animal well-being; suffering is justified in the name of such hedonistic gains as culinary pleasure. The value and presumed excellence of human beings is persistently emphasized as the "natural" justification for the subjugation of non-human animals, and the individual value of other animals, let alone their "liberation" or "rights", are often viewed with hostility and seen as naive, even absurd. Simultaneously, there is little resonation with, or even talk of, the experiences – the pains, fears, frustrations and anxieties – that the animals have to undergo. Also, the most worrying aspect of these personality conditions, the possibility of physical violence, is routinely practiced, as pigs, lobsters, chickens, cows, salmon and elk are killed annually in their billions, often after being reared in conditions that go against their most basic needs.

Although humans have used other animals for millennia, the type of manipulation, control, egoism and disregard for both their subjectivity and moral issues evident particularly in contemporary Western societies points towards a radically different mindset. One could ponder its links to the birth of liberalistic politics and the industrialized, utilitarian approach to life and how – when combined with the old notion of human supremacy that has lingered in Western philosophy in varying degrees throughout its history – these may have bolstered the prevalence of collectively, societally maintained narcissism and even psychopathy towards both other animals and other, more distant human animals. What is significant here, however, are the connections of cognitive empathy and lack of resonation. When the affective counterpart of cognitive empathy, the capacity to be emotively, experientially attuned to other creatures, is missing, the consequences may be catastrophic from the viewpoint of not only our moral ability in general but also our capacity to treat other animals as subjects worthy of moral regard in particular.

It should be emphasized that the claim here is not that individuals with anthropocentric attitudes are narcissistic or psychopathic – rather, it is suggested that anthropocentrism as a collectively maintained belief system is troubled by these traits. Individuals perfectly capable of affective attunement, other-directedness and moral consideration may, then, partake in narcissistic and psychopathic doctrines in their relationship to other animals; it is this one segment of their approach to reality which is affected. The issue does not, thereby, primarily concern personal psychologies but rather the psychopathology of culturally and societally upheld attitudes.[9] It is the nature of those attitudes which is the key focus here and which also ought to be explored from the viewpoint not only of ethics or politics but also of moral psychology. Anthropocentrism includes psychopathic and narcissistic logics, both ontologically (how humans are defined as "extraordinary" in comparison to other animals), epistemologically (how, why and what sort of "knowledge" is used in regard to other species and their members) and morally (how the subjectivity of other animals is ignored) to such a degree that one can speak of anthropathy as an affectively impoverished collective ethos.

Anthropathy concerns human personhood as that personhood is manifested in relation to other animals. If we understand "person" to refer, as it did in Greek culture, to one's having a "mask" or a "role" in regard to others (Midgley 1983), the anthropocentric human "mask" is emotively defective in its conception of non-human animality. Ultimately, it may also be defective in its conception of humanity. One could ponder whether the defectiveness originates from the sort of anxious insecurity paradoxically latent in both psychopathy and narcissism – that is, the hidden sense of not existing as "whole" without manipulating the external world into validating one's importance. When removing oneself from emotional contact with other animals, one enters a very lonely place where one may even feel as if she is not quite real. Perhaps it is such removal and disconnect from the animal realm which has cast a chronic sense of isolation and insecurity onto humanity and which again comes out as the need to dominate the very animals one ought to be reconnecting with.

Yet personal psychologies may be affected as well, for this leads to a related, equally pivotal question which concerns the effects that anthropocentrism may have on our psyches. If anthropocentrism as an ideology is troubled by narcissistic and psychopathic tendencies, could it also impact our personal constitution, our individual psychological make-up? Despite often endorsing an internalistic view of mindedness, within which minds are relatively private phenomena and independent from their surroundings, philosophy also has recognized the rather evident impact that cultural and societal forces have on our individual psyches. For instance, drawing from Aristotle, Amelie Rorty (1997) has demonstrated how societal institutions and belief systems can affect our sense of morality and virtue and how in order to develop and refine our abilities in the latter, the former need to be constantly reworked towards a direction that aids our efforts of cultivation. Similarly, Diego Romaioli, Elena Faccio and Alessandro Salvini have argued that the "mind understood as a combination of nodes within an interpersonal network that is in state of perpetual change, depending on the context and objectives" (Romaioli et al. 2008, 185) ought to replace the internalistic view, and that as such, our mindedness constantly evolves with our surrounding contexts, including socially sanctioned belief systems. The lesson is simple: social and political beliefs and dogma can impact our personal psychologies, particularly when it comes to what sort of capacities we consider valuable and worthy of developing. Could it be, then, that anthropocentrism, with its insistence on egoistic optimization and lack of affective attunement, is moulding our personal psychologies and making us hesitant to meet other creatures via emotive, other-directed involvement?

Anthropocentrism pushes forward and reaffirms anthropathy, and an evident possibility is that it may, again, begin to impact our way of relating to the world on a more general level that bears an effect on personal psychologies. Here, societally maintained dogmas begin to seep into individual sensibilities, whereby they no longer impact just one segment of one's belief system but rather one's broader outlook and thereby ultimately the constitution of one's mind. Although the key emphasis here is on the collective psychopathologies, the possibility that they also can bear an effect on private traits cannot be ignored. Indeed, studies support the claim that the way in which we are trained to approach others may influence our personal levels of narcissism. One example of this is medical students, of whom up to 75 percent suffer from a decline in empathy levels due to the way in which medical school reinforces attitudes of elitist privilege and viewing others primarily as bodies rather than minds (Hojat et al. 2004). Another example is finance majors, who similarly may have less empathy and higher levels of narcissism and in relation to whom the suggestion has been that education plays a pivotal part in this process, as finance majors are subjected to notions of profit maximization, commodification and the use of mathematic models and quantification rather than affective relating as a way to explain and approach human affairs. As a result of the emphasis of this training, emotive participation may begin to appear as irrelevant and irrational (Brown et al. 2010).

One may wonder, if this form of "education" in relation to non-human animals is not continually taking place in various sectors of the society. Ranging from education to marketing, media and the legal system, institutions are "training" us to consider animals via aloofness, elitism, profit, commodification and various mechanical models (as biological production units, faceless representations of species prototypes, etc.), which again may render us ever more detached, self-directed and utilitarian, first in our dealings with other animals and secondly perhaps in our dealings with other humans and the world in general. This would mean that anthropocentrism can fuel the rise of tendencies related to narcissism and psychopathy on a more personal level as well. Anthropocentric ways of perceiving can begin to penetrate the mind and sculpt it anew in the image of the emphases and attitudes inherent to the anthropocentric discourse, as psychopathologies manifested on the level of cultural attitudes and for instance within the languages and actions of animal industries become generically internalized. Here, the human mind continues its evolutionary processes in the context of the institutions of violence it itself has created – they become the surroundings that mould the mind.

This does not necessarily mean that humans are turning into stereotypical psychopaths, with a disconcerting keenness for axes and chain saws or a desperate yearning for adoration and power: ordinary people need not become the classic presentations nor the extremes of narcissism or psychopathy. Rather, the unfortunate evolution may take place quantitatively, as different shades and on differing scales. Indeed, there is a growing tendency to view narcissism and psychopathy as spectrums, onto the lower scales of which many of us err in our more egotistic life episodes. One possibility is that anthropocentrism and anthropathy may enforce these tendencies and bring one higher up on the scales, thereby rendering mild, even accidental episodes of egocentrism and power orientation into actual pathologies that fluctuate between the mild and the severe. Just as the consumeristic society, prone towards celebrations of individual, hedonistic gain and elitist understandings of others, can increase narcissistic and psychopathic tendencies, arguably so can anthropocentrism.

Indeed, anthropathy and consumerism as two culturally produced modes of relating to reality are closely interlinked. Consumeristic, neo-liberalistic societies view the world and many of its entities and creatures as commodities, as potential instruments with which to make ever more profit or with which to gain ever more gratification. Here, the lines concerning which sort of beings are utilizable objects become faint and ambivalent, as in the end we all are potential targets. In such a framework, the anthropathic notion that animals are sheer instruments of hedonism or targets of consumption easily slips into appearing as natural and self-evident, and this, again, may intensify the ethos of consumerism – anthropathy and consumerism fall into a mutually enforcing and supporting symbiosis. Anthropathy lends consumerism a backdrop that endorses and justifies a highly individualistic, hedonistic and optimizing approach to existence.

The effects of anthropathy – both on our individual psyches and on broader, culturally endorsed ideologies – can be vast. It has been suggested that, historically, the instrumentalization of non-human animals has enabled the instrumentalization of other human beings (the historian Charles Patterson has made a bold claim according to which animal agriculture has accentuated our more aggressive, instrumentalizing traits in regard to other humans as well; see Patterson 2003). Perhaps this logic still applies and is more potent than ever. One sign of it is that advancing empathy towards other animals will also heighten it in the human context, as those with pro-animal attitudes tend to score well in their empathic concern for their conspecifics (see, for instance, Signal and Taylor 2007). How we regard pigs can directly influence how we regard other human beings, as pro-animal attitudes are likely to feed pro-human attitudes – maybe equally, then, anti-animal sentiments motivate hierarchies among human beings. Could it be a coincidence that the era which has seen far more institutionalized animal exploitation than any other is also the birthplace of consumeristic disregard for the value of the environment and of other, more distant human beings? And moreover, could it be a coincidence that it is this very era which is witnessing the increase of narcissism and psychopathy? (Studies point out that environments, such as large-scale, faceless societies, can increase these personality disorders – see Glenn, Kurzban and Raine 2011 – which again opens the door for the possibility that our culturally reinforced relations to other animals also may be one environment impacting their prevalence.)

To summarize, although cognitive empathy fulfils an important and even vital function in understanding others, when unaccompanied by emotively attuned dimensions, it can have devastatingly dangerous consequences. Particularly, its self-directedness is antagonistic to moral agency and renders its role – again, when taken alone – in animal ethics both dubious and highly risky. If projective and simulative empathies require more embodied engagement, cognitive empathy thereby is, in order to be morally productive, in need of affective engagement.

NOTES

1. Kant stated, "If nature had implanted little sympathy in this or that man's heart; if (being in other respects an honest fellow) he were cold in temperament and indifferent to the suffering of others – if such a man (who in truth could not be the worst product of nature) were not exactly fashioned by her to be a philanthropist, would he

not still find in himself a source from which he might draw a worth far higher than any a good-natured temperament can have? . . . For love out of inclination cannot be commanded; but kindness from duty . . . is practical not pathological love, residing in the will and not in the propensions of feeling, in principles of action and not of melting compassion; and it is this practical love alone which can be the object of command" (Kant 1964, 66).

2. Arthur Schopenhauer also refers to Kant's notion, according to which emotions will only lead one's moral understanding astray and which stipulates that "the character only begins to have value, if a man, who has no sympathy in his heart, and is cold and indifferent to others' sufferings, and who is *not by nature a lover of his kind*, is nevertheless a doer of good actions, solely out of a pitiful sense of duty". For Schopenhauer, this is "revolting to true moral sentiment" and an "apotheosis of lovelessness" (Schopenhauer 2005, 24).

3. Elsewhere, Simon Baron-Cohen combines cognitive empathy with a sympathetic component: "Empathy is the drive to identify another person's emotions and thoughts, and to respond to these with an appropriate emotion" (Baron-Cohen and Chakrabarti 2008, 216).

4. Psychopathy has also been defined as consisting of three main traits, which are disinhibition, boldness and meanness (i.e., lack of empathy; Patrick, Fowles and Krueger 2009.)

5. Some argue that the divide may not be categorical and hence psychopaths may have some grasp of moral norms, at least to such an extent that they can be considered morally and legally responsible for their actions (Vargas and Nichols 2007). However, this insistence may stem from the unwillingness to recognize them as mentally disabled individuals and from the need to position them as morally culpable.

6. Tellingly, Machiavellianism – a third personality disorder in the so-called dark triad – is close to both and involves the manipulation and exploitation of others, combined with low emotional and moral involvement. Machiavellians are "likely to exploit others and to view others in a goal-orientated manner (they see people as 'means to an end')" (Ali et al. 2009, 759).

7. This term, like "psychopathy", may appear confusing, since "-pathy" originates from "pathos", which again refers to emotion. However, here "-pathy" is used in its more modern sense (again, like "psychopathy"), referring to ailing or suffering with a difficult condition.

8. This is not to say that companion animals can never be kept without overt problems. When the animal's needs are met and she is approached as a subject, the relationship towards her can gain a more ethical dimension. However, even then power often raises its head, and one should keep a note of its potential consequences.

9. It also should be underlined that the meaning here is not to further stigmatize individuals with the relevant personality disorders, for the disorders are likely to cause them much suffering, fragility and anxiety. It is the problemacy of the disorders rather than the individuals affected by them which ought to take priority (see Glover 2014).

Chapter 4

Affective Empathy

David Hume's stance on empathy also gives flight to affective empathy, a state of resonation with the mental contents of others. Instead of coolly detecting what the other creature is undergoing, under affective empathy we instantaneously resonate with her emotions, as if we were a reef moving to the tune of the waves. In Hume's terminology, ideas are transformed into our own impressions – the anguish of another is formed into an idea and then becomes anguish in oneself. As Hume posits, "The motion of one communicates itself to the rest; so all the affections readily pass from one person to another. . . . When I see the effects of passion in the voice and gesture of any person, my mind immediately passes from these effects to their causes, and forms such a lively idea of the passion, as is presently converted into the passion itself" (Hume 1969, 367). Hence, affective resonation is Hume's "reverberation", within which we first observe and form into an idea the emotive states of others and then become immersed in them.

Another philosopher to give a similar account is Arthur Schopenhauer, who describes "compassion" (again, used in a fashion similar to contemporary usages of "empathy") as the following: "[It is] the direct participation, independent of all ulterior considerations, in the sufferings of another, leading to sympathetic assistance in the effort to prevent or remove them" (Schopenhauer 2005, 85). As with Hume, what arises as central in Schopenhauer's definition is our ability to reverberate or resonate directly with the emotions of another – it is this which "direct participation" refers to. Schopenhauer clarifies: "When once compassion is stirred within me, by another's pain, then his weal and woe go straight to my heart, exactly in the same way, if not always to the same degree, as otherwise I feel only my own" (ibid., 85). Once more, we can flow with the experiences of another to the extent that they move us just like our own experiences do. Schopenhauer also echoed Hume in his belief that this process takes place after we have formed an idea of the emotions of the other: "The sufferings of others . . . enter the consciousness indirectly, that is, by the secondary channel of mental pictures, and not till they are understood by experience" (ibid., 89). Therefore, empathy consists of forming an "image" of the mental state of another and directly participating in that state by letting it enter into us to such a degree that we share the experience with the other and are equally concerned over her suffering as we would be over that of our own. We quite concretely feel with and resonate to the tune of the emotions of others. As for Hume, for Schopenhauer this truly is a spectacular process: "No doubt this operation is astonishing, indeed hardly comprehensible" (ibid., 86).

DEFINITION

In contemporary terminology, perceiving emotions in others activates representations of similar states in oneself, which again enables one to affectively "resonate" with the other (for discussion, see Goubert et al. 2005; Jackson, Meltzoff and Decety 2005; Jackson, Rainville and Decety 2006). Following suit, affective empathy is described as a "capacity to understand and respond to the unique affective experiences of another person" on an affective, felt level (Decety and Jackson 2006, 54) and as "an observer's emotional response to the affective state of another" (Baron-Cohen and Wheelwright 2004, 164). A further definition that matches affective empathy runs as follows: "[It is a] particular orientation toward the other, in which agents are attuned and responsive to the affective states of those with whom they empathise" (Hourdequin 2012, 409). Thereby, whereas cognitive empathy remains detached, affective empathy is intrinsically involved and emotive: contra to the former, affective empathy chaperons us not only to note feeling but also to go with that feeling. This is an elemental capacity, and in humans develops around the age of two or three (Hoffman 1990).

Affective empathy is immediate, the typical example being when we witness someone undergoing sorrow and begin to feel tearful. Resonation is not therefore something that we infer but something that comes spontaneously, without effort and often without delay. Hence, even if it involves conceptualization (conceptualizing resonation as the most appropriate response to the situation and further conceptualizing what the other is undergoing), this happens almost instantaneously. Yet significantly, affective empathy differs from *emotional contagion*, wherein we unreflectively confuse the emotions of others with those of our own – for instance, when we yawn and tire in the company of yawning, tired people while remaining unaware of the source of our exhaustion. When undergoing emotional contagion, the distinction between oneself and the other is momentarily lost, as we fail to notice where our emotions originate from – as an example, angry mobs or group hysteria involve individuals wholly absorbed in collectively maintained emotions, ignorant and uncritical of where their emotions stem from. In a state of affective empathy, on the other hand, one knows that it is the other whose emotions one is resonating with, and this disables the origins of emotions from becoming blurred or muddled (Nussbaum 2001; Decety and Moriguchi 2007). Schopenhauer also underscored that the boundaries between self and other are not to be crossed: "The conviction never leaves us for a moment that he is the sufferer, not we; and it is precisely in *his* person, not in ours, that we feel the distress which afflicts us. We suffer *with* him, and therefore *in* him; we feel his trouble as *his*, and are not under the delusion that it is ours; indeed, the happier we are, the greater the contrast between our state and his, the more we are open to the promptings of Compassion" (Schopenhauer 2005, 88). Here, we are "sensible [of the suffering of another] *with* the sufferer; I feel it as my own, not indeed *in myself*, but *in him*" (ibid., 103).

This highlights that the "idea" from Hume's description remains important, for resonation does not consist of an impression in the other directly becoming an impression in the self (which would be emotional contagion) but instead requires that we have an idea that it is indeed the other who is undergoing the relevant experience and whose experience we are sharing. Therefore, affective empathy also rests on theory of mind, although this theory is channelled differently than in cognitive empathy: in the latter, theory of mind entwines with rational reflection and observation, and in the former, it entwines with affective attunement.[1]

Resonation may appear mystical (indeed, for Schopenhauer, it is "mysterious"), but in fact it finds firm bases in our core being. Neurosciences have shed much light on this astounding feature, with reference to mirror neurons[2] and more importantly imitative brain activation, within which neural pathways concerning, for instance, pain in oneself are activated when witnessing pain in another (see Goubert et al. 2005; Jackson et al. 2005). Therefore, affective empathy is something that our constitution is prone to spark: we tend to conceptualize the emotions of others by taking part in them. The biological roots of affective empathy are also supported by primatology. Thus, Frans de Waal (2009), the renowned ethologist who has studied empathy in primates, argues that empathy has a clear evolutionary basis in both humans and their biological kin. He also highlights how this is an inbuilt, physiologically manifested characteristic, as he states that empathy "provides an observer (the subject) with access to the subjective state of another (the object) through the subject's own neural and bodily representations. When the subject attends to the object's state, the subject's neural representations of similar states are automatically and unconsciously activated" (de Waal 2008, 286). Thereby, instead of being a romanticized notion of inter-being connectivity, resonation is grounded in our physiology and our evolutionary roots.

Philosophically, affective resonation does not perhaps go quite as far as Hume suggests, for we cannot ever capture the original feeling of another. Resonation with another's joy does not, thereby, constitute the exact emotion that the other is undergoing – we do not literally "catch" mental states of others, as one catches an apple. Yet it enables us to feel something akin to what the other is feeling, forms an interpretation based on our own subjective landscapes, and thereby when we witness fear in another, we undergo our own personal sense of fear. The sceptic could, of course, ask, whether resonation is accurate or whether we simply assume that the emotions constituted in ourselves resemble those of another, but such questioning remains theoretical. Affective attunement is one of the oldest ways of knowing others, firmly sculpted into our mentation and biology, and is thereby arguably also one of the most reliable sources of accessing others – indeed, when taking into account that there is no wholly "objective" method of constituting knowledge, one of our wisest, most practically prudent choices is to trust our ancient sensory and emotive abilities. In other words, there is no certainty in anything, and this being so, the safest choice is to trust, with a degree of critical reflection, those forms of knowledge which are most elemental to our being.

Affective empathy is quite possible in relation to the most different of animals as well. Research indicates that we also can, on the neural, physiological level, resonate with those who are unlike us and that therefore empathy towards the different and distant is perfectly attainable (see Lamm, Meltzoff and Decety 2010). In fact, affective empathy can be exceedingly germane in relation to non-human beings (Mathura et al. 2016). In its grips, we feel suffering with the crated pigs or the featherless chickens we witness and undergo anxiety with the hunted-down wolves or the beaten-up dogs. These emotions are rarely as vivid, as raw, as they are in the other, but their fainter echoes travel through us, at times with such intensity that we recoil and become highly distressed (or, alternatively, highly exuberant). It is affective empathy that many of those who are shown scenes of undercover footage from a farm are undergoing; it is also affective empathy that many wish not to feel because it can cause acute discomfort, as happens often with those who turn their heads swiftly away when offered a leaflet with images of agonized animals. Of course, as already implied, affective empathy does not only focus on resonating with the negative experiences of other animals and can with ease also extend to the positive. Hence, it can be highly rewarding and make us sizzle with joy when witnessing a cow blissfully kicking her feet up in the air after being released onto a field or when observing an old laboratory chimpanzee seeing the sun for the very first time.

While cognitive empathy is often required if we are to rationally understand the behaviours of another – for instance, when we note emotions in a pig or a dog that do not instantly invite resonation and instead spur bafflement – affective empathy is capable of experientially manifesting the mental states of the other and brings understanding to a different level. Whereas cognitive empathy rests on emotive disconnection, affective empathy does the exact opposite, as it spurs from emotional involvement and thereby offers entirely fresh perspectives into the other. It stands as a formidable, compelling and potentially wounding state which entices us to note bonds and similarities between ourselves and others and invites the desire to exist and even to sacrifice for another, regardless of her species.

The question of whether these truly are non-human experiences that we resonate with, or whether they are our own human projection, may of course be raised, but as suggested above, perhaps affective empathy is the most primal, foundational grounds for knowing another, and therefore perhaps questioning its validity signals questioning our very ability to relate to those around us. Approaching affective empathy with doubt rather than trust may be non-sensical not only in regard to other humans but also in relation to other animals. Resonation stands as a peculiar yet spectacular mode of understanding and as such perhaps ought be not only trusted but celebrated, even if theoretically its validity can be doubted and even though in practice it, too, can at times lead one astray and should thus be combined with reflective evaluation. As Hume (1969, 367) argued, affective empathy is our most "remarkable" attribute due to its capacity to emotively communicate the experiences of others and should therefore be applauded rather than viewed with suspicion – a claim, which can be extended to efforts to understand individuals from other species as well. Indeed, it offers precisely what cognitive empathy is lacking and therefore stands as the fruitful backdrop for the latter, as perception and inference also benefit from the support of affective attunement.

HAPLESS EMPATHS AND DESUBJECTIFICATION

Yet the issue of accuracy can also form a problem. If cognitive empathy unaided by its affective counterpart can spark detachment and even psychopathic, Machiavellian behaviour, diminished cognitive empathy combined with high levels of affective empathy can lead to naivety. It would ensure strong social ties, an almost complete lack of violence, exceptional altruism and a sense of such durable attunement with others that we would be willing to routinely self-sacrifice in order to ensure their flourishing (and do so without judging it as a "sacrifice"). However, lack of cognitive empathy would also render such highly resonating creatures gullible and easily manipulated and deceived, for they would be incapable of judging what lies beneath and beyond the immediate in others (A. J. Smith 2006). The intentions, motives and reasons of others would be at least partially lost, as a singularly affective person would simply resonate with the anger or the cheerfulness of another without noting the possibly complex origins of those emotions – in the extreme, she could haplessly resonate with the joys of her own aggressor, who has hidden agendas. Simply stated, she would thereby weep equally with villains and victims and be generally incapable of spotting the type of intricacies underlying emotions which are not immediately obvious in the other's behaviour; as long as there were individuals lacking her attunement to others in her surroundings, she would exist in a continual state of being potentially controlled, misled and hurt. Therefore, there is a danger of innocence at the core of affective empathy and its reliance on the notion that grasping others is self-evident and beyond doubt. For the master manipulator, the individual capable of pretending emotions, intensely affective individuals are the perfect prey.

Relying solely on affective empathy does not only lead to problems in such a setting characterized by potential abusers, for it also would render difficult the full understanding of those others whose incentives are morally legitimate yet complicated enough to be at least partially hidden from obvious display – again, the highly affective individual would simply resonate, for instance, with fear, without being capable of noting its potentially complex mental origins. In her mode of living in immediacy, she would also be unable to predict the next moves of others or see where their future goals lie, and thereby she would become – even though she is a deeply social creature – a poor judge of both private and social projects. Although we should trust affective empathy, we should not do so without any discrimination, and relying solely on it is problematic (just as is relying solely on cognitive empathy). The issue is not so much that it gives us wrong conclusions but rather that unsupported by a more cognitive, rational counterpart, it may not offer us the whole picture, for those states not easily recognized via resonation would remain hidden.

These are not only theoretical hypotheses, for such individuals do exist. One category formed around them is Williams syndrome – the polar opposite of psychopathy and narcissism. Those with Williams syndrome tend to struggle with developmental delay, poor living skills, lack of concentration, learning disabilities, poor executive functioning (manifested in problems concerning self-monitoring and planning) and a lower-than-average IQ. Yet these individuals also profess a variety of mental talents: they are often verbally gifted, with an ability to use highly attuned, emotive language, and they can be astoundingly sociable, intrinsically prone to both emotively understand and pay heed to others, to offer help and concern and to form tight social bonds. Since they find the concept of theory of mind difficult (even if not impossible), their cognitive empathy levels are low – they struggle to step onto the metalevel in order to scrutinize the intents of others. Simultaneously, it is the exceedingly developed sense of affective empathy which appears to guide those with Williams syndrome towards a stunning intensity of emotional attunement with others. They can resonate acutely with the experiences of other beings, and this sparks high levels of friendliness and altruism, as they may find themselves wholly concerned for others and also willing to support, comfort and assist strangers in need. Yet the downside of this condition is familiar from the above discussion: those with Williams syndrome tend to suffer from social exclusion since the majority of people around them, invested with less ability for resonation, cannot understand their exceeding sociability and kindness and since, due to their inabilities in cognitive empathy, they may also be taken advantage of quite easily. Indeed, they can be so effortlessly deceived and manipulated as to haplessly give all their belongings to help cunning others and hence tend to need a guardian in their daily lives. As a result of these difficulties of coping with others, they may undergo intense states of worry and anxiety, and may be bullied and abused (Mervis and Klein-Tasman 2000; Mervis and Becerra 2007; Järvinen, Korenberg and Bellugi 2013). Their state is paradoxical and even painful: they resonate strongly with others but harbour the eerie feeling of not fully understanding those others.

The problem appears to be this: in a world populated by humans who all show their emotions fully and honestly and who have no underlying agendas or hidden intricacies, affective empathy alone would go far, but in a world inhabited by creatures with complex forms of mentation, often not wholly evident on the surface, it needs further support. Therefore, resting on affective empathy has its limits. More than resonation is often required for a fuller understanding of others; resonation is truly "remarkable" and vital and something to be endorsed, but alone it may not suffice, particularly when dealing with the complexities in others. As the case of Williams syndrome demonstrates, it may be particularly the lack of cognitive empathy which causes problems. In order for one to perceive the intentions and motivations of others, inference and also detached perception are important: successfully knowing others cannot depend on affective empathy alone, for there is much hidden under what is instantly obvious. From this viewpoint, both cognitive and affective empathy are required for the type of understanding of others that dwells deeper than the obvious and becomes neither callously manipulative nor emotively naive: cognitive and affective empathies can form a happy symbiosis, fulfilling the lacks and cracks in each other.[3]

These are also relevant considerations in relation to knowing non-human animals. Although chickens and rhinos do not cunningly manipulate us and fake their emotions, it is easy to misjudge the intentions and reasons behind those emotions. Someone only relying on affective empathy could haplessly, consumed by a flux of resonating care, stroke the wild lion or the alligator who appears sad or anguished and become dinner in the process. She could misread the expressions of other animals by failing to acknowledge their specificity and assume that teeth-bearing dogs are smiling, that rabbits frozen in fear are happy to be cuddled, or that cows rolling their tongues in pain are just happily hungry – her mistake would be to read the expressions of other animals as similar to those of her own. Children typically invested with much affective and little cognitive empathy are prime examples of this, as they may misunderstand the intentions and gestures of dogs and cats and thereby risk needless confrontation and as they may treat their companion animals poorly based on ignorance of what those animals are trying to communicate to them. Such an attitude is arguably pervasive and encouraged in some cultural contexts, as people are urged to simply "love" or "feel with" non-human animals without understanding the unique body language and motivations of those animals; instances of this can be found in petting zoos, where unwilling, often stressed captives are hugged and stroked, or in ordinary zoos, where people enthusiastically take "happy selfies" with utterly frustrated, depressed animals. Even the media is infiltrated by such an attitude, as paradoxically animal products can be advertised by calling for resonation with an animal's happiness in a field or a barn, while in reality the animals in question are often faring poorly – again, the sort of cognitive empathy that could question the true state of the animals is missing, for marketing does not endorse it.

Hence, despite its enormous value, when relying solely on resonation, the underlying complexities and specificity of non-human emotion may remain hidden. This is because resonation relies on what is most apparent, whereas emotions are often complicated and retain many less-than-obvious dimensions, and this gulf is even more evident in relation to members of other species. As Martha Nussbaum argues, we do have a way of understanding other animals which consists of both emotive ability and cognitive, reasoned knowledge: "Although we inevitably lack first-person reports in the animal case, we can come as close to that as possible by focusing on a detailed account of the emotions of particular animals, made by an observer who has unusual empathy and unusual awareness of the specific capacities of the animals in question" (Nussbaum 2001, 92). The latter – rational, perceptive, inferential understanding of the capacities of other animals – is something that cognitive empathy can help us to achieve and which strengthens the accuracy of affective empathy.

Affective empathy is indispensable, but cognitive empathy is, therefore, also needed, for it helps us to question and explore what the emotions of other animals are based on and thereby to map out their nuances. Both perception and inference can aid and be needed in acknowledging species-specific differences, and this becomes ever more significant the further removed the non-human creature is from humans. With affective empathy alone, understanding other animals would be similar to the mentality of Williams syndrome: deeply caring and sociable but perhaps too often misguided over why and what the other animal is feeling. The trick is to combine resonation with cognitive perception and inference and thereby to both reverberate with the emotions of other animals and to inquire into how one might know more about what their expressions and behaviours mean and what lies behind their experiences.

There is also a further criticism of affective empathy worthy of discussion. According to Gallagher, empathy must include three components that render it something quite distinct from sheer resonation. First, narratives, mentioned in relation to simulative empathy, are important and separate empathy from mere immediacy by spurring us to consider the contextual causes of the other's emotions. Second, empathy must include intentionality, which means that instead of mimicking another's emotion, we produce our own emotion towards it based on how we direct our attention to the causes behind it. In simpler terms, we don't feel the suffering of another but rather feel something towards the cause of that suffering – for instance, the pain caused by war may evoke melancholy in the empathizer. Third, via these two factors, empathy becomes a feeling of its own, the "feeling of being with" the other individual (Gallagher 2012, 19). Hence, it is not resonation, the immediate sharing of a mental state or "feeling with", but a separate and distinct feeling of being with the other individual and her emotion. Gallagher clarifies: "One can understand empathy . . . as being its own primary and irreducible affective state – the state of feeling empathy" (ibid., 19). In short, the claim is that empathy does not stem from affective resonation but from directing one's attention to the causes of the other's emotion, forming narratives in order to understand them from her perspective and producing an emotion of one's own, a sense of "being with". Here, affective resonation becomes unnecessary.

There is something quite appealing about Gallagher's account. Viewing empathy non-narratively, non-intentionally and non-contextually threatens to detach and abstract emotions both from the individual undergoing them and from their background contexts. Suffering may become detached from the subject, something viewed solely as "an emotion" rather than as "an emotion embedded in a particular individual, with a particular history and causes". Such an ahistorical and non-contextual stance on emotions threatens to make us less capable of understanding others and of taking action in order to help them. It has even been argued that without contextual knowledge, there is no empathy, for interpreting the emotions of others takes place in relation to their situation (see Barrett 2017). Indeed, it may be this that renders those with Williams syndrome so easily manipulated, for their capacity to properly evaluate the background of the emotions of others is lacking.

The benefit of Gallagher's account is that not only does it enable a deeper understanding of the emotions and their causes, it also facilitates a more in-depth acknowledgement of the subjectivity of both the other and oneself. When empathy emerges as a distinct emotion of its own, the emotion of "being with", which is aimed at the causes of the emotions of another being and her life narratives, we begin to comprehend the other better, see her as more than a given emotional state X – she emerges as a full individual. In affective empathy, the risk is that we only note the emotion, not the individual, and thereby become immersed in, say, the grief and guilt of another without paying full attention to the individual behind those emotions (it is the *emotion* that is empathized with rather than the other being), and the model proposed by Gallagher erases that problem. Simultaneously, the empathizers retain their own agency, for they are not merely flowing with the emotions of another but qualifying their causes and contexts and producing an emotion of their own, thus becoming active subjects and participants rather than passive mirrors of another.

In relation to non-human animals, this would mean that instead of concentrating on resonating with, say, the misery of a cow, one ought to map out the practical and political contexts which explain the sources of that misery and the narratives which lay down methods of grasping the individuality and history of the animal. Indeed, merely resonating may be an unfruitful option when political or moral change is required, for it can detach us from the causes of the emotion and thereby make one weep at the sight of an agonized cow in a slaughter yard while still keeping hold of one's diet originating from such pained animals. Since resonation may be quite non-contextual, unaware of the elements behind the emotions of others, it may also become apolitical, incapable of pointing out ways in which others can be aided and supported. Indeed, one of the downfalls of affective empathy is that it can delay action. Studies demonstrate that affective empathy increases reaction time to dilemmas with regard to how to respond, and reaction times are much longer if individuals are offered emotional rather than neutral material (see Decety and Lamm 2006).[4] This exemplifies how sheer resonation without informative support can also defer political action.

Moreover, resonation may hide the subject behind the emotion. When weeping with the agony of the cow, one may be wholly captivated by the emotion but still fail to see the subjectivity and specificity of the animal – what starts to matter is the emotion, not the individual it is rooted in. This logic is at play when we resonate with the sight of stereotypic images of starving African children: it is the emotion, detached from actual individuals, that takes hold, and non-human emotions also may be reduced to iconic images similar to those taken of pot-bellied babies, void of recognition of the subject behind them. In such a case, the risk is that one may even enjoy resonation and unintentionally render suffering into entertainment – here, one bizarrely enjoys weeping for a while, for it may give one the sense of being virtuous, caring and elevated, while the subjectivity of the being one weeps with is quickly forgotten, together with the political and moral problems and causes of her suffering. It is when we render suffering into a spectacle that even affective empathy can deviate from the individuals it is usually anchored in. (This is related to the aesthetization mentioned in regard to projective empathy; see again Sontag 2004.) Paradoxically, then, in the extreme and when misled by aesthetization, sheer resonation can even aid desubjectification, for emotions take primacy over the individual to the extent that they become as if their own separate entities (faceless "grief" or "joy"), and the individual may disappear from view. Narratives that bring forth subjectivity and individual standpoints are one way to avoid such a scenario.

Ignoring the subjectivity of others links back to being politically unaware and also to politically pacifying oneself. In the latter case, relying on resonation alone may nullify one's own agency by rendering one quite passive and unmotivated to take action in order to rectify what is happening to non-human animals. The passive weeper may feel deeply but still assume no responsibility over acting so as to better the situation of the cow – many weep, and simply move on as if nothing had happened. Gallagher's aid here would be to activate the empathizer by replacing passive resonation with the active construction of a distinct emotion of "being with". Interpreting Gallagher's stance, one would no longer lament with the cow but actively participate in making sense of her situation by feeling, say, anger over her context and treatment, possibly with quite motivating results.

Therefore, there are problems with resting merely on affective empathy – problems also evident in relation to non-human animals. What the critique points out is that affective empathy may not always suffice on its own, not that it is something to be avoided. It can be supported by and benefit from simulative empathy and its methods (contextualization and narrativization): not only does it gain depth when accompanied by cognitive empathy, but it is also made politically stronger by simulative projection.[5] However, none of this should be taken to mean that affective empathy is not a pivotal capacity, for there is no substitute for resonation. Relying solely on resonation can, in relatively rare occasions caused by aesthetization, lead to desubjectification but without any resonation, noting the subjectivity of others is equally threatened. Arguably, resonation is necessary for a full, emotively grasping recognition of subjectivity, and as such is an astounding bridge to fathoming foreign experience. Therefore, we need resonation, and instead of abandoning it, we ought to strive to accompany it with methods that firmly root it in contexts and individuals. Gallagher's suggestions, particularly noting contexts and narratives, can support affective empathy to become ever more capable of demonstrating the subjectivity of others and making oneself an agent capable of taking political action on their behalf.

However, Gallagher's criticism may demand too much. When depicting the consequences of resonation, some of the critique is apt, but when it comes to defining whether resonation is empathy, the same does not apply. First, knowing the causes of others' emotions and mapping out narratives around them asks too much of "empathy". We can meaningfully undergo empathy without any knowledge of why the other being is joyful or anguished, and we can empathize with beings whose life narratives are completely alien to us. Envision walking past a stranger crying on a park bench: you feel sadness with her, regardless of that fact that you have no inkling of her sadness's causes or its narrative ramifications. This is, in fact, a pivotal aspect of empathy: the ability to undergo "feeling with" despite of a lack of further knowledge. It is also precisely the reason why empathy can, with such ease, also extend to perfect strangers (of whom we have little information). Indeed, this is one of the most beautiful features of affective empathy: the ability to focus attention on the subjective states of others, even when those others are otherwise alien to us. This suggests that while contextual knowledge is important, it is not necessary.

Such resonative empathy is evident and common when we consider the plights of distant people or the plights of distant non-human animals whose narratives are difficult or impossible for us to assess and the political causes of whose sufferings we do not always know. An image of a malnourished woman lying by a road will spark empathy even when I do not know the region she is from, the political landscapes and causalities of her misery or anything of her persona and life story, and footage of a hen with a broken leg, even when disconnected from any clear context or narrative, will similarly spur empathy. To suggest that these states are not "empathy" amounts to discarding most of what we feel to be "empathy". Therefore, although Gallagher is right in positing that intentionality, contexts and narratives can help empathy to gain more nuance, he is wrong to suggest that mere resonation is not important or sufficient – it is a distinct variety of empathy, and arguably it is also the core feature in many other varieties.

Sheer resonation also comes with many benefits. Understanding causes and narratives may provoke awareness and action, but it may also evoke biased exclusion based on our own political beliefs and prejudices against individuals with given histories. A prejudiced person who would feel deeply for a malnourished child may quickly halt her empathy when she realizes that the child is the offspring of refugees or from a social class that she views with suspicion or when she learns that the child's life narrative includes crime. Although contextuality and narratives may further empathy, they may also withhold it – a matter that has gained far too little attention. Indeed, without any resonation, simply following contexts, narratives and our own emotion towards them would be a dangerous road, for one could easily overlook (as so many do) the suffering of those whose backgrounds and life stories one has any politically coloured problems with. Again, the same also applies to non-human animals, for the causes of their suffering, and the narratives spun around them, may similarly provoke hostility rather than empathy, as is arguably quite typical, for instance, in relation to various unwanted or rivalry categories of animals, such as large predators, snakes or rats, whose contexts are described via competition and threat and narratives concerning them all too often portray them as aggressive, filthy villains deserving death. Without resonation, such biases are quick to take hold, and this is why resonation must also stay at the root of contextually and narratively informed empathy.

What Gallagher's account leaves out is, therefore, the most spectacular feature of empathy – resonation. Empathy is not an emotion of its own, directed towards the emotion of the other being (this would be something akin to sympathy) but is instead a mode of identifying the emotion of the other or feeling with it, and in the latter case, reverberation with the other is vital. As Tangney, Stuewig and Mashek posit: "Empathy is not a discrete emotion. Rather it is an emotional process with substantial implications for moral behaviour" (Tangney, Stuewig and Mashek 2007, 18). It sparks concern for others, prompts helping behaviour and inhibits negative emotions such as anger (ibid.), and it is precisely resonation that forms the key to this process. As implied here, emotions that the context of the other generates can also be destructive. Some emotions, including contempt, potentially evoked by hearing of the other's narrative tend to be disruptive. Despite its limitations, resonation stands as the key ingredient in preventing these disruptions and ensuring empathic attunement. It can be made more perceptive with the type of tools offered by Gallagher, but it also has its distinct, independent merits which render it into a necessity.

Resonation can lead to a plethora of emotions, and these may strengthen both our understanding of the situation and our resolve to aid others, but there appears to be no reason to confuse them with "empathy" itself. Of course, empathy may deepen and move towards morally loaded emotions such as "care", "solidarity", "awe", or "being with", but it should still be kept as its own distinct category.

AFFECTIVE MORAL AGENCY

The quotation from Tangney and colleagues above leads to the following question: What is the relation between affective empathy and morality? Does it form the necessary criterion for moral agency? As noted in the previous chapter, affectiveness is needed for one to avoid the type of amorality manifested in psychopathy. Whereas the case of psychopathy demonstrates that cognitive empathy alone does not suffice for moral agency, the case of Williams syndrome demonstrates that affective empathy may suffice, even in the absence of developed cognitive ability. As pointed out, those with this syndrome are highly caring, altruistic and sociable, thereby epitomizing the core of what it is to be moral – they are distinctly other-directed and also capable of accepting difference. Moreover, since the case of psychopathy reveals that high cognitive empathy and absence of affective empathy can lead to amorality and since Williams syndrome demonstrates that high affective empathy with low cognitive empathy can spark morality, it appears evident that affective empathy may, indeed, be the key to moral agency.

Affective empathy evokes other-directedness and openness to diversity. First, since the experiences and emotions of others penetrate us via resonation, we often cannot help but become focused on the other – when feeling with the terror of another individual, one is taken over by that terror and is similarly concerned over it as one would be over one's own emotions (those originating from the "self"). This shifts our mode of relating from self-directedness to other-directedness: the other's internal states become our point of attention, the target of our intentions. In fact, it is difficult to imagine a more potent way of becoming other-directed than resonation with the emotions of another, for such resonation brings those emotions into our own subjectivity with experiential vivacity (we feel with them, at times quite intensely) and thereby can force us to pay notice to them. The other enters us, and we cannot avoid becoming attentive to her, even if only momentarily. Therefore, affective empathy indicates other-directedness, for it invites one to notice the other and to become orientated towards her. When we are suddenly engulfed by the sorrow of another, it becomes exceedingly difficult not to let one's intention focus on that sorrow and its source, and when affected by the pain of another creature, we struggle to remain centred on and directed towards only our own egoistical inclinations and our often relatively petty projects – instead, we become concentrated on someone outside of ourselves.[6]

Second, affective empathy invites openness towards the difference of another. To resonate with the experiential state of another creature *is* to become open to that state; resonation *consists* of letting that state enter our own being. In affective empathy the other enters us, fills our own experiential spheres for a moment and becomes known from within – resonation, thereby, stands as a form of merging, wherein the experiences and emotions of other creatures come into us and the atomism and detachment, facilitated by projective and cognitive empathy, are absent. It is this that can spark openness to diversity, for once we reverberate with another, we also become open to noting her differences, uniqueness and peculiarities. Although it comes easier when we are familiar, proximate or similar with the other (a bias that will be discussed later), as Hume (1969) already noted, it can nonetheless extend to dissimilar, faraway strangers as well. In other words, its occurrence and intensity are often higher when it is effortless for us to recognize the body language of those we are empathizing with, but this is not a necessity, for affective empathy can also extend towards difference. The key is that it finds some common ground, some point of reference via which the emotions of the unfamiliar, dissimilar other make sense and thereby tap into us, as is the case when we suddenly note that a human being from a wholly different social class, colour, physique, cultural habit, gender and part of the world shows the same basic tendencies for fear, anxiety, curiosity, love and pleasure as we do.

Hence, one point of reference here is the recognition of similarity under layers of difference, whereby we learn to comprehend heterogeneity via approaching it through shared attributes: it is easier to get to know a refugee in all her cultural and social difference by first resonating with her basic human likenesses. Paradoxically, shared attributes offer the platform via which to explore difference and distinctness (as will be noted at the end of the chapter, such reliance on similarity can also have its costs and limitations, but despite not offering the "ideal" way to knowing diversity, it offers one approach to it).

Another such point of reference is simply learning of the other via alternative means, such as cognitive empathy (trying to figure out differences by observation and inference), which can then enhance our ability to fathom what the beliefs, physiologies or behaviours of the other refer to. In the latter case, cognitive empathy may support and extend the scope of affective empathy – indeed, as noted, for openness towards difference and heterogeneity to be more comprehensively possible, cognitive empathy is required, otherwise we too easily slip into resonating with only that which we easily recognize. Moreover, again the use of narratives and contexts (i.e., the tools of simulative empathy) may be of help as well.

Therefore, affective empathy enhances moral agency by enabling us to become focused on another, and it can also support openness towards heterogeneity and difference – moreover, the moral contrast between psychopathy and Williams syndrome suggests that it may be necessary for such agency. Only by being able to resonate with the emotions of others can we become experientially immersed in the relevance of their flourishing and well-being.

Indeed, without a hint of affective empathy, we simply cannot be moral. If we define morality as an enterprise that involves noting value in the outside world, and particularly in other individuals and their experiences, the relevance of affective empathy becomes apparent. In facilitating access to the experiences of others, affective empathy enables one to perceive inherent value in and feel concern for other individuals – in quite a Humean fashion, just as one's own experiences invite evaluation and concern, so do those of others. We view others as individuals of inherent value because we have had a glimpse into their phenomenality and felt their individuality in a raw, ineffable, immediate sense – in short, affective empathy breaks the spell of an egoistic, self-directed epistemology by opening us to the experiences of those around us. Hence, David Pizarro argues that because affective empathy "sensitizes us to the distress of the other, its presence acts as an efficient moral marker" (Pizarro 2000, 360). Quite simply, affective empathy helps us to note moral relevance: "Empathic arousal is thus a 'first alert', signaling moral relevance" (ibid.). Other emotions or reason cannot achieve this feat, for if one has never resonated with the experiences of others, one's reasoned and emotive responses towards those others remain hollow and superficial, not quite capable of capturing the raw, immediate sense of what it is to be an experiencing, valuable other.

This is also poignant in relation to non-humans. Arguably, it is precisely affective empathy that we need more of in order to note both the subjectivity and diversity, and thereby the moral worth, of other animals and which is often poignantly absent in the contemporary world. To understand and to morally grasp the value of reindeer, octopuses or birds from the broiler unit requires affective empathy – it is the core of being able to comprehend and relate to non-human animality on a moral level.

Other-directedness ensures that we take the cow or the chicken seriously into account and focus on her experiences rather than seeing those experiences as wholly secondary or even irrelevant in comparison to our own. This is a powerful antidote to anthropocentrism, which takes the human as the standard and also places her well-being as the primary target of moral action – within anthropocentric discourse, only human beings are of inherent value, and duties, rights and other central moral notions such as "justice" are seen to apply most fully, or even only, to them. The result is a self-directed morality, where the "self" is the collective formed of *Homo sapiens*. Moral agency is not practiced effectively in relation to non-human animals – if moral agency requires other-directedness, and if the latter is missing, our moral responding to non-humans, or indeed our animal ethics, becomes partial at best. In order to note moral value in other animals and to become moral agents in regard to them, other-directedness is pivotal, and affective empathy is one of the most experientially potent ways of sparking it. When resonating with the experiences of baboons and parrots, we cannot help but note the significance of their experiences and turn our intention towards them, which paves the way for moral awareness and consideration.

Here, the other animal enters human minds and urges humans to accept the relevance of that animal's own mindedness. It is difficult to think of a more fruitful and effective way to entice an anthropocentric individual into becoming other-orientated in regard to, say, pigs than showing her footage of the emotions of a specific, individualized pig (a testament to which is the success of undercover footage used by animal advocacy). The methods of simulative empathy – contextualization and narrativization – can add to the depth of the ensuing understanding, help to maintain focus on the animal subjects and also invite political action, but resonation nonetheless holds open the gate to a cow- or a pig-directed ethics.

In addition, the openness to diversity that affective empathy can spur is significant to animal ethics. Resonation can enable noting the sort of specificity in non-human creatures that anthropocentric cultures often ignore in their tendency to construe and reaffirm generic and stereotypic conceptions of non-human animality, wherein each animal is a more or less faceless representative of her species. Affective empathy demonstrates the subjectivity and uniqueness of each animal, as she becomes a particular creature with particular emotions that we can suddenly resonate with. In order to be morally mindful of other creatures, their specificity and heterogeneity must be acknowledged, and affective empathy can push us towards exactly that track. Following the above, opening towards the specificity of pigs can be focused on similarities, wherein an anthropocentrically inclined person suddenly becomes aware, when engaging with a pig, that she is not a prototypic creature far removed from humanity but rather a being who can experience anxiety, elation and many other emotions familiar from human experience – instead of being perceived via alienating stereotypes, the pig is approached as a being who shares much with humans, and again, paradoxically, similarities open spaces to noting ungulate specificities.

Here, one becomes aware of how utterly different beings can demonstrate subjectivity in ways that one can emotively comprehend and feel with – it is heterogeneity glued together by shared attributes that such openness entails. Yet there are risks to concentrating only on similarities, for it can narrow our attention down to only that which we instantly recognize and prevent us from accessing the ways in which non-human creatures may hold quite distinct emotions and manifest shared emotions in diverse manners, the reading of which requires knowledge and effort. Resonation can extend also towards the different, but it is more likely to do so when accompanied by further forms of understanding. Therefore, again, knowledge concerning the uniqueness of other animals, enabled, for instance, by cognitive empathy, can add to the degree of understanding.

Moreover, affective empathy offers a potent antidote to both egocentrism and anthropathy; hence, even if projective and cognitive empathies can aid it, affective empathy conversely can combat the dangers faced by projective and cognitive empathies. It enables an epistemological shift to take place, wherein humans recognize subjectivity and specificity in animal others and refuse to reduce those others into instrumentalized commodities serving the "human self". Egoism, manipulation and coercion become absurd when others are approached via affective epistemology, for they rest on premises which that epistemology does not recognize. Detachment is precisely that which enables and often instigates such negative ways of relating, for our grasp of others remains overly non-experiential: we "know", as we can know mathematical formulas or note that it's snowing, the mental states of others, but we do not "understand" them, for the experiential level is lacking (we know them only as one can know another from reading a list of her attributes). This is decisive from the viewpoint of moral agency, for only such an epistemological shift permits a broader shift in our collective psychopathologies and ultimately in our moral outlooks. Here, egoism, manipulation and coercion are replaced with emotionally aware engagement, wherein the non-human enters human mentation and species realities entwine on a felt level (how could we value a pig when we do not fathom her experientially, when we never let her into our world and when we never visit her world?). Therefore, affective empathy as an experiential attitude towards others holds the promise of contesting the trends within the contemporary cultures that so forcefully seek to invite an ever wider-scale, industrialized concentration on the human self at the expense of other creatures. If a purely hedonistic, instrumentalizing attitude towards non-human animals is historically related to the rise of self-directedness in the political ethos, perhaps it is via affective empathy that a new politic can be constructed, one that also opens up wholly fresh modes for inter-species existence.

Yet there are limits. As already pointed out, affective empathy tends to primarily concern emotions and experiences familiar to us, for we can only flow with the waves of that which we know at least on some level, and indeed also noting difference via affective empathy is initiated by first highlighting similarities. Therefore, although affective empathy can facilitate openness towards diversity, such openness can be limited due to its paradoxical reliance on similarity, which again narrows the scope of moral regard. Although resonating with a pike is possible if we tune our senses, it is easier to resonate with a pig, and this risk of bias is worth remembering (it will be addressed in the last part of this book).

A related issue is that affective empathy may also invoke the feeling of knowing the other fully: its grip can be so strong that an overt sense of familiarity rises, wherein resonation with the fear or joy of a hen leads to the presumption that we can know and access the hen entirely (arguably, the latter is an issue that at times plagues the culture of "animal loving", for many with intense sentiments with and for dogs and gorillas proclaim to know these creatures completely). Thus, noting and reverberating with similarity X extends to the presumption that the animal is wholly known. Such a sense of familiarity, even when it can engender moral concern, can also be an act of colonializing the animal under humanity. The danger is that the claim to full knowledge over others, even when entirely innocently motivated, easily entwines with power and a sense of arrogant authority or even ownership (see K. Weil 2012).

As Simone Weil has argued: "Justice. To be ever ready to admit that another person is something quite different from what we read when he is there (or when we think about him). Or rather, to read in him that which is certainly different, perhaps something completely different, from what we read in him. Every being cries out silently to be read differently" (S. Weil 2002, 135). When we claim to have a total view into another, to be wholly familiar with her, we easily pose power over her – she becomes a conquest we name and define with the thoroughness of our portrayals. Similarly, Emmanuel Levinas argued that claims of knowledge concerning others all too often fail to do justice to them. Our specificity can never be fully captured by definitions or interpretations, for the latter are too rigid and universalizing to fit the constantly changing flow of experiences that constitutes us. When assertions of knowing another are made, they are always prone to do violence towards that other – a risk that also plagues empathy (Levinas 1961).

Hence, to presume to be resonatively attuned to the whole of the animal can turn problematic, for it can eradicate her ferality, individuality and non-human particularity, which humans can never fully perceive, know or conquer. There is much to the non-human world which is utterly peculiar, partially even alien and in many ways inaccessible to human senses and mentation, and moral agency must be able to acknowledge also these facets of animality. It is on these lines that Levinas was nothing less than cynical over the need for empathy. For him, empathy can lead to hazardous presumptions of sameness, which abolish the uniqueness of the other – empathy becomes a vehicle of power, a "totalization", rather than a method of understanding (Pandya 2012).

These are severe criticisms and perhaps too harsh in regard to affective empathy – after all, resonation also does allow access to the particular experiential movements of the other. Yet they come with a noteworthy reminder, for despite its capacity to follow the experiences of others, affective empathy can also presume too much of its ability to know. Therefore, it enables other-directedness and openness towards diversity but also runs the risk of simultaneously being limited in noting difference and overlooking that which is occluded and even utterly impenetrable in the other. It stands as a foundationally important, vital mode of empathy and a necessary ingredient in moral agency but, like the previous candidates, would benefit from further support. Projective, simulative empathy can lend it contextual awareness, and cognitive empathy can add to its capacity to form reasoned, critical conclusions. However, an additional variety of empathy is needed to bring us closer to truly recognizing peculiarity and opacity in others.

NOTES

1. In order to separate it clearly from emotional contagion, some suggest that affective empathy involves more than mere resonation. For instance, Decety and Jackson argue that empathy is composed of three components: affective response towards another individual, cognitive capacity to perceive her point of view and emotion regulation. The last of these involves, for instance, simulations of a detached-observer position, wherein we strive to evaluate the situation somewhat objectively (Decety and Jackson 2006). Doing so enables a morally desirable response to others, for it pushes us to truly note their viewpoint – it also helps to maintain the boundary between oneself and the other. Like in Hume's approach, the suggestion is that affective and cognitive empathy combine with each other and also entwine with simulative empathy.

2. It should be highlighted that mirror neurons have been researched mainly in relation to goal-directed actions and may be irrelevant to many common empathic situations (Jackson, Meltzoff and Decety 2005) – thus, affective empathy cannot be reduced to them.

3. Here, an odd possibility emerges. As noted above, cognitive empathy tends to entwine with scepticism, for it asks, Do we *really* know the mental contents of another? Does this mean that scepticism is, after all, required for knowing others? A distinction needs to be made at this point. Affective empathy is usually – albeit not always – capable of showing the emotions of others. The main problem is that it may not reveal the motives or the broader reasons that infiltrate those emotions. On the level of experience, affective empathy may be quite astute, perceptive and capturing, indeed arguably more so than any form of inference could ever accomplish; but particularly on the level of intentions and motives, something further is required to accompany it. Scepticism is not, therefore, needed primarily for noting emotions, but critical reflection can enhance noting the reasons and causes behind those emotions (in so doing, it can also deepen our understanding of the relevant emotion). Moreover, two forms of scepticism need to be distinguished here: strong scepticism, which (negatively) doubts the existence of mental states or minds, and moderate scepticism, which (positively) looks for further evidence in order to advance comprehension of the mindedness of others. It is the latter of these which is relevant here, whereas the former tends to lead to the absurd, destructive desubjectification of others.

4. An optimistic view of the matter is that affective empathy can coincide with reflection, which again delays action, whereas the perhaps more realistic stance is that emotions can become overwhelming and hence defer activity.

5. Indeed, Schopenhauer suggests that simulation can help empathy – that is, trying to envision the perspective of another can spark resonation. Therefore, identification with the other is important: "For this [compassion/empathy] to be possible, I must in some way or other be identified with him. . . . Since I do not live in his skin, there remains only the knowledge, that is, the mental picture, I have of him, as the possible means whereby I can so far identify myself with him" (Schopenhauer 2005, 85). Schopenhauer concludes: "Our sympathy rests on an identification of ourselves with them" (ibid., 87) and thereby echoes contemporary studies, which demonstrate that simulating or imagining the viewpoints of others can assist in affective empathy.

6. Now, as pointed out earlier, this process can at times lead to the prioritization of emotion at the expense of the subject undergoing them, and in such occasions, suffering becomes something faceless and generic, an entity almost removed from the being behind it. Yet even such occasions arguably begin with recognition of foreign subjectivity and other-directedness and only begin to falter when aesthetization enters the scene. Therefore, even this does not cancel the other-directedness of affective empathy but rather merely reminds us to avoid combining the suffering of others with entertainment and spectacles.

Chapter 5

Embodied Empathy

The fifth variety of empathy, capable of addressing difference and opacity, is embodied empathy. Its philosophical roots lie in phenomenology, as echoes of it can be found in both early twentieth-century classics such as Max Scheler and Edith Stein and contemporary phenomenologists. Here, it is our somatic capacity to express and read mindedness which is central.

FROM ATOMISM TO EMBODIED ENGAGEMENT

The key to understanding embodied empathy is in recognizing what it is an alternative to – the sort of atomism discussed in relation to projective and simulative empathies. Scheler was a vocal critic of atomism and perhaps the first figure to posit that its impact on projective empathy renders the latter a frail basis for understanding others. For Scheler, projective empathy rested on scepticism and its atomistic stance on minds, according to which we are locked up into the prisons of our mentation, incapable of reaching out towards and entering that of others – following scepticism, we cannot ever precisely know what the mental states of others consist of, for such states are wholly subjective and enclosed into the sphere of private, internal landscapes. Scheler strongly questions this view and rests his critique on shared embodiment. Both oneself and the other are primarily and intrinsically somatic creatures, a unity of a mind and a body, and thus creatures continually expressing mental contents via their embodied behaviours. This shared embodiment forms the basis of how we relate to others and their mental states, for we do not approach others sceptically as unknowable entities, as bodies who are hiding a fenced off mind from us, but primarily as accessible beings, constantly communicating mindedness via their gestures, movements, tones of voice and so forth (Scheler 2009).

In contemporary philosophy, Dan Zahavi (2008) is perhaps the most prominent voice to support the Schelerian stance, as also he suggests that it is our capacity to engage and interact, on a corporeal level, with others that leads to empathy. What Scheler and Zahavi are bringing forth is the importance of letting go of the belief that we are beings encapsulated in our own minds. Their critique is ultimately against self-directedness, the belief that the "self" forms some type of an atomistic unit, wholly separated from others, and stands as the sole reference point of comprehending otherness. The core of their critique is that, if anything, we cannot know the minds of others in isolation, for understanding their emotions cannot arise from standing afar, encapsulated in one's own psyche. Instead of the atomistic model of having and knowing mindedness, the wiser, more realistic choice is to note how minds are constantly made evident via our bodies. Hence, the mind is not hidden within the body but rather manifested and experienced via the body: "Expressive movements and behavior is soaked with the meaning of the mind; it reveals the mind to us" (Zahavi 2008, 520). Such expressiveness is our surest form of knowledge concerning others: "But there is no more direct way of knowing that somebody is in pain than seeing him writhe in pain" (Zahavi 2007, 33). Indeed, it is via our own bodies – our ability to tune into others on a somatic level – that we can understand the mental contents of others. It is this which forms the core of embodied empathy: our ability to express, interpret and understand mental states on account of embodied interaction.

Therefore, getting rid of the rigid distinction between body and mind is crucial for embodied empathy. For Scheler and Zahavi, as for many other phenomenologists, the mind and the body cannot be categorically separated. Rather, we exist as a complex unity of mind and body, wherein the body is expressive of a mind, constantly communicating mental contents, and where the body continually impacts and constructs the mind. Thereby, when we move, frown, cry, touch or look, our being is expressing mental contents to others in an open, immediate fashion, and those others again read those contents via their own corporeal responses.

This was famously underlined by Maurice Merleau-Ponty, who concentrated much effort on tearing down the mind-body distinction. According to Merleau-Ponty, one cannot separate the mind from the body, as the two exist in a state of entwinement or a "chiasm", within which both maintain, direct and express the other. The mind is evident in our bodily movements, and the body affects the mind to an extent that we cannot precisely pinpoint, in the living subject, where one's influence begins and the other's ends. This chiasm is shared by all corporeal creatures and communicates our viewpoint to others. Again, there is no imprisonment, no isolation or solipsistic, hermity entrapment into private mentation, for the body continuously expresses the mind, readable by other embodied beings: "We must reject the prejudice which makes 'inner realities' out of love, hate or anger, leaving them accessible to one single witness: the person who feels them. Anger, shame, hate and love are not psychic facts hidden at the bottom of another's consciousness: they are types of behavior or styles of conduct which are visible from the outside. They exist *on* this face or *in* those gestures, not hidden behind them" (Merleau-Ponty 1964, 52). It is here that we find the roots for conceptualizing and understanding others.

This critique serves as an important reminder. "The problem of the opacity of other minds" is often argued to limit empathy (Hollan and Throop 2011), as it is presumed that the mental states of others are, indeed, hidden into private subjectivity and that any empathic understanding of them is bound to be projective. As suggested earlier, such criticism is also common in the context of other animals, as claims of empathic understanding are often dismissed as pure anthropomorphic projection, wherein one misleadingly transports a human self into a pig or a dog. Here, the human is the reference point against whose image all understanding of non-humans is reflected – the presumption is that we cannot "know" dogness or pigness, and that in claims of such knowledge, we are merely seeing ourselves mirrored in these animals. Such a take on empathy stems from the misconception, according to which "selves" are wholly isolated from others, their inner realms inaccessible. The solution is to replace this misconception with noting that we are, indeed, connected by embodiment capable of expressing and understanding mindedness – something that also applies in relation to other animals. If we follow the logic of embodied empathy, the pig may directly, via her behaviours, express her emotions to us without us having to infer (cognitive empathy) or project/simulate (projective/simulative empathy) her condition – nor do we need to resonate (affective empathy) with her emotions in order to understand them, for direct, instantaneous communication suffices (whereas in affective empathy, we reverberate with the other's emotion, within embodied empathy we conceptualize it, perhaps without a hint of emotion, via somatic involvement).

It should be highlighted that Scheler's and Zahavi's criticism could also be extended to cognitive empathy, which stands as the favourite choice of scientific endeavours into non-human mentation. Here, others are the focus of attention, but by abstaining from emotion, cognitive empathy keeps others isolated from oneself, an arm's width away. Others are not imprisoned in their minds, for cognitive empathy does presume that others can be understood in themselves quite fluently, but the empathizer and her "self" remain so imprisoned, sternly preventing her emotive contents from pouring out and reluctant to directly engage, on a somatic level, with those she is seeking to understand (indeed, doing so is often perceived as an "interference" that distorts credibility, something "subjective" that science ought not tolerate). In other words, with its insistence on emotive detachment, cognitive empathy reaffirms the isolation not of the being one is empathizing with but of the empathizer herself. This partial atomism is an odd depiction of knowledge wherein, first, the knower must deny the relevance of her own corporeality in the act of knowing (the scientist becomes a mythical "pure mind" whose body plays no part in what it is to know the mental states of another), and secondly "knowing" is not active participation *with* another but passive withdrawal *from* another.

This has awkward consequences. By refraining from direct, embodied contact with others, the capacity to read their mental states diminishes, for learning to read behaviour is like learning a new language: one must not only pay attention to those who speak it but also interact and engage with them in that language. Not directly engaging with a gorilla will make it near impossible to learn the nuances of her way of expressing her mindedness – in the absence of somatic interaction, coming to know the more delicate meanings of behaviours will be unlikely. It is for this reason that the scientist, thus far armed with cognitive empathy, ought to escape her isolation by interacting and spending time with those animals she is seeking to understand.

As Zahavi notes, expressiveness, or the "expressive unity" of mind and body, can "present us with a direct and non-inferential access to the experiential life of others" (Zahavi 2008, 518). As a warning against simulation, he refers to Wittgenstein's famous quote: "We do not see facial contortions and make the inference that he is feeling joy, grief, boredom. We describe the face immediately as sad, radiant, bored, even when we are unable to give any other description of the features" (Wittgenstein 1983, #170). Yet cognitive empathy can also be criticized following Zahavi's suggestion, for grasping the minds of others is not anchored in inference. For "theory theory", the approach which accentuates the significance of cognitive empathy as it posits that empathy stems from rationally using a theory of mind, empathy is inferential. According to Zahavi, theory theory implies that those without a theory of mind could not comprehend others – yet the example of small children (who only accumulate a theory of mind at around four or five years of age) clearly proves otherwise. In fact, young children can possess an astoundingly smooth capacity for intersubjective understanding, as they often fluently, without effort, read behaviours of others via learning to engage with them on a somatic level: it is only through vigorous training, a mode of acculturation, that young children begin to see others as a duality of "body" and "mind" and begin to pay less attention to somatic expression while learning to assume the importance of detachment, "pure mindedness" and inference. Perhaps the sceptical scientist, too, is the product of acculturation, which forces her to forsake the body as a trustworthy and necessary source of knowledge and replaces it with bizarre notions of non-physical minds.

Thus, theory theory, just like simulation, is based on faulty grounds. According to Zahavi, the notion of a mere body, potentially empty of experience and something that the mindedness of which must be theorized, is distinctly odd – yet it is precisely the image which accompanies the presumption that the mental lives of others are hidden from view, only to be found via elaborate, aloof inference. As Zahavi posits, "Such a view . . . presents us with a misleading perspective of the mind, suggesting as it does that the mind is a purely internal happening located and hidden in the head, thereby giving rise to the skeptical conundrum" (Zahavi 2007, 33). It is this notion which gives root to cognitive empathy and from which the notorious "problem of other minds", the laborious questioning of whether we can ever "know" (particularly non-human) others and the constant demand for more rational evidence for the mental contents of others, stem from and which ought finally be considered critically. Hence, the suggestion here is that cognitive empathy also stands on a misconceived separation between body and mind, self and the other – a detachment that is non-intrinsic to our earliest constitution and only later, via cultural indoctrination, becomes the presumptive standpoint towards knowing others.

This critique is also important in animal ethics due to the Western prevalence of scepticism over animal minds. Scepticism, already mentioned in the chapter discussing projective and simulative empathies, originates from the problem of other minds and continuously asks for more evidence for "knowing" non-human mentation, up to the point where no amount of evidence suffices, for doubt is always possible (Gaita 2002; Jamieson 2002). Its flaw is in presuming a clear-cut distinction between bodies and minds and between human knowers and animal others – the bodies of animals do constantly communicate their minds to us, and we can access those minds to some extent via shared embodiment, which enables us to interpret and read what is being communicated. Just like wondering whether another human is a zombified body void of a mind, whose mindedness one can only believe in once one has enough evidence for it, demanding evidence in relation to non-human animals can be grounded in a misconceived starting point. Non-human animals are not potentially bodies void of minds but come as a unity of a mind and body, and we are not isolated from them but can learn to understand them via physical, somatic involvement. Here, conceptualizing the emotive states and experiences of a horse takes root from expressive, affective behaviours and gestures.

Perhaps we begin as creatures capable of interacting with and understanding, at least on some level, non-humans, and it is the anthropocentric culture with its emphasis on dualities between mind and body, and humans and animals, which smothers this ability – therefore, embodied empathy is, due to cultural reasons, unduly sidelined, with the result that one important channel for knowing non-human minds is frequently blocked off.

DEFINITION

But what, precisely, is embodied empathy? For Scheler, as for Zahavi, it is a state of perception: one immediately perceives the mental states of others on account of the expressiveness of the body. As Scheler argues: "That 'experiences' occur there is given for us in expressive phenomena – again, not by inference, but directly, as a sort of primary 'perception'. It is in the blush that we perceive shame, in the laugher joy.... We can thus have insight into others, in so far as we treat their bodies as a field of expression for their experiences" (Scheler 2009, 10). We, in a relatively instantaneous manner, read emotions from somatic expressions and this constitutes empathy. Therefore, embodied empathy is perception, which again is a form of conceptualizing what one witnesses. Yet it differs in an important way from cognitive empathy, and this difference originates from its somatic nature. Whereas cognitive empathy seeks to remain detached from physical involvement, embodied empathy originates from such involvement: when we perceive mental states in others, we do so on the basis of bodily interaction, and perceptions are bodily rather than inferential (adrenaline may lead me to read another as angry). Moreover, embodied empathy is also experiential: perception of mental states in others leads to an affective content. Often it is emotions which act as the sort of concepts with which we "read" the presence of the other.

Hence, embodied empathy resists on the type of detachment typical to cognitive and projective empathy: "When I experience the facial expressions or meaningful actions of an other, I am experiencing foreign subjectivity, and not merely imagining it, simulating it or theorizing about it" (Zahavi 2008, 520).

Yet embodied empathy also differs from affective empathy, for the experiences it spurs are not formed of resonation but rather of distinct, even wholly different emotions that the observation of the other's mental contents awake. We do not imitate the emotion of the other but instead respond to it with an original emotion branching from ourselves, and thereby the fear of the other can be met with, say, sadness[1]. Here, one forms emotions as a way of conceptualizing and responding to what the other is undergoing. Moreover, the emotions revolve around noting the subjectivity of the other: centrally, we do not experience what she is experiencing but instead experience her agency, her subjectivity (it is her as a subject, rather than her particular emotion, which is the focus). As Scheler (2009) underlined, in empathy we need to perceive and respond to not only the experience but also the self who experiences. In short, embodied empathy emerges as "an ability to experience behavior as expressive of mind" (Zahavi 2007, 37), and this experience of subjectivity again leads to various emotions in us, as engaging with, say, someone shy and intellectual may arouse gentleness and curiosity.

Hence, embodied empathy consists of the ability to, on account of bodily interaction, directly and affectively perceive mental states as expressing foreign subjectivity. In simpler terms, and in the context of other animals, we interact with dogs by being open in relation to them and letting them also impact our ways of being, and via doing so we learn the emotive nuances behind their expressive behaviours – moreover, we do not perceive their communications in a neutral, detached way but feel something in this process (the curiosity of the dog may arouse joy in us and so forth). At the centre of it all is the experiential acknowledgement that the other is, indeed, a subject capable of responding and being responded to (the dog, thereby, does not remain an object that is observed from afar).

There is a further element separating embodied empathy from affective resonation worthy of notice. Whereas the latter may lead to the impression that one fully knows another, embodied empathy brings forward the opacity and intense difference in others. In other words, it acknowledges that there is much in others which remains both entirely strange and partially hidden. Often, the two go hand in hand: being aware of difference entwines with noting that others are, to some extent, inaccessible. Hence, even though embodied empathy enables communication and understanding, and vehemently resists notions of encapsulation, it also highlights how many of the behaviours of others remain distinct and elusive and thereby brings forth the fact that the other is always partly impenetrable in her specificity. Knowing others is possible, but not in a complete sense. When we engage with someone, there are always behaviours that we fail to read and which offer a reminder of their unique subjectivity. We keep much to ourselves, and even though engaging with someone in depth over long periods of time will increasingly reveal more of their subjectivity, something always remains uncaptured and hidden from view.

This applies also, and perhaps even more evidently, to non-human creatures, whose difference is often staggering, who are always partially elusive and who cannot be completely grasped by the human imagination: indeed, as pointed out earlier, claims to fully "know" risk transforming empathy into an arrogant human ownership of the animal other. When interacting with a pig on a physical, somatic level and getting to know her ways of expressing her mindedness, we will also come to understand that next to similarities lie vast diversities and unlikeness and that there are limits to knowing. I know my canine companions well because I have spent years with them, engaging with them physically each day, letting them impact and read my own mental states and learning, via bodily attunement, the contents of many of their behaviours and the intricacies of their subjectivity, but the more I do this, the more I sense their specific canineness, which is dissimilar to me in numerous respects, and the more I intuit that there is always something that escapes knowledge (paradoxically, this intuition becomes ever more manifest the more I spend time with them). Their particular physiologies and ways of sensing and behaving based on specific evolutionary histories render this distinctness and elusiveness perhaps even more apparent than is the case with other human beings. There are no categorical differences in knowing a human and knowing a dog, but there are shifting degrees of specificity and impenetrability. Recognizing these differences and opacities is an important part of embodied empathy, for they teach us to respect the uniqueness of being dog or being squirrel – the non-human can never be "fully captured", and this in itself is a testimony to her independent subjectivity.

Many other phenomenologists were equally embracive of embodied empathy, and their takes on it further illuminate its nature. For Edmund Husserl, the mutuality of being corporeal, sensing creatures with experiential access to our surroundings, shapes the platform for empathy, as the latter refers to the capacity to experience foreign subjectivity: "I can experience others, but only through empathy" (Husserl 1989, 210). Perhaps the most astute and neglected phenomenologist to speak of empathy was Edith Stein, who dedicated a book to the topic.

Stein used the newly developed term "empathy" but was critical of how it had been coined in German language (*Einfühlung*) as something akin to "emotional contagion", a direct "catching" of the emotions of others. According to Stein, empathy, like contagion, does take place in immediacy, for it contains a sense of the given or the evident (also emphasized by Husserl). Yet this givenness is communicative and hence something much more than contagion, for experiential communication requires that one notes it is another being one is engaging with – the ability to differentiate between oneself and the other separates empathy from contagion.[2] Indeed, as it is for the contemporary thinkers mentioned earlier, for Stein recognition of this difference between the empathizer and the target of empathy stands as central. In her view, empathy consists of three elements – seeking to know another, returning to one's own perspective and accessing the other again. Therefore, we strive to grasp another and return to our own viewpoint before revisiting the other once more. Via this movement, we remain firmly focused on the difference between ourselves and the other: we do not project ourselves into her place, nor do we become flooded with her emotions, thereby losing the feel of ourselves, but instead we keep altering between perspectives, remaining wholly aware of the boundaries between ourselves and others (Stein 1989).

In this process, shared embodiment is important, as is the critique of atomism, for in order to reach the communicative state between two different creatures, we have to approach others as sensing, bodily, experiencing subjects. Following suit, in emphasizing empathy as a process of communicating with the difference and subjectivity of others, and also rendering evident her own critique of the mind-body dualism, Stein asserted that "this individual is not given as a physical body, but as a sensitive, living body belonging to an 'I', an 'I' that senses, thinks, feels and wills. The living body of this 'I' not only fits into my phenomenal world but is itself the centre of orientation of such phenomenal world. It faces this world and communicates with me" (Stein 1989, 5).

Empathy is, then, grounded in shared embodiment and on reading the somatic expressions of another's mind – it also concerns communicating with the subjectivity of the other and noting her distinctness. As for Scheler, for Stein the distinctness of the other is crucial, for empathy is not resonation or "joy-with-him" (Stein 1989, 14) but instead concerns experiencing the other's subjectivity. That is, we do not feel what the other feels but instead feel her existence as a unique subject: again, empathy is not emotion mimicry but rather an affective recognition that it is indeed another subject who is engaging with me.

In relation to non-human animals, this means that in a state of embodied empathy, we approach them as body-minded subjects rather than as purely physical creatures. Moreover, we are continuously aware of their difference and keep altering between our own perspective and recognizing theirs; furthermore, we do not resonate with them nor undergo emotional contagion but instead feel something in relation to their subjectivity. In plainer terms, when interacting with a dog, I do not "catch" her joy or fear but instead build up emotions towards her subjectivity: instead of one specific mental state, she, as this specific dog, is the focus of emotional responding. I also keep moving back and forth between my own way of seeing and her subjectivity, which lays the grounds for interaction in the proper sense of the term (if I were to only focus on myself, or only on her, dynamic engagement would be impossible). Embodied empathy with dogs or pigs, thereby, centres on engaging with them as "an other" by affectively recognizing and responding to their subjectivity.

Indeed, Stein was quite favourable towards empathy with non-human animals, as she argued, "Should I perhaps consider a dog's paw in comparison with my hand, I do not have a mere physical body, either, but a sensitive limb of a living body. And here a degree of projection is possible, too. For example, I may sense-in pain when the animal is injured" (Stein 1989, 59). We can empathize with dogs and geese because we note that their bodies are living entities, intricately bound with and expressive of mentation; and we also note that as corporeal creatures, a sense of mutuality and imminence of grasping between us and other animals can take place. This corporeal being that forms my "I" responds – often before the first thought – to the corporeal manifestations of emotion in others, regardless of their species. Scheler also thought empathy towards other animals to be quite possible, as many embodied expressions are easily recognizable: "We can understand the experience of animals, though even in 'tendency' we cannot imitate their manner of expression" (such as tail-wagging; Scheler 2009, 11). The basis for this is found in shared attributes: "We have here, as it were, a universal grammar, valid for all languages of expression, and the ultimate basis of understanding for all forms of mime and pantomime among living creatures" (ibid., 11).[3]

In contemporary animal philosophy, this phenomenological stance has been favoured by Ralph Acampora. In his seminal and eloquent work on "corporeal compassion" and the non-human world, he has argued – much in line with classic phenomenologists – that it is our shared embodiment which allows us to understand others. Although Acampora's work also draws differences between itself and the phenomenological tradition, particularly when it comes to the ability to escape anthropocentrism, the central emphasis placed on bodily – rather than mental – knowing of others is shared by both.[4] Acampora begins from the critique of atomism and links it to animal ontology. We are not floating in "retro-Cartesian position of species solipsism . . . wondering, as it were, if 'there's anybody out there'" but are rather "always already caught up in the experience of being a live body" (Acampora 2006, 4) with connections to other beings. In sum, atomism combines with anthropocentrism, within which humans detach themselves from other species, whereas acknowledging shared embodiment re-engages us with non-human creatures.

Specifically, Acampora draws from what he calls Merleau-Ponty's "intersomacity" or embodied, dynamic relations between members of different species. Expressed in a less cumbersome manner, this refers to noting how our bodies share the same ability to relate to and perceive the world and each other, allowing mutual recognition to take place. Such recognition, again, opens access to visiting the subjective worlds of non-humans, and it is from here that "corporeal compassion" spurs. Thus far, Acampora follows the model of embodied empathy, all the way to noting its normative implications. Other living animal bodies cannot be mere resources or tools, "heaped alongside hammers and minerals", but due to their ability to "share the same perceptual sphere or scale with humans" (Acampora 2006, 7), they belong to a different moral order in comparison to the inanimate nature. Therefore, it is via their existence as perceiving, embodied creatures that other animals can be related to and also viewed in a moral light.

Yet Acampora goes perhaps slightly too far with his take on corporeal compassion, suggesting that it extends to all living beings. He claims that life is characterized by "having a self-generated perspective" on existence (Acampora 2006, 18) and joins those who speak of plants as demonstrating a capacity to perceive and dwell in the world since they relate to their surroundings by, say, turning towards the sun. Indeed, Acampora maintains that all life takes part in "transpecific intersomaticity" – that is, shared, embodied relating with one another. Here, having a mind becomes both wholly secondary to embodiment and relativized.

Acampora argues that highlighting the mental/experiential is akin to the Cartesian, dualistic ethos and talks of the "prevalent psychocentric bias in favour of mentality's moral significance" (Acampora 2006, 4). However, one could argue that the fault does not lie in recognizing the significance of mindedness but rather in defining it as something that transcends embodiment. Undoing this mistake does not need to include prioritizing only embodiment, as if mental capacities were its insignificant shadows. The somatic level is vital but should not engulf the uniqueness of the capacity intrinsically entwined with it in animals – mindedness. Acampora's account is also at risk of misusing terms. In metaphoric terms, there is agency not only in all life but also in all existence, ranging from how atoms react to their environments to how galaxies shape each other. However, such reacting or responding does not constitute agency or subjectivity in any other than a metaphoric sense, and the same arguably applies to perception and perspective in plants. Plants respond, but they do not perceive in the sense as being *aware*, and it probably is not *like* anything to be a plant (and if it is, it is so far removed from animal experience that we would struggle to comprehend it). The enormously significant element of consciousness, our capacity to feel our existence as something, is most likely missing (although of course future research may prove differently). Without it, there is nothing to relate to, no intersomatic openings to other worlds.

Therefore, whereas Acampora's thoughtful philosophy aims for a biocentric account of compassion, extending it to all living beings, embodied empathy as proposed here focuses on minded creatures (creatures, who have inner subjectivity, the capacity to feel their existence as something).

SOMATIC INTERSUBJECTIVITY

Despite evident similarities with other phenomenologists, Stein also offered criticism, particularly over Scheler's notion of empathy as perception. For her, perception captures the primordial or the "original" (perception of suffering captures the feel of suffering), whereas empathy is non-primordial or representative in a sense akin to memory (in remembering suffering, we no longer capture it). Therefore, Stein suggests that perception may ultimately render empathy into something more akin to resonation – it sparks one to focus on and go with the emotion one perceives instead of forming a representation of that emotion, which one does not enter. Stein's understanding of empathy, on the other hand, does not repeat the original experience in all its authenticity but rather offers us a mediated account of this experience: "While I am living in the other's joy, I do not feel primordial joy" (Stein 1989, 11).[5] Empathy is experiential, but its experientiality concerns, again, not the emotion the other is undergoing but her subjectivity: "Through empathizing do we experience others" (ibid., 18). It is this that the non-primordial sense of empathy stems from, for we do not live with the experiences of the other, but instead we concentrate on her subjectivity, her existence as an "I". In a state of empathy, we are to focus on the subjectivity of others while keeping her experiences on a non-primordial level as faint representations that we can understand but do not feel with. Now, as seen from cognitive empathy, Stein is mistaken in her belief that perception by necessity evokes resonation. Yet she has an important point to make: embodied empathy does not primarily consist of perceiving individual mental states but engaging with the subject as a whole, and when this is accomplished, one's sense of the other's mental states is non-primordial.

But what do such non-primordial representations consist of? Here, contemporary authors who speak of "offline" simulation become a possible tool of mapping out Stein's stance. For them, offline empathy is exclusive of raw emotive content, even if it can become "online" with ease (Gordon 1995). That is, we keep our own emotions unaffected, stay detached from the emotions of the other, even if we can comprehend what those emotions are; we can imagine what it is like for another to undergo fear, but we do not let ourselves become filled with fear. Yet this option is misleading in interpreting Stein. First, the "offline" notion describes something quite disengaged, whereas Stein maintains that empathy is experiential rather than detached. Second, Stein is also critical of simulation, which draws her even further away from such off-line identification. Instead of the offline model, it is worth going back to the movement between oneself and the other, which Stein emphasized. In primordial experience, we grasp the mental landscapes of the other, but for Stein, movement back towards the self is significant, followed by revisiting the other again.

Perhaps it is this movement which leads to non-primordial experiences; when we empathize with fear, we do not merely reproduce that fear as we would were we to stay affixed to the viewpoint of the other, but rather we see it from our own standpoint, invested with our own mental responses. Just as in the act of remembering we see the past experience from our present outlook instead of simply repeating it as it was, in a state of empathy we recognize emotions of others from a particular horizon, which allows us to affectively acknowledge what the other is going through but which also offers us a standpoint that avoids sheer resonation. Here, it is not only the specificity and subjectivity of the other that is accentuated but also that of ourselves: we are not empty receptacles for the emotions of others but our own specific agents who bear our own mark on how those emotions manifest to us.

Therefore, Stein's stance on embodied empathy, like that of Scheler's, underlines that empathy focuses on the other's subjectivity rather than on her specific emotions – yet for Stein, the movement between the self and the other is also important and leads to a state where we do not primarily feel with the emotions of the other but instead make sense of them via our own subjectivity, the role of which is highlighted. (This version of embodied empathy draws further lines between it and affective empathy, for whereas embodied empathy resists becoming attached to specific emotions and the viewpoint of the other, affective empathy is founded on doing precisely so and is thereby highly primordial.)[6]

When feeling Steinian embodied empathy towards a hen, one will not resonate with her distinct feelings but instead will constantly shift between the perspective of the hen and oneself, thereby both forming an understanding of the hen as a subject with her own take on the world and staying rooted in one's own beliefs, emotions and other mental states. I see the hen's excitement or curiosity but do not become immersed by it and instead let my own view on the hen and her emotions help me to constitute intersubjective engagement between us. It is precisely this that allows for there to be two distinct subjects interrelating with each other (rather than one subject mirroring and thereby "losing" herself in the other). In short, the Steinian account makes a subject both of the hen and the human observer.

This meeting of subjectivities leads to an important concept for phenomenologists – intersubjectivity. As for many other phenomenologists,[7] for Stein intersubjectivity stands as pivotal and is inherently entwined with embodied empathy. The latter does not only involve experience, for before such experience can emerge, it is often rooted in preconscious somatic entanglements with others, within which our gestures, looks and behaviours are mutually recognized, interpreted and acted in relation to, to the point where experience is co-constituted. Here, my body-mind responds on the basis of being responded to, and this dynamic field of sensory, embodied mentation, notably referred to by Merleau-Ponty as "flesh" (Merleau-Ponty 1968), as the shared, lived world of corporal sensuousness begins an existence of its own. Intersubjectivity, thereby, emerges as a process, within which one and the other submerge into a flow of continually altering and jointly constituted somatic communication and experience. For Stein, the starting point for intersubjectivity is the recognition of the subjectivity of the other – the fact that there is another "I" in front of us. What matters, again, is not our awareness of *what* the other is experiencing but rather *that* she is experiencing and that she is her own, particular being.

The resulting state is beyond comparison. Thus, Stein argues that "What another person experiences at a certain moment is not directly given to me. But the presence of the other is directly given, and so is the awareness that the other is an experiencing self. This cannot be compared with other modes . . . of experience. The experience of another is unique. This means that other modes of experiencing only are of partial help in explaining how the subjective becomes intersubjective. It also means that there is no doubt about who is experiencing primarily, and who is sharing, or experiencing, the experience of the other" (Stein 1989, 59). We first become aware of our relation to others, the existence of their subjectivity, with which we can interact, and then enter into states of intersubjectivity, which again feed embodied empathy. Intersubjectivity acts as the platform on which to build embodied empathy – very simply put, via engaging with others, we gain a better understanding of their viewpoint and subjectivity.[8]

When reading the expressions of others in a dynamic sense, letting our bodies communicate with the bodies of others, a sense of mutuality takes over as we recognize others as mind-body unities and let our own mind-bodies respond to and interpret their expressions. As a consequence, intersubjectivity is born as a process of co-constitution, wherein we are continually reshaped and reconfigured in response to somatic behaviours of others, and those others again are affected by our own bodily expressions – in other words, how we physically express ourselves influences their mentation, and vice versa, until we form a small, shared world filled with mutual recognition and impact. Intersubjectivity is direct, somatic communication between two or more beings, and supports the emerging of a "we" out of a "you" and "me" – the mysterious yet palpable state of being "more than one, less than two" (a phrase coined by Donna Haraway). Embodied empathy is entwined with intersubjectivity, for it is both enhanced by such states of dynamic interaction and again offers those states something crucial: without tuning into the behaviours of another, there could be no intersubjectivity. Therefore, the sort of "engagement" with others that is being proposed is intersubjectivity, wherein we affect the mental states of others and vice versa. It is this that replaces the dualisms between bodies and minds, and others and us, and sets the foundation for embodied empathy. In the context of other animals, we are then to seek contact with them and let them impact our own mentation – it is then that we may learn to read what their bodies are expressing.

As suggested by both Husserl (1989) and Stein (1989), a core facet of intersubjectivity is the recognition that the world is accessible to others, that it is perceived by other creatures in their own specific manner.[9] This originates from recognizing that others indeed are subjects with their own perspectives on the world, and lends us belief in that very world. For Husserl, the world is sense-making only when one comprehends that it is mentally accessed by also countless others, and by recognizing that the world and we ourselves are accessible to others, to a plurality of sensing viewpoints, we no longer remain within the prisons of our own mentation, forever wondering if the mentation of others is real or just a lonely figment. In the shared act of perceiving, the mutuality of the experiential process, the world and its creatures become manifest, and it is here that empathy takes flight. As Husserl described: "We experience the same things and events, we experience the animals and people there facing us, and we see in them the same inner life. . . . In a certain way, I also experience (and there is a self-givenness here) the others' lived experiences" (Husserl 1989, 208). By becoming awake to the fact that we share the ability to have a perspective on the world with many others, we become not only capable of empathy and noting the experientiality of others but also of trusting our knowledge concerning the world and its beings.

Therefore, again, the importance of desisting scepticism, atomism and the "problem of other minds" surfaces as crucial: instead of approaching others via doubting their subjectivity and pondering whether we are ultimately lonely drifters on this planet, we are to approach them as subjects. Indeed, without intersubjectivity we can have no knowledge. Whereas the sceptic assumes knowledge to stem from isolated minds and their purely internal machineries of doubt, the claim here is that only by noting how others see reality can knowledge be structured: "The only thing I know, I know through intersubjectivity, through verification by other subjects, through the collective 'knowledge' inherent in the summing of perspectives" (Verducci 1998, 339). Isolated minds might as well be hallucinating all that they perceive (a possibility which the father of scepticism, René Descartes, infamously entertained) while minds co-constituting each other, and noting and reflecting on each other's viewpoints, are much more rooted in what they know. For Stein, too, having knowledge of this world rests on forsaking isolation and doubt and replacing them with recognition of foreign subjectivity. (Merleau-Ponty talks of "perceptual faith", the ability to trust one's senses and embodied knowledge, as the key to rooted mindedness, and intersubjectivity gives it one important foundation, for via intersubjectivity we have a sense of certainty in what we see, hear or touch; see Merleau-Ponty 1968.)

Intersubjectivity also goes far in the non-human context.[10] We are to focus on animal subjectivity and non-human ways of expressing mental states via embodiment. Instead of purely theorizing what the mental states of pigs may be, it is more important to pay notice to their somatic behaviours as something that express a mind and reveal subjectivity which we can directly experience and communicate with. Intersubjectivity with other animals renders embodied empathy possible, for it is only after noting them as subjects that we can form the sort of routes into their mindedness that such empathy requires – in other words, with intersubjectivity we come to recognize non-human subjectivity. Intersubjectivity establishes the ontology, the existence, of non-human subjecthood, and embodied empathy offers the epistemology, the ways of knowing, into that subjecthood. Therefore, when we interact with cows and begin to acknowledge that the cow is a subject rather than a biological "thing", we can also begin to cultivate a better grasp of her bovine ways, and the latter again enforces the intensity of intersubjective states.

Noting that elephants and tigers also have a view of the world lends credibility to trusting its existence and our capacity to form specific perspectives of and knowledge concerning it. Intersubjectivity with other animals is thereby a concrete antidote to anthropocentric isolation, which positions humans as the only minded beings and leaves them alone and isolated – it reminds us that we indeed are not alone and that the anthropocentric ideology is, thereby, misled in its very basis. Suddenly, reality is no longer limited to something only humans can notice but is filled with utterly different and distinct viewpoints and coloured with incredible variety, against which we are far better equipped to judge the merits of our ways of knowing. Indeed, as also suggested by Acampora (2006), anthropocentrism is species solipsism, in which the collective "human self" is secluded to her lonely existence, and intersubjective, embodied empathy offers nothing less than a way out of such epistemic misery.

Therefore, both embodied empathy and intersubjectivity are also quite possible in relation to other animals. However, as suggested, cultural influences often diminish them, as we learn to aim for detachment and reason rather than somatic knowledge, and this also impacts human-non-human relations. The situation is made even bleaker by the anthropocentric presumption that crows and cows are not "subjects" – if we do not approach them as such, entering into states of intersubjectivity and empathy becomes unlikely, and we begin to walk past these animals without noticing experiential spheres and without stopping to interact with them in a manner that would entice us to ponder what it is to be a non-human "I". Of course, some embodied empathy does take place in relation to other animals, one example perhaps most commonly mentioned being instances where there is intentional synchrony between the behaviour of the human and the non-human – an obvious case in point being attentive forms of training, such as dog agility.[11] Here, the human is reading bodily cues from the dog, and vice versa, to the point where quite intense and effortlessly flowing moments of intersubjectivity can be formed. (It should be remembered that such instances can also be negative from the standpoint of the animal: they can "read", on an embodied level, the harsh and coercing intentions of humans via, say, raised voices and aggressive gestures.)

Embodied empathy is also used in more ordinary contexts when one is being attentive towards other animals and letting their responses impact how one responds to them. A typical example is a day spent in a park or a forest letting squirrels or magpies approach with curiosity and leave without fear or a day spent at home continually even if mostly unconsciously signalling one's emotions and intentions to a dog or a cat and reading her bodily expressions often quite instantaneously, thereby forming a dynamic, knowing synchrony between two companions.

Yet embodied empathy requires the sort of attunement to the other which consists of recognizing her subjectivity, and often even those sorts of encounters, which use bodily behaviours of other animals as clues to their mentation (think of hunters, farmers or those trainers who approach animals as objects rather than subjects) are wholly disregardful in this sense. In fact, when it comes to the way in which humans approach other animals, embodied empathy is perhaps the most sorely missed and most clearly absent type of empathy in many contexts. Not only is recognition of subjectivity frequently absent, but the willingness and capacity to get familiar with the bodily expressivity of other animals remains relatively rare. Dog "owners" do not pay attention to the bodily expressions of their canine companions, and many are only aware of the most obvious signs of dog language (wagging a tail, baring the teeth) while remaining wholly ignorant of the varieties and nuances of canine expressions – thus, even the animal closest to humans in Western cultures is often sidelined in the arena of embodied empathy (this becomes ever more worrisome when considering that dogs themselves often make an enormous effort to understand human bodily expressions). In general, humans tend to remain astoundingly unaware of the ways in which other animals manifest their mental states, ranging from how farmed animals show their suffering or fear to how wild animals display their affection and play. We are illiterate in non-human languages, painfully incapable of understanding the bodily expressions of cows, pigs, parrots, salmons, frogs and elks and thus all too often remain oblivious to their mental capacities and perspectives on this world. We humans have become poor readers of non-human behaviour, and it is this that poses a vast obstacle to noting the mental contents and subjectivity of other animals.

What is required, then, is more embodied empathy – more encounters with other animals and more attunement and attentiveness to how we engage with them and how they express their own mentation. We need to make an effort to understand non-human behaviour and to let ourselves enter into states of intersubjectivity with hens or foxes. This is all the more important because embodied empathy can enable a process of "becoming" with other animals. Drawing from Merleau-Ponty and Gilles Deleuze, it has been suggested that somatic engagement with other animals opens not only states of intersubjectivity but also states of the sort of mutual co-constitution which shape and form us in the future (Haraway 2003, 2007; Acampora 2006; Toadvine 2007; Ruonakoski 2011; Singer 2015). Here, we intertwine in the present moment, and in forming a mutual reality with the sheep or the rabbit, letting them affect us and us affect them, we begin to shape and orientate each other. Donna Haraway (2003, 2007) has used the example of the co-constitution between wolves and humans and later between dogs and humans, but this is only one option, for such co-constitution can, does and should happen in all sorts of contexts (between, say, pigeons and humans or foxes and their neighbours).

The benefits of this are evident, for were we to truly enter into embodied empathy and intersubjectivity with other animals and allow them to bear an impact on us while making ourselves understandable to them, perhaps we could see a world where humans direct their own futures so as to better advance the vivacity of animal existence, the survival and well-being of members of other species and simultaneously cultivate their own ability to live well. In such a world, we would "become" something novel in our effort to pay heed to non-human life, and in the process that non-human life would alter too – both, ideally, in a direction that supports interspecies flourishing and the thriving of life.

EMBODIED MORAL AGENCY

But what of the link between embodied empathy and moral agency? Will embodied empathy help us to become more morally attuned with others?

Like Husserl, Stein also argued that empathy intertwined with morality: "Every comprehension of different persons can become the basis of an understanding of value" (Stein 1989, 116). Therefore, the claim is that embodied empathy will produce a normatively laden experience of another. A sense of the value of the other is constituted out of recognizing her subjectivity – as soon as we both recognize that the other is a specific, unique being in her own right and become affectively engaged with her, we also (so it is presumed) note moral relevance. Therefore, the suggestion is that the embodied, felt acknowledging of the individuality of another will spark the moral dimension, particularly if one enters into intersubjective modes in which both become open to the other's presence.

A further distinction strengthens the normative bearing of embodied empathy. As a subcategory of embodied empathy, Stein also mentions what is contemporarily called "reiterated empathy"[12] and which consists of moments "when I empathically comprehend the acts in which my individual is constituted for him [the other person]" (Stein 1989, 88). Here, we pay attention on how the other responds to us to such a degree that we see ourselves via her perspective, and thus her responses open the pathway to noting how our own subjectivity is formed in the eyes of another: "To consider ourselves in inner perception, i.e. to consider our psychic 'I' and its attributes, means to see ourselves as we see another and as he sees us" (ibid., 88).[13] As Zahavi notes, Husserl also speaks of moments "where I experience the other as experiencing myself. . . . The absolute difference between self and other disappears. The other conceives of me as an other, just as I conceive of him as a self" (Zahavi 2001, 160). Therefore, reiterated empathy involves two levels: reading the subjectivity of the other and reading how she reads that of our own.

This double-foldedness is significant for moral agency, for surely our ability to notice how our own actions and character appear to others plays a vital role, particularly in the type of moral cultivation emphasized in virtue ethics, the purpose of which is to advance our sense of matters such as "justice", "courage" or "empathy". As claimed by Aristotle, our surroundings do and should impact our moral character via a dialogue wherein we learn from others, and reiterated empathy is an excellent source for the sort of feedback required for training our virtue. Simply stated, in order to treat others with moral regard, we have to acknowledge their subjectivity, but in order to reflect and work on our moral character, we have to acknowledge how others see our own subjectivity (how our actions appear to others, how they affect them, how we, as beings, are experienced by others). Ultimately, such a subcategory allows one to mark not only how others respond or how our responses seem to others but also how our own responses towards others will again affect how we are responded to. When it comes to empathy, this is the ultimate locus of communication: acknowledging how one's expressions are perceived, felt and intuited by those in their sphere and how that again impacts the way in which our subjectivity is constituted for others and with what consequences.[14]

Therefore, embodied empathy holds moral potential, for it focuses on and brings forward the subjectivity of others while also motivating moral cultivation. When observed from the viewpoint of the main constituents of moral agency – other-directedness and openness to diversity – embodied empathy appears equally beneficial. First, in centralizing the noting of the subjectivity of the other, it lays the path for other-directedness. The other emerges as a subject with her own viewpoint, and since embodied empathy highlights the prominence of this subjectivity, it also draws us towards paying heed to the other's well-being rather than merely noting our own.

Second, embodied empathy invites openness towards and recognition of difference. As posited by Scheler and Stein, in embodied empathy we remain aware of the difference of the other being, and in addition a sense of the occluded, the impenetrable, is continuously present, as we acknowledge, next to all that which is recognizable, a whole realm of gestures and expressions which remain distinct and even inaccessible. The other is communicating both her familiarity and her difference, her openness to being known and her privacy, which cannot be entered. She is reachable, often peculiar and always partly uncharted: some of her behaviours we can read even when wholly different, others leave open questions and frustrated efforts of understanding, and some spark respectful recognition of boundaries beyond which one cannot enter. As Scheler argues, there is much which will remain hidden from view: "The other has an individual self distinct from our own, and we can never fully comprehend this individual self, steeped as it is in its own psychic experience, but only our own view of it as an individual, conditioned as it is by our own individual nature. . . . The other person has – like ourselves – a sphere of absolute personal privacy, which can never be given to us" (Scheler 2009, 10). Indeed, noticing and respecting opacity emerges as the paradoxical epicentre of empathy: "The realization that as finite beings we can never see right into one another's hearts, that we cannot even have full and adequate knowledge of our own hearts, let alone other peoples', is given as an essential feature in all experience of fellow-feeling" (ibid., 66).

Opacity may also be the very route to noting difference. When entering intersubjectivity with even those closest to us, there is always something that escapes, and this something bears a constant mark on interaction (also those whom we love the most, know the most, retain opacity to them, and in somatic communication the sense of this remains persistent – I know the other and yet do not know). Much remains un-understood, even alien, and embodied empathy directs us towards accepting this unfathomability, as with access there is a sense of inaccess. The alterity of the other resides here, as this unknown marks the boarder of "otherness". Indeed, for Scheler this opacity and difference is the very basis of subjecthood, for to suggest that others should be known just as we know ourselves would reduce them to a faceless state of sameness, void of subjectivite distinctness (Scheler 2009). This is something that Zahavi also underlines as he borrows a quote from Husserl: "Had I had the same access to the consciousness of the other as I have to my own, the other would have ceased being an other, and instead have become a part of myself" (Zahavi 2007, 35).

Therefore, embodied empathy constitutes the subjectivity of the other partly via inviting recognition of her dissimilarity and opacity. It is precisely as a different, specific being that the other becomes a subject, and this difference and specificity can include also impermeability. It is this that renders embodied empathy a perfect basis for openness towards diversity – in fact, out of all the varieties of empathy, it acts as the best anchor for such openness.

In relation to non-human animals as well, embodied empathy can enhance moral ability. First, noting the inherent value of other animals evidently requires that they are first perceived as subjects, and embodied empathy establishes just this. The pig emerges as a subject in her own right with whom we can interact, and this allows for other-directedness to take place, together with noting value in the pig. As Husserl and Stein posit, a sense of value may emerge from recognizing subjectivity in others, and this also applies in regard to non-human creatures. Indeed, arguably it is often the lack of such recognition that acts as a hindrance to animal ethics: as argued earlier, when pigs are deemed as biological "things", it appears as absurd to assert that they have inherent value, let alone rights, and as long as the culture is resistant to the notion that pigs may be subjects, individuals or "persons", the road towards animal liberation or even genuine concern is blocked. Embodied empathy allows for the sorely missed recognition of the subjectivity of other animals to emerge and in so doing facilitates moral agency in the realm of animal ethics.

Second, embodied empathy allows for the recognition of the alterity of other animals. The anthropocentric ideology has insisted on sameness with humanity as a criterion for moral worth: other animals must possess various factors linked to humanity in order to count as morally significant. Following Scheler, doing so is an evident mistake, for it nullifies the very subjectivity of other animals – they become, at best, little humans, void of their specific animality, authenticity and substance. Embodied empathy reminds us that difference rather than sameness is the grounds of subjectivity and opens the door for the recognition of subjectivity in a breathtaking variety of creatures, all quite distinct, different and even peculiar, yet all invested with the capacity to have a perspective on this world. It facilitates openness towards difference and thereby our ability to be moral agents in relation to those animals who are quite dissimilar to us – in other words, it offers us nothing less than the capacity to become morally aware of animals as "others".

Moreover, embodied empathy also acts as an antidote to the far-too-common sceptical assertion, according to which we cannot note inherent value in non-human animals, for we cannot know their mindedness fully. Such a requirement appears absurd in the context of intersubjectivity and embodied empathy, for others are always partly inaccessible, and this very fact forms the core of their particularity as living, experiencing creatures and hence also entwines with their value. Instead of claiming that pigs cannot be subjects of worth because we cannot know precisely what it is like to be a pig, the claim that embodied empathy can bolster is that precisely *because* we cannot assimilate and thereby fully know the pig she is a subject of worth. The impenetrability and unfathomability of non-human animals – their specific ways of mindedness, unknown to humans – no longer pose an obstacle to recognizing their value but in fact support such recognition, and this further accentuates how embodied empathy can facilitate moral ability when it comes to relations with other-than-human creatures.

Just as embodied empathy is often missing in contemporary culture and its dealings with other animals, so too are these aspects of moral agency. Next to the obvious – lack of other-directedness and openness towards difference and opacity – one of the dimensions mentioned by Stein, reiterated empathy, appears regrettably absent. We far too rarely reflect on how other animals experience us, how the pig in the farrowing crate perceives the farmer and how the dog in the living room corner observes her human companion. We are quite busy thinking of what we can gain from animals, and to some extent we are busied by what we think of them, but we very rarely note what they may think of us, let alone how they emotively interpret and experience us. What are humans to the cows, hens, wolves and snakes of this planet? Not only do human beings tend not to notice how their ways of behaving are felt and interpreted by non-human animals, they are also oblivious to how their often ignorant and violent ways of treating those animals may serve to frustrate and suffocate the animals' efforts to express themselves to humans. When we are unaware of how other animals experience and perceive us, we are also unaware of how our behaviours disable other animals from engaging with us and disable us from understanding them. The pig stricken by fear and unnoted by the farmer will not be able to communicate her mindedness, and the vicious circle of assuming that such mindedness does not exist continues. Simply stated, we cannot properly pay heed to the somatic expressivity of other animals as long as we fail to notice how our own actions prevent and alter it.

To see how a human being appears to non-human animals is one of the greatest challenges on the way to cultivating our moral ability. If we wish to become more virtuous in relation to the non-human world, we first need to notice how it perceives us and what humans are in the minds of whales, hedgehogs and seagulls. Following the Aristotelian way, we are to stop being the hermity species stuck in thinking of and listening only to themselves as if existing in a state of solitude, and we are to start paying notice to what our actions and character are from the non-human perspective. Here, that perspective is the all-important "feedback" we need for the sort of moral cultivation that enables animal ethics to flourish.

But how could embodied empathy support animal ethics when it rests on bodily engagement and when we evidently cannot meet, in reality, all the billions of pigs we ought to have concern for? Moreover, not all animals are likely to want interaction, either because they are solitary creatures, fearful or just not remotely interested in humans. Would relying on embodied empathy not leave them outside of moral concern?

It is important to note that the same problem concerns all forms of empathy, for we equally cannot resonate with, project, simulate or cognitively infer the mental states of all existing animals. However, fortunately, being able to do so is beside the point. Empathy is not something one ought to concretely undergo for all existing individuals, one by one, but rather something we know we could undergo if we were in their company, heard their histories or were otherwise familiar with them: it is an outlook or an attitude that we extend to all those we know it is possible to empathize with. Similarly, as one can claim to have concern towards all human beings or, say, all dogs or cats, one can empathize with all minded animals regardless of whether one knows them individually. Here, one conceptualizes those animals as creatures, towards whom empathy is the appropriate attitude.

What suffices are two things. First, we need to know in the company of which sort of beings empathy makes sense – that is, what type of creatures one can meaningfully empathize with. Since empathy concerns the mental states of experiencing subjects, the answer is simple. We can extend empathy towards all those who have consciousness in the phenomenal sense – that is, all animals who experience existence as something and thereby have subjective mental states (it is "like something" to be a dog or a bat,[15] and hence we can empathize with them). Even when we cannot meet the octopus or the gorilla, we know they are legitimate targets of empathy, and our attitude extends to them, together with moral care.

Second, we can expand our prior experiences of empathy to concern those quite distant to us in a manner that renders the "attitude of empathy" less theoretical and more tangible. Here, we draw guidance from previous moments of empathy in order to map out those individuals who are far removed from us. As it comes to embodied empathy, we learn about the differences and complexities of subjectivity from face-to-face, skin-to-skin contact with various distinct beings, which will allow for the attitude of embodied empathy to become more inclusive and capable of spreading itself towards those we will never physically encounter. Here, embodied empathy becomes a way of perceiving or interpreting others, even when those others are not, nor ever will be, present – we learn it via interaction with those individuals we do meet, and that interaction offers us ways of extending it towards those who are not in our vicinity and whom we will never gain contact with. Simply put, our engagements with others become a type of a store of somatic knowledge which we can also apply to those unfamiliar to us. In relation to non-human animals, the more I interact with members of other species, the larger my store of somatic knowledge and the better my ability for "virtual", imagined embodied empathy.[16]

Yet there are also further difficulties with the link between moral agency and embodied empathy having to do with other-directedness: although embodied empathy can support the latter, it does not do so self-evidently. As seen, Husserl and Stein assume that the mere recognition of subjectivity in others sparks a sense of value, but this may not be the case. Indeed, one can fully note the subjectivity of her enemy and yet pursue that enemy without any moral consideration; equally, a racist may note that people of a different skin colour are minded subjects yet endorse their subjugation. We can skilfully interact on the somatic level, following embodied empathy and intersubjectivity, yet still deem the other as lacking moral worth. Indeed, perfect enemies may engage in such a setting, reading each other's responses, and responding to them, without a hint of moral recognition. This also applies to the non-human setting, as, for instance, a hunter may admit that the wolf she is pursuing is a thinking, feeling subject (even a powerful subject and a "mighty" opponent) and yet remain without any recognition of the wolf's moral worth. Perceiving and experiencing others as subjects is vital, but alone it does not mean that their moral value is acknowledged – there is a gap between subjectivity and its value which is not adequately addressed. Again, it seems that embodied empathy also requires the support of other varieties.

Here we are brought back to the relevance of resonation. Although the emphasis on recognizing the subjectivity of others, instead of merely floating with the specific mental states of those others, is inviting, it is misleading to suggest that resonation holds no relevance. It is precisely resonation that establishes the link between subjectivity and sense of value – we do not constitute that sense when noting and responding to subjectivity alone (something that would happen even between two creatures fighting each other to death) but when we both note subjectivity and can reverberate with its contents. When intersubjectively engaging with others, moments of resonation – the sort of primordiality that Stein opposes – can render the other into something much more significant than sheer recognition of subjectivity would allow for, for suddenly her experiences and perspective are brought so close as to break the barriers of the "self" and render that self acutely concerned for and orientated towards the other.

NOTES

1. Perhaps this is what Gallagher had in mind, when he states that empathy is not resonation but rather its own distinct emotion: "It seems possible for me to forego simulation and E-imagination, and to simply imagine (or see) you in a particular situation and to feel genuine sadness and outrage at the injustice done to you" (Gallagher 2012, 20). However, defining empathy in this way does not mean that other varieties, such as affective empathy, are not relevant.

2. This is something highlighted also by Scheler, who was careful to distinguish fellow-feeling from not only projection, but also emotional infection. In the context of the latter, he uses the contagion of melancholy as an example, and argues that it can "gather momentum like an avalanche" (Scheler 2009, 15). It is due to confusing

fellow-feeling with infection that Nietzsche, according to Scheler, sought to abandon the former (for him, it would lead to the accumulation of misery). In such a state, we lose sight of the other and the origin of our feelings, which in effect renders empathy impossible.

3. Yet Scheler is also (perhaps overly) cautious due to species differences: "The varieties of sensory pleasure and pain in animals are also largely alien to us, and fellow-feeling is no longer operative in such cases. Nevertheless, so far as the various modes of vital feeling are concerned, understanding and fellow-feeling are able to range throughout the entire animate universe, even though they rapidly fall off in respect of specific qualities as we descend the organic scale. The mortal terror of a bird, its sprightly or dispirited moods, are intelligible to us and awaken our fellow-feeling, despite our total inability to penetrate those of its sensory feelings which depend on its particular sensory organisation" (Scheler 2009, 48).

4. According to Acampora, Merleau-Ponty risks remaining anthropocentric, for he focuses on how humans relate to the world (Husserl is also criticized for the same fault, not least because of his suggestion that other animals are lower or less perfect deviations from humanity). Yet Acampora (2006) grants, as does Ted Toadvine, that in his later work, Merleau-Ponty sought to frame a less anthropocentric account of animal embodiment.

5. Although it should be noted that Stein also asserts the following: "Empathy is a kind of act of perceiving sui generis. . . . Empathy . . . is the experience of foreign consciousness in general" (Stein 1989, 11).

6. Of course, it could be claimed that we always make sense of the other via our own perspective; however, the point here is that there are different degrees of remaining so anchored. In affective empathy, the degree to which we become immersed in the other is high, whereas in projective empathy, the degree can be exceedingly low, and embodied empathy stays somewhere in between these options.

7. From contemporary advocates of the phenomenological approach, Zahavi is particularly keen to highlight the links between empathy and intersubjectivity.

8. This is a theme also underlined by Matthew Schertz, who defines empathy as "a form of communication by which human beings interact in an intersubjective gestalt" (Schertz 2007, 186). Indeed, for Schertz empathy enables intersubjectivity, as it forms "an aspect of the event of interaction" and a "primary condition of human intersubjectivity" (ibid.). Here, it is via experiencing others as subjects that empathy becomes possible, not the other way around. Others have also suggested that intersubjectivity feeds empathy, as the claim has been that we must be "intersubjectively open" and have "pre-reflective experience of the other as an embodied being like oneself" before empathy manifests (Thompson 2001, 12).

9. This stance was also brought forward by Hume (1969), who emphasized "apperception", the ability to comprehend that the world exists for others and their unique perspectives.

10. What Acampora (2006) calls "symphysis", a coming together of different bodily beings within which mutual understanding takes place, comes close to it. Symphysis acts as the guide towards moral recognition and care, as we begin to approach non-humans via the Heideggerian notion of "being with".

11. Dog training has been philosophically addressed, for example, by Erika Ruonakoski.

12. Stein uses the term "reflexive empathy", but since it is used differently in this book, the contemporary version is preferred here to avoid confusion.

13. A similar logic can be found in Sartre as well, manifested in the famous keyhole example, wherein one is spying on another and is suddenly woken to realize that the other is also looking at oneself: "I am encountering somebody who is able to perceive and objectify me" (see again Zahavi 2001).

14. For some, intersubjectivity, rather than empathy, forms the foundation for moral agency. Eva Johansson (2007) argues that empathy is not the road towards morality and that instead the much broader notion of intersubjectivity, within which one experiences the good and the bad jointly with others, guides one's moral development as a pro-social, pro-moral creature. However, perhaps the more fruitful stance is that intersubjectivity is one of those enabling elements which add to embodied empathy's moral potential.

15. This definition of consciousness is echoed in a famous article by Thomas Nagel (1974).

16. Of course, such extended application is much less reliable, and both individual and species differences pose various problems, for stretching knowledge from one specific being to another, particularly if these individuals are from different species, is challenging. Therefore, ideally, embodied empathy is grounded in actual physical contact, and the more of that contact we have, the more reliable it becomes. One way to fight these risks is to gain as much information of the other creature as we can – what her physiology and environment are like, how she behaves and so forth. I will probably never engage with wild gorillas, but these sorts of cues will feed me some ability for embodied empathy with them, albeit with limitations. Another way is to strengthen embodied empathy with the other varieties: projection/simulation, inference and resonation all help to bolster and broaden embodied empathy's scope by offering additional perspectives into animality.

Chapter 6

Reflective Empathy

Projective, simulative, cognitive, affective and embodied forms of empathy all emphasize quite distinct elements and have differing implications from the viewpoint of both moral agency and human-non-human relations.

To summarize the distinctions between these five varieties, it is helpful to think of their underlying epistemological movements. Within cognitive empathy, there is no movement between oneself and the other, as we maintain a state of detachment; the other is an object who is evaluated from afar, without going towards her nor letting her come towards oneself. Within projective and simulative empathy, there is movement from oneself towards the other, as the self is projected or simulated into her being: the observer seeks to transport herself into the place of the other. Within affective empathy, the other moves towards the self, and even enters us, as we begin to flow with her emotions and become immersed in them. Within embodied empathy, the movement takes place in both directions, as we impact the other and she impacts us – there is a dynamic, co-constituting movement at the borders between self and other.

Although these different types of empathy can be both conceptually and practically separated from each other (they are distinct mental states, with their differing scopes and consequences), they can of course support and feed each other. One can practice each of them without the other ones (for instance, I can enter cognitive empathy without any hints of affective resonation, projection or embodied intersubjectivity) but often they come in altering combinations (for instance, when embodied or projective empathy lays the path for affective resonation and begins to overlap with the latter). Empathy is a complex phenomenon, with distinct, often mutually contradictory types which nonetheless may take place at the same time and which often entwine and constellate together while pulling in different directions.

Each variety has its limitations, with moral implications. Cognitive empathy can fail to support genuine other-directedness, for it may remain wholly self-centred and detached from the emotions of the other, thereby enabling even immorality and amorality, which depict the other as an object to be instrumentalized. For this reason, it benefits from the support of other forms of empathy, and particularly affective and embodied empathy, which enforce an experiential sense of the experiences and subjectivity of the other. Projective empathy similarly fails in other-directedness, remaining ignorant of the subjectivity of others while also struggling with acknowledging diversity. Even the more other-directed simulative empathy will often struggle with a type of unrootedness, originating from the manner in which the empathizer is left to rely on her imagination. Again, projective and simulative empathies also benefit from the other varieties (in fact, from all three of them) as background support – projection and imagining "the other" can be useful but need to include a more tangible connection with her alterity. Affective empathy enables one to enter the mental states of others – or at least sparks the feeling of gaining entry – but alone it fails to accommodate a grasp of that which is not obviously present or which cannot be entered, and for this reason both cognitive and embodied empathy are useful backings for it, for via them one does not focus only on the shared feeling but also gains information about the differences and nuances of the other. Embodied empathy accommodates openness to diversity but may fail in spurring genuine, morally regardful other-directedness, and here affective resonation with the emotions of the other can offer a vital reminder.[1]

In regard to non-human animals, all of these varieties are useful, and particularly so when used alongside each other. Cognitive empathy can offer factual information on cows and pigs and is especially beneficial when we should not become overwhelmed with emotion but rather remain levelheaded (for instance, when seeking to comprehend the underlying, more intricate experiences, motivations or needs of the animal). Simulative empathy can help us to imagine the perspectives of farmed animals or fishes in trawling nets and therefore may open pathways to both moral awareness and further forms of empathy. Affective empathy enables the astounding feat celebrated by David Hume – flowing with the emotions of another – and thereby anchors us to the well-being of other animals on a very elemental, experiential level. Embodied empathy reminds us of the nuances, differences and opacities in cows and pigs, thereby bringing forth their subjectivity, and warns of the dangers of assimilating them to the human self.

Hence, all of these varieties are useful in different ways. Attention should be placed on their particular limitations and strengths in a way that cultivates moral ability and ensures a holistic, morally aware understanding of non-human creatures: we should practice the more positive aspects of these varieties while keeping an eye on and limiting their negative implications. This requires that we advance our ability to recognize the different varieties and our capacity to include their more fruitful dimensions in our dealings with other animals.

Yet there is also a sixth option which ought to be considered. It rests precisely on bringing forward the best elements of the previous five and on reflective cultivation of our empathic ability. Here, Edith Stein's stance on empathy is once again useful. As noted, Stein (1989) suggested that empathy consists of movement between the self and the other. We could interpret this further and posit that empathy can, ideally, consist of a first-order level, where we identify the mental states of the other or feel with them, and a second-order level, where we intentionally position contents from the first-order level in relation to our other experiences, emotions and beliefs, thus enabling a reflective viewpoint. This form of empathy will here be called "reflective empathy".

DEFINITION

Reflective empathy consists, first, of perceiving or feeling the emotions and subjectivity of another – that is, the content of the five types of empathy mentioned above. Second, it spurs from intentionally reflecting on them on the basis of our own emotions, attitudes, beliefs, intentions and other aspects of our own mental repertoire. The important thing to note here is that we do not simply let those emotions, attitudes and beliefs affect the contents of empathy (which they always will, to some extent, as the experiences of others are coloured by those of our own and are interpreted in light of what we feel, what we know and how we perceive), but we participate in this process *reflectively*, paying attention to what we know of or feel with another and what sort of mental contents of our own impact our judgement or experience. In short, we empathize and then adopt a metaperspective into the process of empathy.

Hence, in the first part of this movement, on the first-order level, we perceive what another feels or reverberate with her, thereby acknowledging or sharing mental states as they originate from the other. In the second part, these contents are met with reflective interpretation, elucidation and sense making. We note the sort of emotions that arise in us and the sort of beliefs and attitudes that affect how we interpret the other, and we reflect on their nature and relevance so as to render more fluent our ability to know her. We are never cut off from the other being but instead move between a first-order and second-order level, between immediacy and a metaposition, between inferring, simulating, feeling another and evaluating how our own mentations impact the whole process. As a consequence of this movement, we form "an affective sketch" of the mental contents of another and our own relation to her – affective and sketchy because those contents are perceived via our own emotional and intellectual interpretations.

To give an example, a cow's terror can cause resonative terror in us, but when we move on to the metalevel, it manifests as being mixed with various emotions such as melancholy, rage or guilt; attitudes such as care, apprehension or detachment and beliefs concerning, say, the morality of treating cows in a specific way. The task is to reflect on both the content of resonation (what we are feeling and why) and our responses to it (Why do I approach the situation via rage? How does my detachment affect my interpretation of what is happening? How do my beliefs impact my capacity to empathize? and so forth). By moving back and forth the first- and second-order level, between the immediacy of empathy and the metalevel of reflection, we gain a clear perception of the situation and may cultivate our ability to further understand both the experiences of the cow and the causes behind our own responses to those experiences. It is important that both levels are indeed kept in the picture and that there is movement to and from, for otherwise, if we stay only on the metalevel, there is a risk of over-intellectualization, abstraction and even alienation, wherein we lose grasp of the contents and immediacy of first-order empathy and thereby our grasp of the other being. In such a case, we would simply ponder, say, our beliefs concerning the terror of cows and become withdrawn from the actual perception of or feeling with that terror and the subjectivity behind it – as a result we could no longer speak of "empathy" but merely of "reflection" or rational analysis. Both first-order contents and second-order reflection must take place for reflective empathy to occur.

The crucial benefit of reflective empathy is that it enables awareness of with whom, why and on what grounds we empathize. It points attention to the process of empathy in itself and helps us become aware of the limitations and benefits of the other types of empathy mentioned thus far – in short, it renders one more appreciative of the nature of first-order varieties of empathy and offers perspectives into how to cultivate them further so as to ensure a better comprehension of others. It is precisely the plurality of the different types of empathy, and both their respective limitations and potentialities, which makes reflection so valuable, for in its most ideal, morally educational form, empathy notes its own distinctive varieties, learns from its faults and seeks to develop its strong points. It also helps us to better understand how our own perspective, together with its emotions, beliefs, attitudes and other mental states, affects the different types of first-order empathy and our interpretation of others – as a result, it enables us to cultivate our ability to focus on the other by, for instance, pointing out obvious biases or prejudices that may impact our ability to identify and feel with.

As a result, reflective empathy enables alteration in one's perspective on others. In a state of reflective empathy, we do not only let our beliefs, attitudes, emotions and other factors impact empathy, we also allow the contents of empathy – what we learn of others via empathy – to impact our own constitution. Both take place critically, with aware intent. In other words, when approached reflectively, empathy may teach us that our beliefs, attitudes or emotions concerning others have been maladapted and ill-informed and need to be altered accordingly, and thus it may cultivate our ability to reconfigure and better match our responses to others according to what those others are like. Reflective empathy opens a pathway to noting the impact of attitudes, beliefs and emotions and as such enables us to evaluate them critically and (ideally) alter them accordingly. The metalevel that emerges from movement between one's own internal states and those of another demonstrate not only our own grasp of the other but also our own characteristics and our approach to her – it signals what we are as beings in our efforts to understand. When such reflection is rehearsed, we may note our own self-directed attitudes, culturally adopted beliefs and often negatively coloured emotions that direct and muddle different modes of empathy; more importantly, we may become more capable of altering these attitudes, beliefs and emotions in a direction that allows more realistic and attuned takes on the other to emerge.

In the context of non-human animals, this means focusing attention on whether one is projecting or, say, resonating, what sorts of factors may remain hidden with the type of empathy one has chosen and how inference or embodied engagement could add to the situation. One may also become aware of how much one projects humanizing notions onto animals or how emotionally detached one seeks to remain, how given emotions (say, contempt, love or fear) or attitudes (say, the desire to benefit from them) impact the decision to empathize only with given types of animals and how beliefs (say, a belief in species hierarchies or, at the other end of the spectrum, species equality) bears an effect on how much (or little) importance one is willing to give to the contents of empathy. The resulting awareness may prompt the cultivation of one's ability and willingness to empathize with other animals in a more varied, honest, extended, well-grounded and holistic way and enable the noting and eradication of various, often culturally produced prejudices that disable empathy towards pigs, bees and goats.

There is much need for this, for other animals are often approached via mental contents which distort our ability for perceptive or emotive attunement. As mentioned above, self-directedness, for instance, can muddle understanding of non-human animality and skew empathy in a manner that reduces it to a process of anthropomorphism or even manipulation; here, our hedonistically or culturally orientated gains from other animals can nullify genuinely animal-regarding modes of empathy. In a similar fashion, culturally adopted and re-enforced beliefs concerning other animals may smother our capacity to pay heed to the contents of empathy and even the very capacity to empathize. In the latter instance, affective resonation with the suffering or joy of a cow may be downplayed due to the false belief that cows are mentally undeveloped creatures whose place in the "order of things" is to be used for human consumption, and thereby one struggles with the internal conflict between resonation, which points towards the inner complexities of cows, and beliefs, which downplay the existence and/or significance of such complexities. This is arguably a common obstacle in the way of empathy. We empathize on the one hand but on the other harbour beliefs which downplay that empathy and as a result often are left in a state of unsolved ambivalence and confusion over whether to trust what resonation or embodied engagement tells us of the mental states and subjectivity of other animals or whether to follow the culturally dominating beliefs which view those states and subjectivity with scepticism and disregard.

The role of emotions should be highlighted here, for they may also distort empathy. Although there has been a tendency in some animal philosophy to celebrate emotions as a purely positive element capable of guiding us towards a more morally sound way of relating to other animals, many emotions capable of impacting our moral judgement are, in fact, quite negative. As demonstrated by studies in social psychology, emotions such as disgust, anger and fear often guide how we perceive others (Haidt et al. 1999), and arguably they also often influence the different varieties of empathy. We may simply not enter into resonation or embodied intersubjectivity because we feel, say, contempt for the other, and empathy is left as a rather helpless alternative, incapable of breaking through emotional barriers. Again, this is pertinent to animal ethics, as emotions such as disgust and contempt can impact our ability to empathize with other animals, and when left unchecked, lead to misleading takes on what type of creatures pigs or sheep are (see Fischer 2015). When we perceive a pig via disgust, it is unlikely that we will easily, without external coaxing, resonate with that pig, and our negatively laden emotional responses towards pigs may be of such calibre that even coaxing is futile. For these reasons, it is highly beneficial to critically explore what type of emotions are affecting empathies and how they could be reshaped in a manner capable of supporting rather than hindering the effort to comprehend animality.

Reflecting on background assumptions and emotions comes with the benefit of also noting the social and political underpinnings of empathy. As argued in the introduction, empathy is a form of conceptualizing the emotions of others, which again is partly culturally learned. By taking an active role in evaluating and reshaping empathy, obvious social or political misconceptions can be erased, thus making conceptualizations more reliable.

Therefore, reflective empathy is also transformative. It includes movement towards oneself – how one ought to redirect one's own background beliefs and other mental contents in light of the other. In this movement inward lies empathy's interruptive potential: it can shock us to alter our pre-fixed, preordained wants, belief systems, stereotypes and misguided emotions. We become exposed to how we think and feel, as the other being and her experiences force us to come face-to-face with our preconceptions and patterns of emotive responding. Thereby, empathy can interrupt us enough to spark alteration within our constitution – it does not merely point towards others, dwelling on their mental lives, but it also lets the other bear an impact on the self. I affect the pig, and she affects me and enters not only my emotions but also my belief systems.

Reflective empathy, then, includes an element of cultivation. It is not sheer immediacy, which is left to exist as if outside one's own worldviews, emotions and belief systems, but it requires alteration, change and aware reconfiguration of those features in oneself. Cultivation allows us to note how empathy works in us, the type of impacts and actions it leads to; it enables the process of becoming increasingly aware and being able to respond to others more appropriately. It also lends potency to empathy. Empathy may surprise and shock us, interrupt our existence, force us to note others and push us to explore our own constitution. This is made possible by the metalevel, which evokes reconfiguration and critical examination of how we approach and relate to others.

To summarize, within reflective empathy, one becomes aware of not only some of the contents and causes of the emotive states of others but also how they fit with or revolt against the self-directed needs, belief systems and emotions that one holds and how one may cultivate oneself to become more capable of understanding the other.[2] This renders evident its normative potential and the manner in which it can guide the development of moral agency, for it is, in its ability to reflectively note the other, both other-directed and open to heterogeneity and, more than this, capable of enticing us to critically evaluate the biases and distortions that may impact and limit these elements – it not only enables other-directedness and openness but also facilitates their development. Moreover, it is not plagued by the difficulties met by the other forms of empathy – it does not invite egoistic manipulation or anthropomorphism, nor does it spark presumptions of knowing the other "fully" or fail to render evident the link between subjectivity and moral value. This is because it makes use of all the other five categories of empathy and hence combines, with awareness, the best elements of perception, projection, simulation, resonation and embodied engagement: others are approached with enough richness to avoid the pitfalls that these categories face when taken on their own. As such, reflective empathy offers the morally most viable option.

But what does this mean in practice? When approaching other animals, we should scrutinize what type of empathy we are following and why and how we may also benefit from adding other varieties into the mixture. We should make use of the sort of perception and inferential knowledge that cognitive empathy entails but also combine it with affective resonation so as to avoid detachment. We should seek embodied engagement with other animals when possible so as to further our capacity to note opacity, difference and subjectivity in them. And when it is evident that we are lacking in empathic ability, we should try and make use of simulative empathy and actively imagine the viewpoints of pigs and chickens. Furthermore, as argued above, the task is to notice how our background assumptions, needs, beliefs and emotions effect our grasp of animality and how to alter them towards a more empathy-accommodating form. It is this whole process, the movement between first-order level types of empathy and second-order level reflection, which constitutes reflective empathy and enables the cultivation of empathic, moral ability – in relation to both humans and other animals.

Arguably, we all sometimes use reflective empathy. It is not a theoretical formulation but something we do in practice, particularly when suddenly confronted with possible biases in our thinking. However, it remains regrettably rare, as the need to pay attention to our empathic abilities and to develop them further is seldom mentioned, especially in Western contemporary cultures. Reflective empathy is the prescriptive ideal, which we therefore should aim to advance – its kernels are in us and deserve to mature.

Before continuing, it should be noted that Lori Gruen's "entangled empathy", designed for animal ethics, has some similarities with reflective empathy. Gruen describes it as "a type of caring perception focused on attending to another's experience of wellbeing . . . in which we recognize we are in relationships with others and are called upon to be responsive and responsible [towards the other]" (Gruen 2015, 3). In entangled empathy, we imagine ourselves in the other's situation, reflect on how the context she exists in is impacting her, emotionally respond to her and seek to rework our relationship with her so as to be able to support her well-being.

Entangled empathy is intertwined with ethics and guided by the search for responsible relationships with others. Gruen talks of moral perception, which she links with empathy and which enables us to distinguish what is morally significant in each situation. The task is to dwell, via the use of both reason and emotion, deeper into our perceptive ability in order to form responsible interactions with creatures surrounding us. Since we by necessity exist in relation to other beings, the aim should be to cultivate our aptitude to be more perceptive and responsive in regard to them. Empathy becomes an expansive project which includes developing our relationships with others towards ethically viable directions. Such empathic expansiveness comprises reflection and change. We are to assess the other's context and our affiliation with her and to correct our empathic responses when they are inaccurate, which again will reshape us and allow us to review how we want to live in relation to others. In her hope-aspiring, bright and persuasive account of empathy, Gruen (2015) uses the example of Emma, a chimpanzee she knows and who has altered her outlook both on animals and on her own work to a point of remaking her.

Therefore, entangled empathy includes reflection and willingness to alter oneself, and it is these elements which it shares with reflective empathy. However, there are also marked differences. First, the sort of reflection included in entangled empathy appears to be primarily aimed at learning more of the other, whereas reflective empathy's aim is primarily towards learning more of oneself in order to know the other. Second, entangled empathy is laden or married with ethics, whereas reflective empathy seeks to offer a stepping stone to ethics while remaining distinct from it. This is an important difference. If a given notion of ethics is built into empathy – if we are aiming towards a particular way of existing in relationship with others – the latter risks becoming relative to it. Gruen's ethic entails equality and solidarity, but what if a different ethical stance – one built, for instance, on conservative values and hierarchies – is chosen? It is due to this risk of relativity that reflective empathy and ethics are linked yet clearly distinct. Third, whereas entangled empathy focuses on engaging with ethics and is therefore primarily normative, reflective empathy underscores the significance of a metalevel of mindedness and is hence primarily epistemic in nature.

CULTIVATION AND ATTENTIVENESS

In the process of cultivating reflective empathy, a specific mode of epistemology concentrated on mindful awareness and attentiveness and endorsed by the philosophies of Simone Weil and Iris Murdoch is of help.

In order to make sense of it, a distinction between two levels of knowing others is again important. On the first-order level exists the content of knowledge concerning the other, and on the second-order level, knowledge concerning that content – we can believe that the other is joyful, and we can form beliefs concerning our own capacity to know the joy of others. Simply put, there is a separation between knowledge, on one hand, and insight concerning that knowledge, on the other. Whereas knowledge on the first-order level may appear as a fact, as something undoubtable and permanent, second-order insight may help us view it as just one form of belief among many alternative candidates which fluctuate. Hence, our beliefs concerning others alter, as do our emotions, and we are to pay heed, on the second-order level, as to why this is so and how to respond to others more succinctly. The task is to keep an eye on the way in which one's own mental states may be colouring perceptions concerning the other: for instance, the belief that the other is joyful may be marked by one's own positive affect and hence be unreliable as a "true report". In short, second-order reflection enables scrutiny on why and how we form beliefs of and emotions concerning others and in so doing may offer more clarity.

Usually, second-order thought has been celebrated in philosophy as something rational, wherein it consists of reasoned analysis over one's first-order beliefs. However, such a philosophically traditional way of approaching the second-order level offers just one option. Another alternative is to define it as something experiential, where it is not only rationality but primarily an experienced mode of clarity which forms the backdrop against which first-order beliefs and other mental contents are explored. The relationship towards a given mental content alters depending on how we can, on the level of experience, relate to it. This enables a process wherein we perceive the mental contents to be dispensable events of the mind, rather than the unescapable truth – that is, experiences offer the same reflective standpoint as reason, via which we become aware of the contextuality of our mental states (Teasdale 1999). It should be emphasized that the relevant experiences really do take place on the second-order level: they are not the constantly fluctuating and often ambiguous, even chaotic first-order experiences and emotions, which come and go incessantly, but instead mental states that loom beyond this first-order level with some amount of permanency and lucidity and which are grounded in training one's mind. Hence, the second-order consists of affects, which are relatively clear and calm.

Here, the concept of "mindfulness", which despite its trendiness can hold serious moral potential, enters the scene. Mindfulness, a method of aiming towards clarity practiced in Eastern philosophies for twenty-five hundred years and increasingly used also in Western psychology, refers to a practice where one seeks to cultivate second-order reflection in its experiential form.[3] The aim is to strengthen one's sense of background affects and thereby to cultivate one's abilities to experientially reflect on first-order mental contents. In a state of mindfulness, one will undergo these contents while noting their impermanency and contextuality from the second-order level, whereby the individual learns that her thoughts do not constitute "her" or the "reality" but instead are just alternating interpretations. Thus, with mindfulness one takes a step back from the immediate workings of the mind: "The essence of mindfulness is to use intentional control of attention to establish a type of alternative information processing configuration" (Teasdale 1999, 154). In practice, it consists of focusing on a particular bodily state (for instance, breathing) while letting the contents of mind come and go, and as a consequence, a greater insight into or "feel" of mental contents emerges, together with the recognition of misleading and distorting mental processes.

Literature defines mindfulness as a "process of drawing novel distinctions" (Langer and Moldoveanu 2000, 1). It enables sensitivity to one's context and awareness of one's own perspectives while at the same time allowing one to have a "heightened state of involvement and wakefulness or being in the present" (ibid., 2; see also Brown and Ryan 2003; Coffey, Hartman and Fredrickson 2010). In other words, attention becomes sharper and more amplified, as one is more fully awake to thoughts and experiences as they fluctuate. The reflective process consists, therefore, of an experienced sense of metalevel attentiveness to one's own mental traits and contents: instead of rational analysis, it is this experiential attention that enables a succinct awareness of how contexts and mental events influence how we relate to our surroundings and which facilitates a finer grasp of both our own mentation and ultimately, if we apply this to bettering our empathic skills, that of others.

A significant aspect of mindfulness is "attention" (Semple 2010). Here, paying attention does not refer to something akin to focusing or concentrating on a particular thing but rather involves both the capacity to step back from first-order mental contents and the ability to navigate through them. Crucially, mindful attention is not, therefore, the sort of logical focus second-order rational thought is often depicted as, wherein we take one "problem" and extensively and logically explore its different facets – indeed, it may not be inferential at all. Instead, it prioritizes a "nonalgorithmic dimension of thinking" (Langer and Moldoveanu 2000), which escapes standard calculative forms of analyses and which refers to the existence of background experiences and affects capable of instantly sparking intuited, non-propositional surfaces for reflection. In this sense, mindfulness is "being" rather than "doing" (Teasdale 1999): it is not an act of analysis, rather the attention and insight it provides consist of the manner in which the metalevel of our experiences and affects is allowed to form the wall against which first-order thoughts and emotions can be witnessed. We navigate through our mental states because we have become aware and attentive of their contextuality, limitations and movement and because we can witness them from a more stable, fixed position. A common metaphor is that of a sky, wherein moving clouds form first-order mental contents and the background colour of relatively still blueness forms the second-order experience of attentiveness.

One way to explicate mindfulness is by reference to its opposite – the state of "mindlessness". Mindlessness rests solely on stereotyping and as a result rests on ready-made schema, various standard explanations and depictions, concerning reality. In so doing, it fails to do justice to contextual and individual variation or more broadly to the specificity and particularity of individual beings and events (Langer and Moldoveanu 2000). In short, we accept cultural norms and stereotypes, preconfigured definitions and regurgitated "truths" and apply these to make sense of ourselves, our surroundings and other beings while leaving critical evaluation of these schema, together with reflection on their nature, outside of our focus. It is as if we are offered lists of pre-made beliefs and emotions and simply followed the list as "true" without applying our critical capacities or agency. There is no second-order level in a state of mindlessness, for one simply accepts first-order beliefs and emotions, continually circulated in the predominant culture, as "evident".

This means that mindlessness can entwine with collective normative prejudices, which rest on misleading yet fixed definitions concerning the world and which all too easily lead to excluding and subjugating given groups of individuals – thereby, it can be an extremely destructive force. Next to having an impact on how we perceive others, mindlessness also bears an impact on our own being, for it tends to lead to a state of boredom and even numbness, which stands as the consequence of following ready-made and thereby somewhat mechanical thought processes and emotive responses throughout one's lifetime. We become inattentive to our own mental states and their origins and simply follow norms related to how we ought to think, feel and act – in a way, we lose our sense of agency over our own mental states and actions and become partial receptacles for preconfigured beliefs, needs, attitudes and emotions offered by our surroundings and reaffirmed by our own unaware willingness to adopt them. Thus, mindlessness comes close to the sort of alienation which existentialist philosophers such as Simone de Beauvoir underlined and which consists of uncritically following socially created norms and leads one towards melancholic or anxious withdrawal.

Mindfulness, on the other hand, resists ready-configured schema and other culturally stereotypic explanations concerning the world – indeed, it is inherently oppositional to mechanized, prescribed mentation and is instead characterized by "high curiosity with a low need for order" (Langer and Moldoveanu 2000, 7). In a state of mindfulness, we become open to not only our own mentation but also the presence of others, without the need to fit them into preexisting definitions and categories. Moreover, the type of hierarchies that often follow mechanical categorizations of beings (exemplified in stereotypic thought-patterns such as racism or sexism) are replaced with meeting and responding to others as specific, particular subjects, and thus it is concluded that "loosening our cognitive commitments to certain stereotypes and archetypes can stimulate personal development and increase the potential for interpersonal learning" (ibid., 8). Therefore, mindfulness enables us to witness others beyond and outside of generic schema and stereotypes in a more authentic state that allows them to manifest their subjectivity, nuance and particularity.

Moreover, when mindful, boredom is replaced with the curiosity of second-order reflection, continually keeping us alert to what is taking place (Langer and Moldoveanu 2000; Coffey, Hartman and Fredrickson 2010). In other words, whereas mindlessness limits one into a state of rather monotonic drowsiness, mindfulness allows creative, awake modes of being. We become more vigilant to both our own mental states and those of others and thereby regain a sense of clarity and agency. (In more philosophical terms, mindfulness may enable "conation", a state of spirited participation in life, emphasized by philosophers such as Baruch Spinoza and linked to nothing less than joy. Within conation, we have a strong sense of vitality, enabled by inner clarity that critically evaluates and monitors the beliefs and emotions offered by the external world – as Spinoza underlined in his *Ethics*, when public opinion is seeking to engulf us with ready-made conceptualizations and emotions, a state of lucidity, formed of both rationality and emotion, spurs us into joy, which again supports our willingness to pursue life.)

Therefore, mindfulness promises to avoid generic, numbing conceptualizations and stereotypes and thus to enable us both to notice specificity in ourselves and others and to become more active, alert, joyful participants in life. Importantly, in all of this mindfulness may also be pivotal from the viewpoint of practicing empathy skills, particularly reflective empathy. It provides one route to forming the metalevel required in reflective empathy and hence offers a perspective on our more immediate emotions, beliefs and attitudes concerning others. Here, we learn to note how first-order mental contents (beliefs, needs, emotions and so forth) impact our take on others and how we may navigate through them in order to become more attentively present to the other, more succinctly aware of her own being and thereby more skilled in empathy. The experienced sense of attentiveness *is* the metalevel, which assists in the refinement of our approach towards others and of our capacity to pay heed to their mental contents. In order to practice reflective empathy, we therefore need to practice the type of attentiveness that is linked with mindfulness and aim for the sort of "being" that allows us to gain more clarity over both our own mentation and that of others.

However, when it comes to mindfulness, there are also pitfalls to be noted. It has been celebrated in Western countries, particularly in the past two decades, and at times such celebration may be uncritical and even naive. On a practical level, the meaning of "mindfulness" can remain conceptually elusive, and researching its actual benefits is challenging (see Flanagan 2013). On a more philosophical level, mindfulness has been linked to the overaccentuation of "presence", currently manifested in Western cultures. We are told to be "here and now" and to stay attached to the "present moment", as if this were a magical cure to our creativity, psychology, well-being and even business decisions. Indeed, "presence", and with it mindfulness, have become something we are marketed by various sources – they have become their own commodities to be purchased (Rushkoff 2014).

Such an obsessed focus on presence and naivety over mindfulness can distort what reflection stands for. In its more productive form, reflection does not stay merely in the present moment, as if floating in "what is" sufficed, but it also, even primarily, aims towards the future by seeking to cultivate our own being towards something more capable of recognition and epistemological clarity. That is, cultivation is the aim of reflection, and it is always directed towards the future – it orientates itself towards rendering our capacities more attentive and able. This means that reflection has a moral component, as it seeks "what should be" instead of merely agreeing with what is. These are worthy reminders for reflective empathy as well. Although it benefits from the sort of second-order attentiveness that mindfulness at best brings forward, the aim is not to stay in the almost mythical "presence", nor "accept" everything as it is, but rather to use awareness of presence for the cultivation of future ability. In other words, being in the present moment is not the end goal in reflective empathy but instead a means via which to develop our capacity to reflectively comprehend ourselves and others more succinctly.

As Alasdair MacIntyre (1984) has rather famously argued, modernity has been plagued by the tendency to concentrate on only what we are here and now while overlooking the need to orient and shape ourselves in a manner that allows for our potential to flourish. These are important reminders for reflective empathy, for it must continually be grounded in the notion of such reshaping and avoid the pitfalls of reducing the metalevel into sheer acceptance of presence. Here, the role of rationality may be of help. Although the metalevel ought to consist primarily of attentiveness instead of endless logical algorithms, rationality can and does have value as a secondary, supportive element. It offers tools with which to distinguish between different mental states and with which to offer propositional content to our conclusions. Spinoza, who spoke of clarity as joy and "conatus", underlined the relevance of reason, and its role must not be overlooked in reflective empathy, even when priority is given to second-order attentiveness. Rational reflection is particularly good at driving in the importance of "what should be", for it can spur the noting of mistakes in our perceptions and remind us of the need to aim for future development – it does not merely "flow" with what is but seeks to find optimal ways of being and as such pushes towards alteration. Therefore, it should not be prioritized, but neither should it be completely forgotten.

In the context of non-human animals, the above stands again as relevant. Attentiveness serves as a way of distancing ourselves from the type of stereotypic, preordained descriptions concerning other animals that the culture is exceedingly keen to celebrate. Arguably, the state of mindlessness is dominating human-animal relations, as non-human creatures are usually defined and related to on account of various standard categories, often originating from anthropocentric preconceptions. Thereby, they are approached as representatives of their species or via categories based on their use-value – specific animal subjects become generic, faceless copies of "pigs" or "farmed animals", and their uniqueness becomes utterly lost. Often these stereotypic takes on animality are mechanistic and hierarchical and undermine animals' mental ability and subjectivity, and as such we become increasingly alienated from their specificity. This mindlessness also has a bearing on our use of our own faculties, as we become detached from and uncritical of how and why we respond to and make sense of animals. Metalevel, second-order reflection is by and large lacking, as elks and crocodiles are described and responded to on account of first-order, predefined and socially learned beliefs and emotions, which one is not even fully aware of. In the process, we risk losing our grasp of our own agency and subjectivity, as we follow ready-made schema without having an active, mindful, aware and reflective input into how we make sense of other animals, and this again can lead to rather zombified, numb relations with the non-human realm (the very realm which holds the potential of igniting vibrancy, colour and vitality by introducing us to its richness). In order to combat mindlessness in human-animal relations, and in order to foster empathy by facilitating metalevel reflection, it may therefore be vital to cultivate attentiveness.

Within an attentive outlook on animals, one seeks a comparably lucid and calm affective state via which to observe beliefs and emotions concerning other beings. Those beliefs and emotions are no longer evident "truths", and one can begin to understand their contextuality, relativity and alteration: it becomes evident that they are mere interpretations which one can learn to guide. This can spark a sense of being alive to animals, a feeling of vital awakefulness as one animal among many others, and can coax one to leave stereotypic, mindless explanations. Becoming more attentive to how we relate to other animals may even ignite elevation and joy as calm, bright mental states, capable of illuminating evermore of what it is to be an animal.

However, such attentiveness should not be approached naively. The task is not to merely observe and accept the current state, nor simply linger in "presence", but rather to cultivate our ability to become more attentive towards non-human mentation, more capable of noting beliefs and emotions concerning other animals and ultimately to enhance our empathy skills and moral agency in the future. Although rationality is not the key component here, it, too, holds evident importance, for it can help the evaluation of one's own approaches and expedite the analysis of culturally produced beliefs and emotions concerning animals, together with their underlying dogma, in a manner that is necessary for reflection and development of empathic, moral ability.

Philosophically, mindfulness has been explored as a state of attentiveness. The two most notable philosophers to have investigated attentiveness are Weil and Murdoch, both of whom may help to shed further light on how to advance reflective empathy.

Murdoch spoke of alienation and mindlessness in length. For her, they were based on following preordained lingual categories and conceptualizations without critical evaluation and on letting cultural, publicly created meanings and beliefs to dominate us to the point where we lose touch with personal experiences, perspectives, and agency. Thus begins a rather robotic existence, which in Murdoch's opinion resembles the shadows in Plato's famous cave allegory, wherein prisoners of a cave concentrate on shadows on the cave's wall, thinking they are the reality while overlooking the source of light causing the shadows. In such a state, we lose our moral agency, which leads to a lack of freedom and ensuing anxiety as we simply follow – often indecisively and monotonically – given pre-fixed beliefs and emotions. As Murdoch describes: "The lonely tortured 'will' of which we are conscious at such moments is not the agent of our freedom and our morality, but rather a symptom of lack of freedom and moral strength. It is indeed not solitary but appearing like a flickering flame before a darker background of habits, principles, ideals, ideas, desires, memories" (Murdoch 2003, 457).

The way forward is to become attentive, which Murdoch sees as the path to recognizing the light and the world it reveals, demonstrated in the cave allegory. Attentiveness offers moral vision, the metalevel required for noting ourselves, the world and its beings more authentically and realistically and therefore with greater moral clarity. Attentiveness, again, stems from entering the "presence" within us – our experiential states and the way they render the surrounding reality manifest. What is pivotal here is the avoidance of generic, externally produced meanings and beliefs in interpreting our own experiences, for they would simply lead back to the shadows: instead, we are to aim for pure experience, beyond lingual descriptions. It is from such pure, raw experience and presence that agency stems and which offers the metalevel from which to observe things. In other words, only by going back to our raw experiences in the present moment, by becoming attuned to them, can we clear ourselves from the cacophony of socially produced dogma and stereotypes and gain a sense of both clarity and agency. In this vein, Murdoch argues that, "our present moment, our experiences, our flow of consciousness, our indelible moral sense, are not all these essentially linked together and do they not *imply* the individual?" (Murdoch 2003, 153). It may seem paradoxical that we gain a metalevel to our first-order mental contents by first diving into the immediacy of experience; however, with "presence" Murdoch is not referring to our constantly changing, most obvious emotions and thoughts but rather the more permanent feel behind them, the steadier sense of alertness and affect.[4]

But how is attentiveness achieved? First, borrowing from Zen philosophy, Murdoch emphasizes training and argues that we are to continually seek to break free from old habits of the mind which keep on pushing forward generic descriptions and cultural dogmas. The aim of such training is not merely to resist old thought patterns but also to learn to cope without constant reference to them – a task much easier said than achieved and one that therefore requires continuous effort. A more important element, however, is "unselfing" – a process within which we are to become freer from our usual, egoistic tendencies to view the world via concentrating on how we may benefit from it. According to Murdoch, such egoism reduces reality and other beings all too easily into objects in whom we only note those aspects which serve our own interests and which renders them two-dimensional, lacking nuance, complexity and exceptionality. Unselfing requires that we let go of these egoistic tendencies as much as we can and begin to perceive ourselves and others without judgement and use-based, instrumentalizing criteria. Neither our own mental states nor other subjects are to be approached as objects evaluated via egoistic lenses, but instead we are simply to observe our experiences and those of others beyond both premade, cultural schema and ego-orientated desires. A helpful tool here is to pay attention to ordinarily trivial-seeming things, such as rocks, so as to navigate the urge to only witness that which gives us gratification. Another helpful tool is to approach attentiveness as if one were looking at art – we do not grasp art if we look at it merely in order to benefit from it and can only enter the aesthetically appreciative zone when we set aside ego-orientated, objectifying criteria (Murdoch 2003).[5]

Therefore, on the practical level, we are to simply be still, go with our experiences, concentrate on our surroundings without ready-made descriptions and categories, let go of self-directed urges, desist objectifying reality, let our attention rest on things we would otherwise fail to notice and approach reality as we would approach art. Such practicing will develop attentiveness and break through new ways of relating, rested on a metalevel of perception and experience rather than our immediate beliefs, wants, attitudes and emotions. According to Murdoch, attentiveness will offer clarity towards both our own mental states and those of others and thereby helps us to comprehend subjectivity more lucidly. Moreover, as already implied above, it also has moral dimensions, which Murdoch greatly emphasizes. For her, the collectively produced beliefs and emotions dominating Western cultures tend to accentuate utilitarianism, which locates value only in that which is of use and thereby calls forward rather nihilistic ethics, incapable of noting inherent, non-instrumental value. Attentiveness can help us to steer away from such a state of moral disregard, for it is a morally laden epistemology, enabling us to perceive reality in the light of value. This is simply because experiences – when separated from the sort of culturally produced beliefs that tend to focus on egoistic and utilitarian purposes – point towards value (as Murdoch argues, consciousness is "soaked in value"; Murdoch 2003, 167). In other words, they are not neutral but rather make us deem the world via notions of what is good (for instance, when I experience love, I perceive inherent value). In a state of attentiveness, we become more capable of judging different varieties of experience and more centred on what truly is of importance: it therefore offers nothing less than moral lucidity.

The form of experience which Murdoch links with both attentiveness and greatest moral insight is love in its agape (i.e., selfless) form – attentiveness facilitates noting the reality of others, which again she deems to spark love towards them, and it is love which again pushes to acknowledge value. The example of art is of use once more, for perceiving things and other beings as one would perceive art eradicates selfish, utilitarian desires and assists in recognizing the other thing or being as she is in herself, and it is this which sparks the feeling of love and ultimately value: "Great art teaches us how real things can be looked at and loved without being seized and used, without being appropriated into the greedy organism of the self . . . selfish concerns vanish, nothing exists except the things which are seen" (Murdoch 1971, 64). Therefore, a sense of realism, a concentration on how things or beings are in themselves, is the pathway towards love and morality – indeed, the latter two linger in witnessing the world via truths. Thus, Murdoch claims that "love is truth, truth is love. My moral energy is a function of how I understand, see, the world" (Murdoch 2003, 293).[6]

In a Platonic vein, "real", "truth", "love" and "good" become quite synonymous in Murdoch's writing: noting things in light of truth and realism spurs love and a sense of the good to the point where these dimensions are interchangeable and thereby difficult to define with precision.[7] The task in life is to move, via attentiveness, towards greater clarity, which enables one to gain access to reality, love and the good: "The good and just life is thus a process of clarification, a movement toward selfless lucidity, guided by ideas of perfection which are objects of *love*" (Murdoch 2003, 14). This is the realm of intuition, resistant to language and ordinary reasoning. Murdoch explains: "At the border-lines of thought and language we can often 'see' what we cannot say: and have to wait and attempt to formulate for ourselves and convey to others our experience of what is initially beyond or hidden. We look out into the abyss, into the mystery, intuiting" (ibid., 283).

Simone Weil, a significant source of influence for Murdoch, had a similarly Platonic approach to attentiveness. For her, attentiveness was a way of witnessing reality that enables authenticity and realism, an antidote to the misleading constructions and interpretations largely based on human ego and cultural conceptions; thus, the cave allegory finds frequent use in Weil's philosophy as well. Like Murdoch, Weil argues attentiveness to be the source of both perceiving matters more realistically and having a moral approach to them, and thereby, again, attentiveness emerges as both a descriptive and a prescriptive vehicle. Via attentiveness, we can learn to note truth and value and see the world and others in light of Plato's sun. The core of attentiveness is once more love, the ability to notice others as they are and to exist for them (S. Weil 1973, 2002). Again, cultivation is also vital, as Weil emphasizes how attentiveness must be continually practiced. Indeed, attentiveness is not something one "has", it is not an essence of our minds but rather something one must constantly aim for. She explains, "Love is a direction and not a state of the soul" (S. Weil 1973, 81).

Similarities between these two philosophers do not end here. Weil argues that attentiveness can be achieved by emptying ourselves as far as possible from self-directed wants, aims, emotions and beliefs, for it is only then that we can begin to pay attention to things as they are, stripped bare of those fantasies and misconceptions our egos are all too willing to construct. As Weil notes, we ought to truly become receptacles for the other to enter so that she can be understood as she exists beyond our own interpretation: "Attention consists of suspending our thought, leaving it detached, empty, and ready to be penetrated by the object. . . . Above all our thought should be empty, waiting, not seeking anything, but ready to receive in its naked truth the object that is to penetrate it" (S. Weil 1973, 62). Indeed, we are to let go of all expectation and interpretation, truly become as if empty in front of the other whom we are seeking to understand: "The soul empties itself of all its contents in order to receive into itself the being it is looking at, just as he is, in all his truth. Only he who is capable of attention can do this" (ibid., 65). Therefore, not only are we to detach ourselves from focusing on what we can gain from others – we are also to detach from even harmless presumptions which seek to veil the other with our own interpretations. The "self" in us needs to be pacified so that we may become open to that which is external to us. Weil clarifies: "'I' has to be passive. Attention alone – that attention which is so full that the 'I' disappears – is required of me. I have to deprive all that I call 'I' of the light of my attention. . . . Not to try to interpret them, but to look at them till the light suddenly dawns" (S. Weil 2002, 118, 120).

However, next to "unselfing" Weil also underlined solitude as a method. Since attentiveness includes questioning not only egoistic aims but also culturally and socially regurgitated beliefs and interpretations, one needs to step outside of the social doxa, and indeed society itself. Referring again to Plato's cave, Weil argues that "society is the cave. The way out is solitude" (S. Weil 2002, 165). The noise of the society fills us with preconceptions and self-directed aims, which renders it difficult to empty oneself and become open to the other; therefore, one is to detach from it all for a while, seek to rid oneself from the social machinery of beliefs. Yet a further method of attentiveness is suffering, or "affliction", as Weil calls it. Suffering enables us to become empty of egoistic and social contents, for it pushes us towards a void, a sense of bareness that renders the "ego" and social hubbub wholly secondary, even irrelevant, and opens us towards the other as she is in herself. In a state of affliction, we notice our own insignificance, gain perspective and our void can become filled with attentive love, capable of noticing the other.[8]

For both Weil and Murdoch, attentiveness is therefore something that emerges out of unselfing, a process of eradicating egoistic, socially reinforced ways of conceptualizing others – it is also something that can be practiced and cultivated by either focusing on the seemingly insignificant aspects of reality or approaching that reality as one would do art, and it may be rehearsed by solitude and even affliction. The aim is to become empty to such a degree that the other may penetrate us and manifest her own reality. Via unselfing, we notice the "truth" of others and enter states of love, which will assist in noting value and impels us to become reflective moral agents.

Now, the strong metaphysical and epistemological underpinnings of Weil and Murdoch – their idea of objectively existing "good" and their notion that we can access wholly truthful understandings of others – would warrant more discussion, as would the issue of to what extent it is beneficial or even possible to eradicate all self-driven interests and interpretations, let alone our "self". However, what suffices here is a more moderate interpretation of their stance, which is the claim that via eradicating as many of our egoistic, social conceptions as viable, and via becoming as attentive as possible, we will gain a clearer comprehension of ourselves and others and also of moral issues. The point is not, therefore, whether we can achieve a completely truthful comprehension of others or find objective value but whether we ought to strive to be as truthful and morally lucid as possible within our limits. Here, "truth" is not presumed to be objective but is rather defined as affective clarity. Moreover, the aim is not to lose our "selves" but to precisely understand ourselves more cogently by setting aside the egoistic, often distracting elements within us.[9]

Most importantly, attentiveness serves, again, as a metalevel against which to practice reflective empathy. Weil's and Murdoch's methods offer the second-order approach, which may enable us to better understand our own empathic responses, limitations and strengths and to develop the ability to know another as realistically as we can. Weil's and Murdoch's notion of love also further explains the ties between reflective empathy and moral agency, for it is precisely the reflective, attentive metalevel dimension which feeds other-directedness and openness to diversity to such a degree that others manifest as "real", even as objects of love.[10]

In relation to non-human animals, all these claims hold importance. As already discussed, there evidently is a tendency to favour human needs, or a type of cultural egoism, in anthropocentric attitudes towards other animals, which may spark anthropathy and wholly distort and limit our capacity for attentiveness and ultimately empathy. Perhaps we ought to "unself" in relation to chickens and cows, which consists of seeking to lessen the impact of our wants and aims in understanding them and of limiting the way in which socially reinforced beliefs continually bear an effect on our animal imagery. The aim should be to approach them with attentiveness, as the sort of "seemingly trivial matters" whose true value we have thus far failed to notice; here, one could simply sit still and observe a cow in a field, take pause to witness her movements and behaviours instead of hurrying past. One could also approach deer or dogs as one does art, without wanting anything out of them and simply being in awe at their existence.

A further element could be solitude, although perhaps with non-human company. Detaching for a while from human society and its constant overload of indoctrination and information and withdrawing into quiet spaces with non-humans can teach attentiveness. Here one is in the company of non-human ways of existence without constantly being reminded of how "the human world" stereotypically defines them, and as such gaps may open via which we become "empty" enough of cultural, societal preconceptions for animals to penetrate our being. Yet a further method may be remembering one's own affliction, being open to suffering instead of always blocking information concerning it away, so that one may learn something from it, the foremost important thing being our own vulnerability, the relativity and ultimate insignificance of our "egos" and our connectedness, via that vulnerability, to other, experiencing beings.

Adding to Weil and Murdoch, wilderness experiences may also help in cultivating attentiveness in regard to other animals. Time spent in nature has been proven to transform our conception of ourselves and our relation to wider surroundings – simply put, it can alter our ontology, our view of the world and its order. The human self begins to seem less significant and the surrounding reality more prominent, even elevating, and a sudden sense of awe and value tends to be connected with such experiences (Ashley 2007; McDonald, Wearing and Ponting 2009; Hinds 2011). Here, the anthropocentric "ego", who is used to perceiving natural environments as sources of raw material and other usage, may suddenly view those environments as entities of inherent value whose presence indicates holistic interconnectedness, within which humans are not "centres" of existence but rather one species among many. The emerging ontological and moral epiphanies can be quite transformative and long-lasting (Ashley 2007; McDonald, Wearing and Ponting 2009; Hinds 2011). Such experiences can be linked to attentiveness (Aaltola 2015) and may also be quite fruitful in cultivating attentiveness in relation to non-human beings – after all, natural environments are teeming with members of other animal species, who form a significant part of what we call "wilderness".

Other animals' presence is often entwined with noting interconnectedness and the insignificance of human "egos", and they may present themselves in such environments much more freely and fluently than in human-made habitats, for those environments are the birthplace of their evolutionary, genetic constitution – their "world". Emptying oneself of self-directed, socially constituted prejudices and coming open to the presence of other animals, witnessing the latter as one would do art, taking part in solitude and thereby becoming more attentive to why one approaches animals in a given way, may take place quite effortlessly in wilderness settings (or even in parks supportive of animal presence). Here, feelings of awe and elevation and the ensuing moral epiphanies may take place – indeed, perhaps such instances can, at their best, spark nothing less than Weilian, Murdochian love.

Via such attentiveness, reflective empathy can gain its metalevel, as we learn to pay more notice to why we conceptualize and feel towards other animals in given ways and what those animals themselves may be like were they to be witnessed more realistically or authentically. As such, it can facilitate cultivation, a process of transforming our own emotions and beliefs concerning pigs and pikes, and noting those animals with greater clarity. To use Plato's cave allegory, perhaps it is often our egoistic ends and cultural beliefs which are the shadows of our animal imagery – the mistaken and distorted understandings of, say, pigs, which claim them to be mere sources of bacon or cognitively incapable, filthy "beasts". Attentiveness can bring the "truth" of other animals closer, and they may thus be perceived in Platonic "light". Such attentiveness can feed love, which again spurs the sense that cats, bats and elephants are beings of inherent value – thereby, they may further aid our moral agency in the realm of animal ethics.

As Weil notes, this is a constant process, a direction towards something. Reflective empathy, too, is such a process, an aim for a more cultivated understanding of our own approaches to empathy and other animals: it is not a "ready" thing, which we either have or don't have, but instead a direction to aim for our whole lifetimes. Misinterpretations, errors and omissions will often muddle the way, and on those occasions it is important to simply refocus. As Murdoch advises: "Try again. *Wait*" (Murdoch 2003, 506).

NOTES

1. The latter two forms of empathy allow one to see others via two equally pivotal perspectives – similarity and difference; hence they are both required when seeking to

grasp the mental realms of others. Without difference, similarity threatens to become reducible to the demands of prototypic sameness, and without similarity, difference risks leading to moral detachment, wherein we recognize subjectivity but fail to see moral worth in it.

2. It should be emphasized that reflective empathy helps us to grasp the relevance of the second-order level, the level of interpretation and positioning, without eradicating the first-order level. Immediacy is not lost, even when it is evaluated and responded to in light of our own mental terrains.

3. As Jonathan Haidt (2003b) points out, when it comes to articulations of moral emotions and practices, much is to be learned from world philosophies and religions (he uses the example of agape love and meditation). He discusses the Hindu notion of "*sama*", which refers to serenity or calmness. It is reached via meditation and forms an important moral emotion, as it is "good not only for one's spiritual advancement, but for the health of the cosmos as well" (Haidt 2003b, 16), perhaps precisely because via it we can become more aware of ourselves and our surroundings.

4. Murdoch notes that for much of Western philosophy, the notion of escaping socially and culturally produced lingual categories and stereotypes appears as naive, as we are seen to be captives of language. However, Murdoch sees this as the crucial mistake made by such philosophy, for there are other levels to human mentation than that which is collectively and lingually constructed. She therefore asks, "Can we not see a little beyond those transcendental barriers [of language as our world], do we not have intimations, gleams of light, glimpses of another scene?" (Murdoch 2003, 36). It is precisely this scene, the "it" which we cannot quite describe precisely because it escapes language, which lends us a metalevel and a way towards attentiveness.

5. Also, for Arthur Schopenhauer, limiting the impacts of the ego is essential, for the ego sees others as objects to be used for one's own advantage rather than as subjects in their own right: "To the Egoist all other people are uniformly and intrinsically strangers. In point of fact, he considers nothing to be truly real, except his own person, and regards the rest of mankind practically as troops of phantoms, to whom he assigns merely a relative existence, so far as they may be instruments to serve, or barriers to obstruct, his purposes; the result being an immeasurable difference, a vast gulf between his ego on the one side, and the non-ego on the other" (Schopenhauer 2005, 142).

6. Here again noticing the seemingly insignificant particulars in others sparks love: "We do not lose the particular, it teaches us love, we understand it, we *see* it" (Murdoch 2003, 497).

7. This difficulty, according to Murdoch, is simply to be accepted, for it demonstrates the complexity of reality. Thus, she talks of the "infinite difficulty of the task of apprehending a magnetic but inexhaustible reality" (Murdoch 1971, 41).

8. Affliction is particularly important because it allows becoming open to the affliction of another. As a consequence, we may begin to truly note others, to be lovingly attentive towards them. Yet Weil notes: "The capacity to give one's attention to a sufferer is a very rare and difficult thing; it is almost a miracle; it *is* a miracle. Nearly all those who think they have this capacity do not posses it" (S. Weil 1973, 64).

9. Having a sense of "self" should be distinguished from egoism and is central to our mental and societal well-being. As Gruen posits: "I think it is easier for those

who have not struggled to develop and maintain a self to be ready to dissolve it. For many whose subjectivity, agency and experiences have been undermined, questioned or denied, the maintenance of a self-identity is an achievement and not one that they are willing to give up so readily" (Gruen 2005, 10).

10. Where Weil points out that giving attention to another's suffering is rare to a point of being a miracle, perhaps it is precisely empathy which can guide us towards it.

Chapter 7

Criticisms of Empathy

Empathy is haunted by various criticisms and problems, which deserve attention – naive belief in empathy's omnipotence should be resisted, for like any aspect of our moral psychology, varieties of empathy come with their challenges.

The most dangerous, even if least discussed, of these is the manner in which empathy can aid in the manipulation and control of others. As pointed out in relation to cognitive empathy, empathy can be used aversively by utilizing information about others in order to benefit from them (Decety and Lamm 2006, 1159), which points towards the unpleasant aspects of empathy connected to immoral or even amoral behaviours and manifested in psychopathy and narcissism. One does not need to suffer from a personality disorder for this to happen. In general, cognitive empathy has been linked to crimes such as rape (Day, Casey and Gerace 2010), and indeed it can enable any form of subjugation. For this reason, some cultures have adopted an antagonistic stance towards empathy, believing that it is best to hide one's inner realms and mental states from others lest they be detected via empathy and used against oneself. Following suit, anthropological studies manifest that empathy can have its social downsides, as empathy can be viewed with hostility, precisely because it can be used to manipulate others, to scan for their weaknesses or to simply hurt and embarrass them: "Many people fear how others will use intimate knowledge of them and may go to great length, consciously and less than consciously, to block such knowledge by others" (Hollan and Throop 2008, 390).

As a result of this "flipside of empathy" (ibid.), people appear to be just as eager to conceal their mental states as they are to open them up for others, and correspondingly there are many cultural contexts where looking away and not knowing the mental states of others – rather than seeking empathic engagement – are considered the morally soundest act. Specific examples are, for instance, a Micronesian community wherein opacity, privacy and emotional control are highly esteemed and which remains clearly hostile towards empathy (Robbins and Rumsey 2008) and a Mayan community within which distrust of others persists because empathy is viewed as an act of intrusion, capable of sparking Schadenfreude (Groark 2008).[1] Empathy can thereby be used to serve surprising motivations, such as coercion and the maintaining of societal hierarchies.[2]

Now, as stated, this problem is also highly relevant in the non-human context, as mind reading the mental states of other animals is constantly used against them in animal agriculture, hunting and other exploitative arenas. Following the anthropological model, it can be used to maintain the hierarchies of anthropocentrism, as understanding the weaknesses and vulnerabilities of non-humans can serve to emphasize, justify and sustain their subjugated position (here, "the laws of nature" thinking comes into play, as the human capacity to manipulate is perceived as a sign of "might makes right"). These ill uses of empathy must be taken into account if a realistic image of empathy is to be achieved: "empathy" is not a straightforward and generically positive state, only capable of enticing us towards moral consideration and accountability but also something that comes with risks of immoral and amoral behaviour, in our dealings with the non-human world as well.

As stated, this problem mainly concerns cognitive empathy and can be remedied by bringing forth other, exploitation-critical, other-directed forms of empathy, particularly emotive resonation (affective empathy). Thus, Frans de Waal argues that it is cognitive empathy which acts as the potential darker side of empathic reactions and that we need the affective component in order to escape its risks: "Perspective-taking by itself is, of course, hardly empathy: It is so only in combination with emotional engagement. . . . Without emotional engagement, perspective-taking would be a cold phenomenon that could just as easily lead to torture as to helping" (de Waal 2008, 285, 287).[3] Simply put, without the emotive component, it is difficult to see why we would care about others, and because of this, the way out of the potential amoral dimensions of (cognitive) empathy is to increase the levels of resonation.[4] However, reflective empathy also holds vast potential in guiding us away from manipulative aloofness, as it forces us to explore how and why we approach others – indeed, since it makes evident the nature of our empathic responses, it can also illuminate when we should be resonating more and mind reading less. Therefore, next to increasing emotive engagement and affective empathy, following reflective empathy can also answer the problem of coercion and manipulation. In such a state, we note our withdrawn, even calculative neutrality, become aware of at least some of its cultural causes and aim to open it up to flowing and moving with the emotions of another:

the farmer recognizes that she approaches pigs from a disconnected position, locates how the surrounding culture and its animal imagery encourages doing so and strives to become more apt in comprehending animality.

Another criticism concerns the motivations of empathy: perhaps empathy only serves to make us feel good about ourselves and thereby offers a type of sentimental, egotistic reward for us, which again renders it less than altruistic and less than morally applaudable. One simple answer to this is the distinction between primary and secondary reasons, which forms the classic reply to the cynical view, according to which people only do good deeds in order to feel better about themselves. Even if on a secondary level we receive gratification from behaving in empathic ways, the primary motivation may be the well-being of others; in short, gratification comes as a surplus benefit but does not constitute the actual impetus for empathic, moral behaviour. To suggest otherwise is to simply misunderstand what "empathy" means, for if we follow other-directed types of empathy, we are by necessity orientated towards the welfare of the other being rather than stuck on serving our own egoistic needs.

This distinction has also been offered an evolutionary backing, as it has been claimed that the evolutionary role of empathy may be very different from its immediate reward (in such a context, the distinction is said to concern "ultimate" and "proximate" causes). As maintained by de Waal, altruism and co-operation have evolved in order to enable fluent social relations, and they act as the ultimate cause for empathy, while empathy's more immediate motivation may be something altogether different (for instance, one may feel good after the release of oxytocin). However, these immediate rewards or proximate causes do not counteract the more fundamental motivation, which is the maintenance of social bonds and the benefits they disseminate to all parties (de Waal 2008). Moreover, in relation to both causes, one still remains other-directed, for it is the other who forms the core of both pro-social behaviour and the more instant feel-good factor.

These are not the only risks faced by varieties of empathy. Further problems include, for instance, the potentially biased nature of empathy, compassion fatigue, the primacy of rationality and the primacy of other moral emotions, such as anger, each of which will be discussed below.

BIASED EMPATHY, BIASED ETHICS

Perhaps the most prominent, frequently repeated criticism of empathy concerns its presumed biased nature. As already noted by David Hume, we tend to feel empathy most towards those who are like us, proximate to us or emotionally close to us: "We sympathise more with persons contiguous to us, than with persons remote from us: With our acquaintance, than with strangers: With our countrymen, than with foreigners" (Hume 1969, 631). Jesse Prinz has argued that the bias stems from the way in which empathy concentrates on victims instead of the crimes – that is, it places all focus on the sufferers of harm rather than the act of causing harm, and when concentrating on victims, it is easy to become influenced by their closeness or similarity to oneself. The problem of bias, therefore, originates from paying excessive attention to individuals at the expense of actions: when individuals becomes the sole or even primary focus, factors such as their similarities will begin to appear significant. Following suit, Prinz maintains that we ought rather to focus on actions, which again means that empathy becomes not only surplus but a phenomenon we should steer clear from: "The most reliable method of achieving impartiality actually involves bracketing off thoughts about victims, and, thus, empathy might actually be something we want to avoid" (Prinz 2011, 228).

This criticism has been reiterated by many (see de Waal 2008) and put forward recently in the popular book *Against Empathy* by Paul Bloom (2016). As briefly noted above, it has also gained popularity in the context of animal ethics, as one of the questions most ardently pushed forward when discussing empathy and non-human animals is whether such empathy could ever amount to anything more than anthropomorphic, biased and partial projection (see, e.g., Holton and Langton 1998). A critic of empathy in animal ethics, T. J. Kasperbauer, posits that empathy is inherently biased, as it is felt most towards those who we are similar or familiar with. It is localized, something that depends on who we are closest to, which renders it into a particularly poor basis for animal ethics due to the differences and distances that separate humans from many other animals: "The only way in which empathy can assist animals is if they possess physical, functional, or phylogenetic similarity to humans, or if they are made honorary ingroup members through domestic companionship" (Kasperbauer 2014, 10). Here, Kasperbauer borrows from Prinz: "We can no more overcome its limits than we can ride a bicycle across the ocean; it is designed for local travel" (Prinz 2011, 229).

These are not unfounded criticisms, for empirical research points towards the risk of bias. One's relation to the other often influences whether or not empathy is aroused, and its impact on, for instance, affective empathy is demonstrated by how we feel less with those with whom we compete (see Goubert et al. 2005). The pain of co-operates is viewed aversively, while the pain of competitors is even viewed with Schadenfreude (gloating at the suffering of others, also documented among chimpanzees; see de Waal 2008). Therefore, whether one relates to and likes another individual or not may determine whether one feels empathy towards her (Decety and Lamm 2006). Such risks are evident from the viewpoint of evolutionary history as well.

As de Waal notes, empathy is prone towards bias: "Generally, the empathic response is amplified by similarity, familiarity, social closeness, and positive experience with the other" (de Waal 2008, 291; thus, among rats, too, empathy is more likely experienced within one's own group – those with whom rats are familiar – and less probably with strangers).

These issues are all frighteningly obvious in animal ethics, signalled in how those non-human creatures who are viewed to "compete" with or nuisance humans ("vermin", street dogs, predators such as wolves, etc.) are often wholly left outside of empathy and even met with Schadenfreude in the form of deliberate, gloating sadism (as when hunters post grim, power-orientated images of the wolves or lions they have killed) – this also explains why companion animals are often seen as legitimate, deserving targets of empathy, while animals (such as farmed animals) unliked by or unknown to many will elicit little empathic response. Empathy can be endorsed and manipulated so that mainly those animals who are similar, familiar or cute are noted, while others are left outside of moral attention. Moreover, following Prinz, perhaps there can be too much focus on individual animals, while the practices of using them remain without due attention: the "animal lover" may mourn the individual cow she has seen while staying unaware of the moral problems plaguing industrial farming. The focus remains on individuals and victims, not actions, which threatens not only to spur bias but also to redirect consideration away from moral wrongs.

Does empathy, then, have any hope of offering a reliable compass for moral agency? Indeed, considering its biased nature, can empathy be anything but a hindrance to moral regard for different and distant others, and as such a considerable risk to animal ethics?

Cultural Diversions

First, it is important to notice how biases may not originate from empathy but rather from cultural causes affecting empathy: they are not "written into" empathic responses and instead are frequently culturally produced. As argued by Sarah Ahmed (2004), emotions are social and political, and our surroundings evoke them with their particular belief systems and discourses. Put simply, we come to signify given sorts of beings as existing beyond the scope of empathy because cultural imagery encourages us to do so. Fishes evoke little empathy in many not only because they "objectively" appear so dissimilar with and distant to human beings but also, and perhaps primarily, because cultural depiction of fishes continuously tells us that they are dissimilar and distant. Fishes are defined as "fish", creatures who are not individuals but rather a faceless, vast mass; they are not killed but "fished", as if being killed was an inherent part of their fate; and they are spoken of not as sentient, minded, cognitively capable subjects but as species and flocks, kilograms and tons. The way that language denotes them is based upon facelessness, quantification, masses, food and death, which erodes their subjectivity and simultaneously disinvites empathy. It is little wonder, then, that they evoke less empathy than most other animals, for they are culturally defined by dissimilarity, unfamiliarity and distance. Thereby, much of the bias stems from culture rather than empathy itself and may be alleviated by paying attention to and replacing the cultural preconceptions that prevent us from also seeing similarity, familiarity and proximity in fishes and other frequently desubjectified creatures.[5]

In order to resist the urge to only empathize with those culturally depicted as most like us, and most familiar and approximate to us and in order to desist the temptation to feel with only dogs and cats, elephants and dolphins, one is to stay focused on the animal. She – instead of our cultural, pre-fixed and often biased notions or indeed our emotions and beliefs anchored on personal needs – must continually remain the reference point of inquiry. If cultural influences thwart empathy, it is them rather than empathy which must be critically assessed and set aside and empathy which must be reaffixed on the animal. We are to seek interaction with other animals, and when this is impossible, envision from all the information and experience we have concerning them what they may be like outside of cultural stereotypes. To position the animal as the reference point of empathizing– the animal stripped as naked as possible from cultural stereotypes – and to position oneself as other-directed and open to diversity are the key to evading biases.

Therefore, when reduced to relying on cultural preconceptions, empathy has lost its foundation and reference point: the animal. It comes to be guided by presumptions, mediations and stereotypes which often support bias and as such transforms into something superficial, crooked, ill-conceived and baseless, a phenomenon defined by the absence of the very factor that ought to define it – the other being. Much like Emmanuel Levinas (1961) urged us to meet others naked and stripped bare from the "totalizations" of language, the stereotypes that enforce misleading preconceptions concerning others, one ought to approach empathy by maintaining a critical focus on cultural animal imagery and by seeking to meet the non-human as clean as possible from preconceptions and prejudices. (Of course, as cultural creatures, we cannot escape cultural influence altogether, but we can try to remain critically aware of the most obvious prejudices and partialities. There is a long way between being culturally influenced and uncritically accepting of cultural dogma.)

Hence, biases often originate from cultural preconceptions – we view given sorts of animals as distant and different not because they objectively are but because culture depicts them as such. The failure, then, does not stem from empathy but rather from culturally produced animal imageries.

Another source of biases is politics. Studies show that power and hierarchies lessen or even erase empathy. We are less likely to have empathy towards those whom we have power over and who have a lower social status (Van Kleef et al. 2008; Hogeveen, Inzlicht and Obhi 2014). Power feeds a sense of superiority, which again easily reduces the "lesser" others into objects or resources one feels entitled to make use of. Power, then, comes with a sense of privilege, which also hinders one's ability to recognize subjectivity in others. Hierarchies include a similar danger of disregard for the experiences of the "lower ranks".

This applies quite evidently to everyday animal ethics, as arguably many forgo empathy towards snakes, chickens and badgers on account of having power over them or a higher social ranking. Human-centred worldviews by necessity endorse such power-orientated, hierarchical notions, and thereby our cultural, social environments are prone to reducing one's ability to empathize with non-human beings. This is an important thing to notice: power is antagonistic towards empathy, it diminishes our ability to identify with others, and this acutely dangerous phenomenon also negatively impacts our take on other animals. Perhaps it is this which explains the macabre undercover footages from animal industries, all too often displaying sadistic forms of abuse – when workers have complete power over animals in slaughterhouses or farms, empathy may be replaced by sadistic, banal violence. As with other cultural prejudices, the antidote is the animal herself. Instead of power and hierarchies, the animal ought to stand as a reference of point, not only stripped bare of stereotypes but also viewed outside power and hierarchies.

But how to position the animal as a point of reference? One evident route, implied in various parts of this book, is societal, political alteration. If cultural, social, economic or political presumptions and relations are hindering empathy, they should be critically reviewed. Therefore, if power limits empathy, presumptions of power and hierarchy within our societies and worldviews ought to be curtailed. In plain terms, anthropocentric and anthropathic notions, which prevail over most social institutions, should be challenged and those institutions changed so as to question species supremacy and hierarchies. For instance, education and the legal system should finally take non-human animals seriously, offer them a standing as subjects worthy of consideration and in so doing normalize empathy towards them.

Once more, reflection is helpful, for it is reflective empathy which will invite one to pay attention to the other being as she is, stripped bare from prejudiced stereotypes, and which will also help us to notice and confront the cultural influences which distort empathic attention. Reflective empathy will persuade one to undertake explorations of the causes of empathizing with dogs while ignoring chickens and offers a way of clarifying and making sense of the underlying cultural beliefs – it also coaxes one to develop empathy skills so that they more readily extend to those animals who traditionally have been positioned as different and distant. The metalevel of attentiveness provides a perfect backdrop for focusing on the animal herself as a subject, and for thereby situating her as the reference point of inquiry, for it allows one to both acknowledge the usual thought patterns and emotions which affect our take on other animals and to note the presence of those in animals in a more authentic manner.

Indeed, reflection forms the key answer to criticisms concerning empathy's bias. Following in the footsteps of Hume, Martin Hoffman notes that empathic affects become weaker with unfamiliarity and distance. We feel less for strangers and those who are not in our vicinity, and as a result, empathic affects may struggle with impartiality. However, Hoffman (1990) argues that the situation can be remedied by acknowledging that reason is also of relevance: that is, although empathic affects are foundational for morality, they alone do not always suffice, and rationality may enable the assessing and structuring of empathic affects towards a more impartial direction.[6] In addition, other studies have posited that reflection can also enable empathy towards the different and distant, exemplified in our capacity to empathize with non-human animals. The argument is that reflection allows for plasticity in how we empathically relate to others and opens up doorways to variance: "This flexibility is a cornerstone of our ability to empathize with diverse others—from animals . . . to people from different cultural backgrounds" (Lamm, Meltzoff and Decety 2010, 374). Hence, contemplation enables empathy to avoid the snares and pitfalls of partiality and bias. We are to reflect upon empathy, to use reasoned analysis as its support and thereby to bring forward more inclusive, impartial realms wherein proximity and similarity cease to matter. Empathy does not need to exclude reasoned reflection, nor should it.

This, again, underlines the role of reflective empathy. Whereas Hoffman appears to position reflection outside of empathy, as if it were an external help one can use in order to avoid bias, reflective empathy renders reasoned awareness into an elemental part of empathy – it does not stem from the outside but rather entwines with the empathic process. Reflective empathy is inherently prone to reveal and rebel against biases, for it involves the evaluation of one's motivations to empathize with particular sorts of beings – it reveals biases and their causes and seeks to approach the other as impartially as one's human faculties allow. When we fail to empathize with a real pig or when we empathize strongly with a cute animated piglet, cultivating reflective empathy will help to monitor where these failures and responses stem from and how to channel them so as to do justice to the being in front of us. As such, reflective empathy will not only help to fight culturally induced biases but also assist in alleviating biases that stem from biological or psychological tendencies to favour familiarity.

Something similar was proposed by Hume, who suggested that biases can be overcome via an emphasis on impartiality or "disinterestedness". We are to aim for a general, universal look on things and thus avoid partiality (Hume 1969). This implies the notion of a judicious spectator who aims for a general point of view (see Rick 2007). As Hume clarifies, we can use "approbation" to view strangers equally, despite the biases of empathy, and this is grounded on both our having "moral taste" and a viewpoint of the universal "judicious spectator" (Hume 1969, 632). As an end result, our partialities evaporate: "In order, therefore, to . . . arrive at a more stable judgment of things, we fix on some steady and general points of view. . . . Experience soon teaches us this method of correcting our sentiments" (ibid., 632, 633). This comes quite close to the metalevel, emphasized in reflective empathy, as second-order attentiveness is partly founded on withdrawing from our most obvious mental states and witnessing things from a more considered standpoint. As it comes to the non-biased take on cats, we are therefore to move beyond the purely human-orientated view and broaden our horizons so as to become more inclusive of feline interests, wants, needs and emotions. Disinterestedness can be learned through stepping away from the immediate towards a more comprehensive and calm perspective.

However, according to John Rick, Hume appears to rest too much on the metaphor of visuality, as if impartiality amounts to clearing one's view – a more fruitful option might be to emphasize the search for further information concerning and mapping out additional attributes of the other being and thereby gaining a more detailed understanding of her. According to this approach, impartiality includes not stepping on some universal pedestal from which to observe others but the effort to become more knowledgeable in those others. In relation to non-human beings, this would require spending more time and effort in expanding the knowledge base covering particularly those animals most different from and distant to us and thereby getting familiar with fishes, cockroaches, squids, reptiles, "farmed animals" and so forth.

Are we to follow Hume's "the clarity of perspective" approach or Rick's "expanding information" take on things? Both are important, and indeed they support each other. Stepping to a metalevel allows for a more considered foundation for gathering information on the other, and gathering such information again helps to maintain a "clear perspective". Both can be combined with reflective empathy and its aim to clarify our takes on animality. Hence, not only should we reflect on the reliability of cultural stereotypes, but we should also replace them with informative beliefs that have been gathered with methods capable of doing justice to animality. Indeed, Rick's claim entwines with the aforementioned need to place the animal as a reference point of examination: avoiding bias necessitates forming various forms of knowledges (biological, behavioural, environmental, geographical, historical, and so forth) that seek to authentically map out the other as she is, not as we wish to witness her.

Therefore, reflection supported by the gathering of further information forms one gateway away from (at least the most obvious of) biases. Hume also suggests that bias may be avoided by avoiding self-directedness: "Avarice, ambition, vanity, and all the passions vulgarly, through improperly, comprised under the denomination of self-love, are here excluded from our theory concerning the origin of morals, not because they are too weak, but because they have not a proper direction, for that purpose" (Hume 2007, 161). Here, he acknowledges that it is often egoistic desires and emotions which lead towards bias and thereby dim the ability for empathy and moral agency. This is a valuable addition. Just like cultural beliefs, our self-directed propensities may impact empathy and render it biased, and the task is to critically scrutinize how one's egoistic desires and emotions govern empathic choices and how to limit their influence. The questions that follow can be simple: Does one not feel empathy towards real pigs because one wants to keep on eating their flesh and harbours various emotions, such as contempt, which support this desire? And does one feel empathy towards cute cartoon animals precisely because they make no demands on the empathizer? Reflective empathy also supports this move away from self-directed bias. The sort of attentiveness it contains is, as seen earlier, largely founded on "un-selfing", the stepping away from blatant egoism. As such, reflective empathy offers the perfect remedy against egoistically driven desires and emotions, which may muddle and misdirect empathy.

Reflective empathy likewise provides an answer to Prinz's critique of victims versus acts, for as long as we remain reflective over the situation, ultimately it is noting the harms suffered by individuals, "the victims", which provides the foundation for becoming aware of the wrongness of the act. That is, even though acts deserve ample focus, their moral nature is determined by their impact on individual beings, and here reflective empathy plays a crucial role. Simply put, we deem given acts as immoral because of their influence on individuals (we do not judge killing to be a moral wrong as an abstract act but because it harms individuals), and reflective empathy allows us to identify that influence on an experiential, considered level. We first need to empathize with the victims of the acts in order to become aware of how and why the acts are unjust – although only noting an individual animal may not spark political understanding of the injustices of the meat industry, not noting her at all will fail even more miserably. Therefore, attention should not be moved away from individuals to actions, making empathy redundant. Rather it should stay on the individuals in a reflective fashion, mapping out the whys and hows pertinent to the situation, for only then will the morality of the action become apparent.

Moreover, it should be noted that bias is not a fault exclusive to empathy. First, as argued above, it is often external to empathy, stemming from cultural influences and egoism, and second, it plagues not only empathy but our moral psychology in general. Indeed, any moral emotion, and any moral use of reason, is prone towards bias. We feel anger the most when those close to us are wronged, we feel elevated the most when our kin are salvaged, we often most love those proximate to us and we tend to note, analyse and choose reasoned moral arguments on account of how convenient they are from the viewpoints of our own lifestyles and aims. Hence, most emotions are deeply partial, and not even reason escapes this pitfall, for we often use it differently or give different importance to its content depending on whom we are focusing: we may, for instance, adopt a utilitarian, use-orientated logic in regard to distant beings while favouring virtue ethics in regard to those individuals with whom we are familiar, and we may be more likely to pay heed to rationally produced principles such as "do no harm" when it comes to beings we recognize as similar to us. In fact, as Hoffman (1990) importantly recognizes, reason can interlink with egoistic motivations, wherein one begins to prioritize those norms which best serve one's own interests (in moral argumentation, the privileged emphasize status, desert, etc., while the less privileged emphasize vulnerability, equality, etc.).

Singling empathy out as "the source" of bias is therefore ill-conceived, for any method of moral decision making, any emotion or reason may be influenced and motivated by various partial interests. If anything, empathy holds the promise of combatting biases. It enables one to choose norms from a non-egoistic viewpoint and offers the motivation to follow and act according to chosen norms, regardless of personal gain (Hoffman 1990, 2001). Particularly, and as already underlined, reflective empathy allows a person otherwise guided by partial emotions and biased reasoned arguments to pause and explore the basis of her own approach to others and to thereby arrive at a more inclusive and considered conclusion. In practice, a privileged individual influenced by emotions such as contempt or "reasons" such as a highly optimizing outlook on social issues will, when in a state of reflective empathy, more likely notice her own biases and alter her conduct accordingly. Our moral psychology would, therefore, benefit from reflective empathy when it comes to eradicating biased tendencies.

Necessary Partialities?

But should impartiality even be the aim? One view is that striving for complete impartiality signals the loss of political and historical situatedness. The problem with such a loss is that it lessens empathic ability, for understanding others requires that we acknowledge both our own and their contexts – that is, the political, historical positions in which we are by necessity embedded. In this vein, Reidar Pedersen has argued that various readings on empathy assume that an unbiased, neutral grasp of the mental contents of others ought to be our aim and that in so doing these readings fail to recognize how both the empathizer and her target are historically positioned creatures. Instead of seeking to escape such situatedness, understanding others should take it into account. Pedersen criticizes how empathy is often likened to visual perception or the automatic motion of mirror neurons, as if we could somewhat neutrally detect the experiences of others, while the subjects and their wider attributes and contexts are ignored: empathy becomes independent and "pure" from other influences, including the empathizer's previous experiences. He calls for taking the broader context into account and accepting our partiality instead of escaping it: "Empathic understanding is always influenced by experience, knowledge, expectations, and possible actions" (Pedersen 2008, 329). In short, we are contextual, biased creatures, and this must be included in rather than eradicated from empathy.

A similar critique has been presented by Eva Johansson, who reminds us of the relevance of culture and context in our empathic, moral make-up, and who endorses the phenomenological viewpoint, according to which our life-world has to be taken into account. Individuals develop in relation to the world, culture and others, and there is no "neutral" or "detached" perspective to be found (Johansson 2007).[7] A hermeneutic stance influenced by Heidegger and Gadamer provides one foundation for such an approach, where empathy by necessity includes one's own life-world. In order to achieve a situational outlook, the empathizer and her target are to enter into a reflective dialogue that pays heed to their background beliefs and past experiences. Here, empathy becomes an ongoing process where we constantly locate the contexts of our empathy rather than a "true" and static representation (Pedersen 2008, 332).

Therefore, the claim is that the sort of contextual considerations highlighted in regard to simulative empathy should be both endorsed and acknowledged as reasons to avoid efforts towards impartiality. We are inherently biased and can comprehend others only when accepting this facet of our nature. There are two aspects to be noted here: awareness of the context of the other and awareness of one's own context. In relation to the first of these, Hoffman has also posited that empathy comes in different degrees and that the most developed of these take into account the historical, political and personal contexts of others. For him, "empathy for another's life condition" is the most advanced form of empathy and allows one to relate to others in their wider life settings and historicities (Hoffman 1990).[8] The underlying claim, already hinted at in regard to simulative and affective empathy, is that when offering exclusive prioritization to experience in the here and now, empathy risks becoming politically innocent and succumbing to an ahistorical slumber where societal, historical and political power plays and mechanisms are marginalized or wholly hidden from view. Here, political nuances, or even obvious power politics, may remain concealed from attention, and empathy can even facilitate political atrocities, as it invites us to only focus on specific experiences rather than the forces that spark their existence. In the non-human context, an example of such an apolitical stance would be the animal lover immersed in a state of intense resonation yet ignorant of the power mechanics that cause the suffering she witnesses and therefore incapable of noting their moral problemacy and taking action. As a consequence, the moral dimensions (noting moral wrongs and the ways to correct them) of empathy can become vague.[9]

However, more importantly, what Pedersen brings forward is that the contextuality of the empathizer also needs to be considered and accepted. This is a valuable claim, for understanding others requires comprehending one's own contextual embeddedness – the fact that one is never a universal observer but instead a creature influenced by various biological, historical, political, cultural and personal factors which go on to build not only our sense of "self" and agency but also our approach to others. Indeed, unless one is willing to endorse abstraction, there is no "pure" experience, wholly disconnected from the external and internal contextualities of individuals undergoing them. In light of this claim, the Humean strive towards a judicious spectator appears misinformed, for we neither can nor should seek to purify ourselves from our partialities – indeed, doing so amounts to eradicating our "selfhood". Empathy should recognize and accept its biased limitations as signs of our human subjectivity and ignore calls for abstract, universal perspectives.

Yet the critique should not go too far to the opposite end of the spectrum and suggest that "anything goes" when it comes to biases. We may not be wholly objective universal observers, but neither should we be completely sunk in whatever partialities we happen to have, thus becoming ever more egoistic and aloof in relation to the other. There is a midground between abstraction and ignorance. Hence, acknowledging situatedness does not mean that we should simply accept biases; rather, it means that we must be careful to understand them and navigate them in ways that permit us to become open to otherness. We will never achieve neutrality, but neither should we just go with whatever flows our embeddedness happens to push us towards (which would allow an anthropocentric person to declare in the relativist ethos that she has the right to approach pigs as meat automata) – instead, we should try and better understand the hows and whys that are influencing our contexts and direct them in a manner that is capable of doing justice to other beings. As Sarah Harding (1991) has pointed out, we will never achieve "objectivity", but we can nonetheless try and cultivate our epistemic abilities by examining and becoming aware of the contextual backgrounds affecting our knowledge.

One model for a midground is recognizing contextual impacts and evaluating them on the grounds of how well they afford space for the subjectivity of others to manifest. We are conceptual creatures, making sense of things on the basis of previous experience and contexts and understanding others' benefits from mapping out their situatedness, but we can avoid those contextual factors that block rather than enable the acknowledging of subjectivity and experience.

Here, again, reflective empathy is of use, for it will offer precisely the sort of a metalevel that is required for awareness of one's own contextuality. When moving between first-order varieties of empathy and second-order noting of our beliefs, emotions and attitudes, we become increasingly aware of what the latter are, how they impact the former and which of them we wish to remain affixed to. In so doing, reflective empathy opens a platform on which to both accept and critically evaluate biases. We are to recognize our contextuality, eradicate those aspects of it that are confused or unjust and keep in mind those partialities that we by necessity are influenced by so that we remain attentive to how they impact our empathy and understanding of others.[10] Here, "universal observers" become "attentive observers".

This means that we will always be tied to our human bodies and senses, which already limit our capacity to comprehend the lives of whales, dogs, flies, pikes or ants, and that we will always be impacted by our cultures, histories, personal narratives and psychologies to such an extent that fully and neutrally knowing another animal (human or animal) is impossible. Yet we can always better our ability to understand by eliminating the most obvious and ill-informed biases and by becoming aware of the ones that we cannot get rid of. What makes us distinct subjects or "selves" is the fact that we have unique, specific physiological, environmental, evolutionary, cultural, historical and personal contexts from which we arise, and respecting this situated subjectivity forms a part of empathy and particularly intersubjectivity with others, for there is no empathy without an empathizing "self". However, it does not mean that we should let go of our effort to constitute knowledge that is capable of also noting the uniqueness and reality of others. There is a middle path between neutral access and biased inaccess, and reflective empathy is capable of pointing in its direction.

Species Divides: Can We Know the Mind of a Bat?

The final question concerning biases highlights species as the boundary of understanding. What if we simply cannot know non-human animality? This is a common critique of empathy and one related to situatedness, as the claim is that due to our human context, we have no access to other animals. Any claim of knowledge will be merely another biased sketch, not an accurate, true account of what raccoons or wombats are, for we simply cannot escape our partial nature, our biological, evolutionary and psychological embeddedness in humanity. Therefore, inter-species empathy is futile.

In this vein, Richard Holton and Rae Langton argue that "we have no idea what it is like to see the world this [non-human] way – and no amount of sharpening our sensitivities could ever help us find out" (Holton and Langton 1998, 15), before concluding, "the method of imaginative identification has achieved nothing" (ibid). This claim has surfaced many times in the history of philosophy, from Ludwig Wittgenstein, who posited that we cannot understand the lion even if she were to speak and whose words have wrongly been interpreted to mean that there is no access to non-human mentation[11], to Thomas Nagel (1974), who asserted that we cannot know what it is like to be a bat. It forms the core of the sceptical outlook on non-human mindedness with its eagerness to posit that even if other animals have minds, we cannot ever truly understand them.

However, this sceptical stance is far too extreme. As already mentioned, the problem of other minds, which has been haunting Western philosophy for centuries, does not only concern other animals – it also concerns other humans, particularly when culturally different from us (on the latter obstacle to empathy, see Stueber 2006). If we adopt the position, according to which we are encapsulated in our specific contexts, we cannot know anybody's mindedness and will remain in a state of solipsistic loneliness. As argued in relation to embodied empathy, this notion of encapsulation stems from a faulty conception of mindedness and should be replaced with awareness of how we constantly communicate mindedness to others and read the mental contents of those others via the various contexts that we do share, the most elemental of them being our embodiment. It is only via presuming rigid, generic categories that one can speak of abysses between humans and other animals, and these categories need to be particularly unyielding for them to support the claim that "we" cannot know "them", that there is "nothing" that can be achieved via empathy and that "they" remain completely, utterly unattainable and unknowable.

Even species categories do not exist in such a strict form, and they constantly entwine with each other – for instance, in moments of embodied engagement and environmental overlaps, which again enable comprehension of the mental states of others, even if such comprehension is never "total" or fully "neutral". That is, even if we are context-bound creatures, many of those contexts are interlinked with those of other animals, and such overlays (for instance, that we all are physical, breathing, feeling, aware creatures capable of suffering, wanting and intending, living in complex, risky environments) form foundations on which to build empathic understanding. It is here that the sort of intersubjective encounters also mentioned by Pedersen, within which we dynamically interact with another, become relevant. The pigeon or the fox in the park can, through a joint living environment and similarities of embodiment and basic needs, present herself to the human walker, and the walker can stop to observe and express her own intentions to the point where dynamic, even dialogical forms of understanding begin to take place.

Moreover, as stated earlier, although theoretically continuous doubt over the accuracy of empathy may be possible, pragmatically it lacks credibility, for the sort of physical, sensing, socially intelligent, intersubjective beings that we are must rely on empathy as a valid form of knowing others. "Certainty", therefore, gains a different meaning – it is not grounded on blocking away all causes for theoretical doubt but rather on accepting and attuning with our own affective, social ability. Here the thought of Wittgenstein (1969), who had much to say about "certainty", is valuable, as he pointed out that we do not infer the mental states of others nor project them but instead approach others as the sort of beings we can understand. Simply stated, asking for theoretical certainty is asking the wrong question, for we are to trust those methods of knowing that bear basic meaningfulness in our lives and which root from how we conceptualize reality (a similar view was offered by, for instance, Merleau-Ponty with his previously mentioned "perceptual faith").

Following suit, although theoretically it may be possible, as Daniel Dennett (1999) has sceptically maintained, that perceiving mindedness in other animals is grounded in an "intentional stance" wherein we project human mental contents onto chickens and lions, seriously entertaining this notion on a pragmatic level is absurd. We are not alien creatures, divided from other animals to such an extent where knowing them is impossible, but instead share many aspects of our embodiment, senses, capacities, environments and evolutionary histories and even contemporary contexts and concepts with them – we have evolved next to and often in relation to them and are thereby beings who, to use Maurice Merleau-Ponty's words, share a "strange kinship" with other animals (see Toadvine 2007). This kinship forms the grounds for engaging with and understanding seagulls, rats and reindeer – grounds which are strengthened by our capacity to trust our most pivotal senses, including empathic responses.[12]

Again, reflective empathy can help in the process, for via it we come to recognize shared or entwined contexts that can ease understanding others – it can indicate how similarities in basic needs or evolutionary traits support efforts to access foreign mentation and how even the most different of beings have some overlap with our own situatedness (hence, a lizard feels pain and strives to maintain her life, even if her other contexts differ greatly from ours). It can also clarify varieties of empathic ability, deepen their reliability and point out the need to trust them in the appropriate situations. In sum, it paves the way to identifying how species share much more than they are separated by and how instead of doubting, we often should be cultivating our empathic skills.

EMPATHY VERSUS REASON

A further critique of empathy concerns its moral relevance. Highlighting the role of empathy and emotions as key factors in moral agency poses a challenge to rationalism, which has dominated much of modern philosophy and which posits that morality is founded on reasoned analysis. This trend is antagonistic towards the role of empathy, which is not, in comparison to reason, seen to offer an adequate foundation for moral agency. The claim is that instead of empathy, one must ground moral judgement and action in rational analysis, for only such analysis can amount to deliberated and thoroughly considered morality.

The point made by rationalists is simple: morality must underscore reason, for any other foundation, including empathy, is too flimsy. Only reason will manifest what we ought to do, all things considered, and in the most impartial light possible, whereas emotions are often frivolous, ill-considered, ambiguous, biased and utterly subjective. Such a stance also appears pertinent in animal ethics precisely because our emotions often support anthropocentrism and are hopelessly unreflected and partial, whereas reason can manifest what we ought to value and do when we adopt a more considered and disinterested perspective. Is the case for empathy's moral significance not, then, wholly exaggerated and misjudged?

First, as seen in the beginning of this book, not everyone agrees with the rationalist dismissal of emotion. What is significant in the sentimentalist claims is that emotions or empathy are not seen as oppositional to reason, as if we had to choose one or the other, but rather interlink with analyses and form the often neglected yet necessary counterpart in morality. A concise summary of this position comes from Sabine Roeser, who demonstrates how positive feelings spur one to endow objects with higher value and who repeats the claim according to which emotions and reason should not be viewed as opposites but rather as intertwined, with both factors required for moral judgement: "In order to have moral knowledge, we need to have emotions" (Roeser 2006, 699). Even if the relevance of reason is not sidelined, emotions are positioned as a necessary constituent of moral deliberation: "Purely rational reflection would miss out on important evaluative aspects . . . only beings with the appropriate ability to have emotions can make justified moral judgments" (ibid.). Similarly, Victoria McGreer argues that affect plays a critical role in moral agency: "Valuing certain ends is fundamentally rooted in the depth and quality of one's affective life" (McGreer 2008, 247); "All forms of human moral agency are rooted in affect" (ibid., 251). Therefore, affects and emotions are inherently entwined with value constitution, and without them moral decision making is an impossibility; moreover, emotion and reason should not be viewed as an "either/or" choice but as two forms of mentation that support and impact each other.

But why favour empathy? As this book has sought to demonstrate, empathy can enable other-directedness and openness towards diversity, two crucial elements in moral agency. It also allows us to note the subjectivity of others, to feel and communicate with it, which is necessary for us to have an authentic grasp of the inherent value of other beings. In short, varieties of empathy pave different forms of access to the subjectivity of others and as such help to constitute the notion that others are indeed creatures of value, independent of their instrumental use. When perceiving, feeling and communicating with the inner realms of others, we come to see them as worthy.

Yet there are contemporary rationalists who maintain that the role of empathy and emotions is overstated and for whom reason still acts as the primary, necessary constituent of morality. Their key thesis is that "genuine moral judgments are those that are regulated or endorsed by reflection", for moral judgements "are or invoke reasons claims" (Kennett and Fine 2009, 78). What are the merits of this criticism? Are empathy and emotions overly accentuated?

Psychopathy, Autism and Disordered Moralities

In order to map out what, on the most elemental level, constitutes morality in us, it is beneficial to explore those groups of human beings who act in amoral ways and struggle with grasping what "morality" means, for investigating what these groups lack next to moral ability may also point out what it is that enables one to be a moral agent. The most obvious of these groups are psychopaths, discussed in detail earlier in this book. They are defined as self-centred, manipulative, coercive, deceptive, impulsive and morally irresponsible, hedonistic, incapable of remorse or guilt, prone to follow only their own immediate reward and unable to note the moral value of others (Kiehl 2006; Mullins-Nelson et al. 2006; Book, Quinsey and Langford 2007; Blair and Blair 2009). As seen, psychopaths are capable of both rationality and cognitive empathy but lack affective empathy. Since they are the prototype of a "moral monster", lacking in moral ability but even excelling in reasoning ability, it seems that it is indeed absence of affective empathy which signals the loss of moral agency, while reason alone does not suffice to restore that agency – in other words, at least affective empathy may be vital (and much more vital than reason) for our moral ability (Aaltola 2014a; Aaltola 2014c).

This claim has gained popularity. As McGreer posits, psychopaths do not have meaningful emotions beyond their own interests, and it is here that their moral agency fails: "They have limited capacities for making any affective investment in ends that transcend their immediate and parochial interests" (McGreer 2008, 254). Shaun Nichols (2002) concentrates on the relation between reason and moral motivation and argues that psychopathy manifests rationalism to be mistaken, for according to the latter, agents who make reasoned moral judgements are also motivated by those judgements (that is, one cannot be a rational amoralist) – since psychopaths are not so motivated, their existence points towards an error in moral rationalism.

However, contemporary defenders of rationalism argue that psychopathy does not prove that it is affective empathy rather than reason which acts as the guardian of morality. One point of reference here is a category of people who are low on empathy, high in reasoning ability and capable of moral agency – their lack of empathic ability, combined with good reasoning skills and morality, appears to demonstrate that moral capability is grounded in reason rather than empathy. Such a category is autism, and, for instance, Jeanette Kennett (2006) claims autistic people to form a proof of the primacy of rationality in moral agency. Autistic individuals are often keen on the rational order of things and use this ability to locate what they consider to be the morally sound way of behaving, which means that they are not "dependent on the operation of empathy, but rather on the application of a more explicit practical concern to do the right thing" (Kennett 2002, 352). Hence, those on the autism spectrum can be moral agents despite of their lack of empathy, which offers a counter-case for psychopathy's amorality and supports the rationalist stance.

Indeed, for Kennett autistic people manifest a Kantian rather than Humean approach to morality, as they seek rational principles instead of resting on empathy or other emotive foundations. Kennett even suggests that it is the lack of empathy in these individuals which may render their moral agency so conscientious: "Deficits in empathy, so typical of autism, may make possible a kind of moral purity not available to the rest of us" (Kennett 2002, 350). Empathy does not muddle things for autistic individuals, it does not make them prone to emotional upheavals which could distort their view and lead them to favour, say, those most familiar to them. In short, not only is empathy not necessary for moral agency, it may even hinder it, as "moral purity" is possible via the use of detached reason. Partly on these grounds, Kennett concludes that "only individuals who are capable of being moved directly by the thought that some consideration constitutes a reason for action can be conscientious moral agents" (Kennett 2002, 357; see also Kennett and Fine 2009). Empathy is irrelevant, for what matters is our ability for reasoned reflection, with the implication being that the latter forms both the necessary and sufficient criterion for moral agency.

Yet the case of autism may not prove as much as Kennett hopes it does. This is because the type of empathy under discussion is not specified: What sort of empathy do those with autism fare poorly in? In order to prove that affective empathy is irrelevant to moral ability, the rationalists would have to demonstrate that it is precisely affective empathy which morally capable autistic individuals lack. Perhaps the most popular study exploring autism and empathy comes from Simon Baron-Cohen (2011), who unfortunately does not sufficiently separate whether he is referring to cognitive or affective empathy, and a similar omission in many other studies may have led to a distorted view, which generically denies the empathic abilities of autistic individuals. What remains without adequate attention is that the generic "empathy" defects in this context may be defects in cognitive empathy, while affective empathy is intact (see Rogers et al. 2007). That is, autistic people may fail in the former and master the latter, thus presenting quite an oppositional situation in comparison to psychopaths (who do well in cognitive empathy and fail in affective empathy).

As seen earlier, high cognitive empathy and low affective empathy lead to Machiavellian behaviour, filled with charm and social fluency on the surface and ruthless exploitation of knowledge concerning the mental states of others below the exterior (A. J. Smith 2006, 2009). On the other side of the spectrum, high affective empathy and low cognitive empathy are thought to lead to pro-social behaviour, emotional attunement and inhibition of aggression. However, it may also have downsides, as some individuals guided by this combination may be socially clueless in their inability to cognitively mind read, and they may also be painfully sensitive to others' emotions. In the latter case, oversensitivity and the inability to read and cope with the emotions of others may lead these individuals to minimize their social contacts, to "block others away", with the consequence of appearing socially insensitive, withdrawn and even empathically incapable (A. J. Smith 2006; Dziobek et al. 2008). Whereas psychopaths typify the first of these options, being socially skilled controllers, perhaps autistic individuals fit the last option, exemplifying socially awkward, superficially insensitive individuals who resonate with others underneath it all.

Indeed, it has been argued that autistic people may have exceptionally low cognitive empathy and unusually high affective empathy (Jones et al. 2010), which leads to frustrations in cognitively understanding the minds of others and to such emotive resonance that it causes them discomfort and pushes them to withdraw from or at least limit social contact, which again makes them appear socially aloof and disengaged (A. J. Smith 2009; see also Vignemont and Frith 2008). This argument is supported by research which suggests that autistic individuals can resonate with facial expressions (Blair 1999) and the distress of others (Corona et al. 2008) and that people with Asperger's syndrome have as much affective concern for others as do control groups (Rogers et al. 2007, 714). Following suit, James Blair (2008) – a scholar who has researched both psychopathy and autism – criticizes those who group these personality types under the same category in their empathy capacities and overlook how they exhibit very different forms of empathy. Other scholars have also made the same distinction in the empathic abilities of psychopaths and autistic individuals: "The pattern of low cognitive empathy in the presence of normal emotional empathy in individuals with autistic conditions seems to be the mirror image of what has been reported for individuals with psychopathy, namely low emotional but intact cognitive empathy" (Dziobek et al. 2008, 471).

Therefore, autism offers a poor way to prioritize reason at the expense of empathy or emotions, and instead it lends support for the claim that affective empathy is crucial for our moral ability, for perhaps its existence (rather than its lack) is precisely what renders autistic individuals capable of moral agency. The rationalist criticism is, for this reason, unfounded.[13] The downside of affective empathy, also manifested in autism, is that too much of it, unaccompanied by cognitive support, may push us towards emotive withdrawal; however, this withdrawal should not be taken to mean that affective empathy is not crucial for moral agency but rather that it also requires, as noted earlier, the support of cognitive mind reading.[14]

The defenders of rationalism have also sought other ways to support their stance. One claim is that instead of empathy, attention ought to be placed on rational ability, which in their view is hindered in psychopaths and present in autistic individuals. Therefore, it is the ability for rational thought processes that separates the two personality types and renders only the latter capable of moral agency; instead of a lack of empathy, it is a lack of reasoning ability which undermines the morality of psychopaths (Kennett 2006). In short, psychopaths "don't appear to understand that moral claims are reasons claims and so it can be argued that they are not capable of genuine moral judgment" (Kennett and Fine 2009, 86). Kennett brings forward research which suggests that psychopaths have an underdeveloped ability for evaluating their own thinking, behaviour, long-term goals and internal conflicts; thus, they are incapable of reflective analysis concerning their own mentation and prone to seeking immediate rewards. Since moral agency, according to Kennett, requires reasoned evaluation, psychopaths fail the morality test. Their ability for executive control, which comprises second-order self-evaluation, regulation and planning, is weakened, and it is this which undermines their moral agency: "These rational capacities are as critical to human moral agency and moral judgment as the more basic capacity to recognise and respond affectively to distress in others" (Kennett 2006, 78). Another author to put forward a similar claim is Heidi Maibom (2005), who argues that psychopaths have a rationality deficit, evidenced by their impulsive, poorly thought out behaviours, and who suggests this limits their moral ability.

Is it, therefore, lack of rationality rather than empathy which impairs psychopaths' moral agency? The crucial thing to pay attention to here is the difference between antisocial personality disorder and psychopathy. The two are often mixed and seen as synonymous, but there are important differences. Antisocial personality disorder is characterized by failed executive functioning, lack of self-control and long-term plans and poor intellectual ability (Morgan and Lilienfeld 2000; Kiehl 2006), and thus they are the sort of explosively irrational individuals with poor reflective ability whom Kennett and Maibom discuss. Whereas those with antisocial personality disorder are frequently ill-tempered and impulsive, which places obstacles in the way of having ordered lives, the so-called primary and successful psychopaths in particular can be quite capable of leading successful, well-structured, controlled and reflective lifestyles. The difference here is that such psychopaths do not suffer from limitations in their executive functioning, rationality or self-regulation (Kiehl 2006; Mahmut, Homewood and Stevenson 2008). In fact, some research posits that those psychopaths who fare well in life have a heightened ability for executive functioning, inclusive of reflection and planning (Ishikawa et al. 2001; Glenn, Kursban and Raine 2011). Following suit, the psychopath's ability for manipulation and deceit appears to go hand in hand with good lingual, creative and analytic skills, and the narcissistic tendencies in psychopaths are particularly evident in their links to high cognitive functioning (Fontaine et al. 2008). If anything, the psychopath emerges as a highly rational creature.

Therefore, deficits in rational inability do not appear to offer a valid explanation for the moral misgivings of a psychopath – on the contrary, the case of psychopaths demonstrates how rationally capable beings can be morally crooked and incapable, which undermines the rationalist argument. Simply stated, the limitations of psychopaths' moral agency cannot be explained via reference to rational disability, and on the contrary, optimizing rationality bolsters the manipulative capacities of those very psychopaths who do the worst damage. Whereas "secondary psychopaths", at times grouped with antisocial persons, are impulsive and reactive yet capable of some remorse and emotional engagement (Meale 1995), "primary psychopaths" are rationally optimizing and not impulsive (Hicks et al. 2004; Skeem et al. 2007) and are the most manipulative and emotionally detached of all. It is precisely the latter who in their systematic planning epitomize a moral catastrophe much more than the antisocial hotheads or the secondary psychopaths do.[15] Since such individuals are characterized by high rationality and executive functioning combined with emotional detachment, lack of reason cannot be the cause of their amorality, whereas lack of emotive resonation again emerges as the likely culprit. Indeed, one could even claim that the primary psychopath is the perfect rational individual, for she can follow her motivations optimally without being affected by the emotions of others – and since she is also the epitome of amorality, she exemplifies how reason alone cannot make us moral.

The manner in which limitations in rational ability do not necessarily lead to limitations in moral agency also manifests in a group of people who are in many ways the opposite of psychopaths. As explained earlier in this book, Williams syndrome is a condition which includes learning disabilities, poor executive functioning, and problems in detached mind reading and cognitive empathy. Individuals with this condition also display rich emotional lives, are exceedingly sociable and have exceptionally high levels of affective empathy. Most importantly, they have a strong need to help and demonstrate heightened concern for others (Mervis and Klein-Tasman 2000; Mervis and Becerra 2007). Therefore, whereas primary psychopaths, defined by rational aptitude and a lack of affective empathy, fail the moral test, Williams syndrome combines low intellectual and rational ability with high affective empathy and moral agency. This difference positions the latter as the perfect counter-case for the rationalists' argument: whereas those with high reasoning skills may fail morally, those with diminished reasoning abilities can, if affectively empathic, be morally quite capable, even saintly.[16]

Unempathic Values

Yet rationalists have more criticism to offer. Maibom (2009) continues her critique of empathy's primacy by pointing out that morality is culturally variable and that many instances of it rest on something other than empathy. Examples of this include moral considerations revolving around "purity" and "natural order". Hence, the claim is that some important aspects of morality simply do not involve empathy (something also exemplified in anthropocentric ethics, which links the moral value of cows to beliefs concerning the "order of nature" rather than empathy).

This claim is supported by studies suggesting that morality finds five psychological foundations (harm/care, fairness/reciprocity, in-group thinking/loyalty, authority/respect and purity/sanctity), of which only the first concerns empathy. Therefore, for instance, matters related to allocating societal resources concern notions of "fairness" or justice rather than empathy, and societal norms related to sexual behaviour often go back to religious presumptions revolving around "purity". On these grounds, Jonathan Haidt and Jesse Graham (2007) posit that various cultural and historical contexts have offered empathy a limited role in morality, one example being the moral codes of the Old Testament, and maintain that this is still evident in contemporary society, where empathy is only one factor among many. Empathy may be central to Western liberalistic ethics, but its relevance is limited when viewed against a wider historical and cultural background and conservative ethics. (Maibom argues that even within such liberalistic ethics, there are various moral wrongs that do not involve empathy, one example being the act of killing in such a manner that the victim is taken by complete surprise and undergoes no pain – here, there appears to be nothing to empathize with, yet we deem the action to be wrong. See Maibom 2009, 490.)

This critique also remains unconvincing. First, it does not demonstrate the primacy of reason. Quite the contrary, it shows how moral norms are often wholly unrelated to reason and stem from cultural traditions, ideologies or religions – in other words, they can follow dogma rather than rational analyses. Therefore, the argument offered not only goes against the relevance of empathy, it also goes against the relevance of reason.

Second, its ability to downgrade the significance of empathy is limited, for various moral codes which on the surface appear to include no empathy may nonetheless be grounded on it. For instance, rules concerning "purity" and the "natural order" are heavily influenced by our identity and integrity in the eyes of others: we want to appear acceptable in the face of the community by following given norms and standards, and in order for us to do so, we have to be able to use the previously mentioned "reiterated empathy" (Wallace 2001) – that is, empathy wherein we identify with how others perceive us. Maibom refers to "cultures of shame" as one instance of culturally influenced morality, within which empathy holds little relevance, but it is precisely such cultures that require large doses of reiterated empathy, as they rest on wanting to appear a certain way in the view of others. Indeed, arguably morality always concerns reiterated empathy, for it is, following Aristotle, a deeply social phenomenon, by necessity partly rooted in how we perceive others to deem our actions. Hence, the empathic component may be always present in moral decision making simply because morality is a social phenomenon and concerns our "selves" and actions in relation to and in the eyes of others.

Furthermore, although there are various norms which do not require empathy on the immediate level and which are, for instance, culturally learned and internalized (Prinz 2011), even they may be ultimately based on the variety of empathy most elementally linked to moral agency – that is, affective empathy. To take Maibom's example of painless, unexpected killing: even if there is nothing to empathize with on the immediate level, our sense of the wrongness of the act is constituted by our recognition of the personhood of the victim, and this again rests on our ability to affectively resonate with others. In other words, we note the value of personhood because we can reverberate with the experiences of others, and this spurs us to view killing as a moral wrong.

Arguably many, if not most, norms concerning individuals[17] can be traced back to affective empathy, including norms seemingly far removed from it. We have adopted a whole variety of norms, superficially unrelated to empathy, precisely because behind them stands our ability to affectively note value in the experiences of others. Even ethics grounded on "natural order" may be partly motivated by a cultural tendency to resonate more with those like or close to us, which paves the way for the belief that they have more value – a belief which again is justified via reference to the "order" of things. Norms concerning justice, purity, loyalty, respect and other seemingly non-empathic issues repeatedly trace back to resonation, for they all revolve around our wish to see at least given groups of individuals treated well, and resonation sparks this wish. Hence, when we call for justice or respect for someone, we are calling for their recognition as worthy beings, and a sense of this worthiness arrives from our ability to affectively engage with them.[18]

Of course, other factors also impact judgements, as our various beliefs and emotions often twist and bend them in directions that appear quite unempathic. This is the reason why catastrophically prejudiced or callous judgements can still involve a hint of empathy: they combine resonation with utterly non-resonative beliefs and emotions, with odd and frightening results. The problem is not that empathy has no role but rather that its role remains ambivalent and limited and frequently hidden under the layers of other, quite opposite factors. The racist resonates with those of her skin colour but forms alienating and subjugating judgements of those who do not resemble her – the grain of empathy is there, but it has to compete against the weight of other elements, often becoming nearly drowned out by them or let to flourish only on their terms.

This leads to the most important point. Even if descriptively, as things stand, some values do not incorporate empathy, this does not mean that prescriptively they should not do so. Moral psychology all too often makes the mistake of assuming that *how* we value is how we *should* value and thus ignores the way in which the purpose of morality and moral agency is to continually aim for something better, to cultivate our ability. Following the descriptive stance, we should simply accept that since some moral decisions are grounded in purity and related emotions such as disgust, there will be those who morally abhor homosexuality, female sexual freedom, extramarital sex and so forth, and nothing should be done about the matter. In the non-human context, where notions of "natural order" and hierarchies are strong, emotively coloured motivations, we should simply posit that since humans tend to evaluate non-humans as creatures who are subordinate on a mythical order of things, the state of affairs is to be accepted. Such cynical descriptiveness would be a depressing end to the tale of morality, as moral agency requires that we constantly pay attention to how to advance our ability – it forces us to question whether matters such as purity and disgust should have a role to play in moral decision making. Paying attention to empathy rests precisely on this prescriptive element, as the main claim is that even if empathy is not fully utilized in morality, it *should* be so utilized, and it *should* be made much more central in our dealings with other beings.

The defenders of the rationalistic stance have sought still further ways to support their case, aimed at disproving that empathy is the core feature of morality. Kennett suggests that even when emotion appears to hold a primary position, rationality can be found underlying it, for emotions linked to normative responses spring from previous reasoned deliberation (for instance, we have reasoned that killing is wrong and hence have a strong emotive reaction against killing). Following suit, Kennett maintains that rationality is the "grounding motive of agents as such" (Kennett 2008, 262; see also Kennett 2006). She supports her case by pointing out, as Maibom did, that ethics often involves issues which have little to do with affect, and as an example she mentions the judgement that other human beings have value – according to Kennett, instead of from affect, it can "arise from a more disinterested contemplation of the complexities and capacities of the 'piece of work' (to quote Hamlet) that is man" (Kennett 2008, 263). As claimed above, there are many instances of morality that seemingly do not include emotive responses. Indeed, Edward Royzman, Robert Leema and Jonathan Baron (2009, 171) talk of "affect scarcity", which points to the fact that there are many acts which are considered morally wrong yet which are not linked to any clear emotive responses (think of tax avoidance).[19] Now, as also claimed above, such instances may ultimately be grounded on emotion and empathy after all.[20] What makes Kennett's argument interesting, however, is that she posits that behind the emotion stands reason – that we do not perceive other persons as valuable primarily because of affective resonation but feel such resonation because we rationally infer their value.

Therefore, perhaps it is reason which originally rendered one moral, and perhaps reason is even behind our emotive, empathic responses. Such a stance is also supported by Huebner, Dwyer and Hauser (2008), who posit that there is not enough evidence to suggest that emotions constitute moral ability; the existing data merely manifests that emotions are associated or correlate with moral judgement, not that the latter is *based* on the former. Indeed, it could be argued that even if emotions are, by default, involved in *all* instances of morality, they are not the basis of moral agency, for rationality may form their ultimate underlying cause.

This hypothesis gains strength from the fact that next to affect scarcity, we can talk of "affect abundance". There are many moments of, say, anger (think of road rage) which are not morally relevant and which concern one's ego or convention more than morality. This consideration is significant, for if the same emotion can be morally relevant and morally neutral, there must exist a further factor that enables an emotion to move from the latter category into the former. That is, we quite simply need to explain what makes an emotion morally loaded, and reasoned judgement offers one such basis: morally pertinent emotions are those which follow not mere reactions to contextual considerations, such as an injury to one's ego, but rational reflection. Moreover, as virtue ethicists such as Plato fully understood, and as Buddhism still teaches, there are many occasions in which morality requires the control of emotion: a virtuous person will be able to resist sudden bursts of anger before arriving at her moral judgement. Here, rationality surfaces as a necessary constituent of moral decision making.

The claim that morally relevant emotions are sparked by prior rational deliberation has much merit and lends support to the thesis that rationality is the constitutional factor underlying moral agency. When I feel anger over the fact that a passer-by insults a homeless person on the street, my reaction appears to be – at least partly – based on prior, rationally formed moral beliefs in equality, the inherent value of all cognitive individuals and so forth. Therefore (or so the argument goes), we would feel anger, love, disgust and, significantly, empathy precisely because of having a rationally grounded normative conviction. In support of this stance, studies demonstrate that we can quite easily teach ourselves new emotive responses via internalizing a new rational judgement (see Kennett and Fine 2009), that emotions are often based on reasoned judgement and vary greatly according to the latter and that reason can have an impact on emotion via appraisal and regulation (Monin, Pizarro and Beer 2007). These are relevant phenomena in the context of morality as well, wherein emotions are frequently affected by preexisting moral beliefs (Pizarro 2000). Therefore, although research shows that we are, in day-to-day life, largely "automated" in our moral, emotive responses, this does not prove that these responses were not originally derived from rational deliberation (Kennett and Fine 2009). Reasoning may have taken place two or twenty years earlier; in fact, it may have taken place only once, and we may no longer remember it, but it can still play the key role in our emotions and moral decision making.

However, it appears unrealistic to suggest that all moral emotions stem from reasoned analysis. Rather, it is quite probable that they often originate from cultural beliefs and dogmas. As demonstrated by Haidt (2001), for a vast amount of our morally laden emotions, we simply fail to find any rational justification beyond ad hoc explanations. We feel disgust, anger, love, even empathy because of underlying or interlinked cultural beliefs, but these beliefs are not based on rationality, and when put on the spot by a critic, we often struggle to rationally defend them. Modifying Kennett's example, we may therefore choose to affectively resonate only with other humans because we view only them to have inherent value, and this is not due to a rational judgement but because we have uncritically, even unconsciously adopted this belief from our culture, which again may have been influenced by religious doctrines ("humans are the image of God, therefore humans have unique value"). To see how non-rationally motivated this belief is, we only need to do an easy empirical experiment and ask others to rationally explain why human beings are of special value: anyone who has done this experiment knows how quickly people will struggle with their justifications and how rapidly cultural and religious "that's just the way it is" dogmas begin to surface.

Therefore, this rationalist defence fails as well. Rational deliberation may be behind some morally relevant emotions, and, as argued in the introduction, reason and emotions to some extent support each other. Moreover, reason of course is of strong importance if we want to maintain a critical, analytical hold on morality. Yet analysis does not always govern emotions, and if anything highly non-rational, unreflected beliefs are the birthplace of many such emotions. Frequently, we cannot offer any rational defences for our emotions, including empathic responses pertinent to morality. Morally loaded emotions can be wholly unrooted from prior reasoned analyses, for such analyses never took place, and while we like to think our responses to be rationally motivated, often their origins are far removed from reason. This is particularly significant from the viewpoint of empathy, for Kennett's argument would have rendered it into a mere by-product of reason (it is also significant due to the worrying trend mentioned earlier: empathy can be biased when it follows ill-conceived, non-rational dogmas). Hence, emotions can come first. As argued by Haidt (2003b), studies demonstrate that reason is often an epiphenomenon which is used to justify emotions after they have occurred. This also applies to empathy, for it can occur quite spontaneously – for instance, when we suddenly resonate with the suffering or joy of another. We may, after the event, seek to explain it with reason, but despite such post hoc ponderings, the moment of empathy came to existence independently of analysis.

The rationalist criticism also fails because it cannot explain the moral agency of individuals, such as those with Williams syndrome, who are relatively non-rational, highly empathic and highly moral. These individuals do not build their empathy on rational inference, and yet they are acutely morally aware and concerned, to the point of being exemplary to the more rational majority. They are the individuals whom Kant would have deemed as incapable of moral agency (empathic yet non-rational) but who appear to be more moral than most of us, and particularly far more morally apt than the Kantian ideal of moral agency (which, to restate the case, resembles nothing less than psychopathy). Empathy (most importantly affective empathy) can come prior to reason and make us into moral creatures without fully developed rational ability. Due to this, affective empathy – our capacity to emotively resonate with others – is a necessary and sufficient basis for the core of moral agency. It can be advanced by other varieties of empathy and reason, but without it morality cannot take flight. Hence, it does not merely correlate with moral ability, it also spurs it into existence.[21]

Rationalizing Reason

There is one further obstacle to be crossed. The rationalists have argued that the nature of moral judgement simply requires and rests on the use of reason. Karen Jones has spoken of "reason trackers", who can instantaneously, even automatically acknowledge and follow reasons without paying attention to their accuracy, and "reason responders", who respond to reasons as reasons and thereby partake in deliberation.[22] Reason trackers follow reasons without noting their content, they adopt them from the surrounding society and follow their lead without critical assessment, often wholly unwittingly, while reason responders concentrate on that content and approach their own rationality from a second-order level, seeking to do what is most reasonable and logical. Importantly, affective responses are often reason tracking, whereby one simply follows a reason without being able to offer further analysis of why one's actions are right (Jones 2006). Resting on Jones's distinction, Kennett and Fine claim that only reason responding counts as "normative", for mere automated responding facilitated by emotion does not constitute moral judgement in the true sense of the term. They summarize: "Genuine moral judgments must be made by moral agents and moral agents must, as a matter of conceptual necessity, be reason responders and not merely reason trackers" (Kennett and Fine 2009, 85; see also Maibom 2005).

Therefore, the claims is that moral judgement is, by conceptual necessity, something derived from reasoned analysis. There are two things to be noted here. First, it is true that "judgement" is often defined as a rationally considered conclusion on a second-order level; however, this is only one of its definitions. The word "judgement" fits a wide variety of meanings and also can be used to refer to evaluation and discernment on the first-order level, prior to second-order analysis. Therefore, I can judge that it is raining regardless of whether I have considered, say, the reliability of my own rationality – indeed, most animals (human and non-human) continuously judge things on a daily basis without any sort of second-order scrutiny on the nature of it all. Emotions and empathy are one basis for such judgements and thereby routinely fulfil what it means to judge. Simply stated, Kennett and Fine favour a definition that includes higher-order deliberation, while one could also favour a first-order definition which allows us to call an emotion-based evaluation "judgement".[23] Moreover, even if we define moral judgements as "decisions concerning whether or not the immediate situation should be under the jurisdiction of higher-order moral beliefs" (Pizarro 2000, 360), emotions can fulfil the role: for instance, I can instantly decide that a given principle applies to non-human animals after I have felt care or empathy towards them. That is, empathy acts as the reason for allocating given things under the jurisdiction of given principles, as happens when I resonate with a beaten cow and categorize the act of beating as unjust. It remains unclear why only analytic reason responding constitutes morality and why one cannot respond to reasons emotively, thus letting empathy decide which reason to follow.

Second, reflective empathy allows for reason responding. The critique presented often assumes empathy to be a highly unreflective phenomenon clearly distinct from reason, but this depiction is simplistic. Particularly, reflective empathy includes a metalevel viewpoint into things and indeed constitutes an exemplary combination of second-order responding and first-order tracking. Whereas the sort of analytic reason advertised by Kennett and Fine risks alienating us from the latter and leading to intellectual abstraction far removed from both lived experience and the phenomenality of our moral psychologies, reflective empathy facilitates the coming together of a pragmatic, experiential metalevel on which to judge.

Yet as pointed out, moral agency is something to be cultivated, not something that ought to be descriptively accepted as it is. Could we not therefore think that even if morality is descriptively, de facto founded on empathy, prescriptively or ideally it ought to be anchored to reason – would moral agency not grow into something more nuanced if we were to base it more on rationality (see Kennett 2006)? That is, instead of empathy, maybe it is reason which should be nurtured as the moral ideal.

As Kennett demonstrates, empathy may not offer solutions to internal and external conflicts – that is, situations where different emotions or beliefs are contradictory. According to Kennett, it is here that the role of rationality becomes evident, as she borrows from Kant: "It is not until sympathy fails and the man, for the first time, deliberates on whether he nevertheless is required to help those in need . . . that his judgment and actions count as moral" (Kennett 2006, 79). Therefore, we need reason in moments of conflict (internal conflicts, where two emotions such as empathy and anger conflict, or external conflicts, where we emotively disagree with the emotions of others). Indeed, even though empirically the great majority of moral decision making is based on emotions and intuitions, reason is utilized particularly in cases of internal and external conflict (Greene and Haidt 2002, 517; Prinz 2006). Reason can enable the sort of impartiality that emotions may muddle and offers tools with which to evaluate and analyse both emotions and beliefs and explore their relevance and consistency in cases of conflict.[24] It also offers a method for practical decision making. Empathy can at times offer little pragmatic guidance, as it can point out that the other being is of value but may not render evident how precisely one ought to respect that value (after resonating with the plight of a pig, how precisely should we bring our concern to the level of concrete action?); we may also feel empathy for all individuals in a given context (for instance, both the villain and her victims) and become overwhelmed and conflicted over how to proceed (whose well-being should we promote and in what way? see Hoffman 1990). Therefore, empathy may not always be enough for us to know what to do, and in such conflicts reason serves an important role.

But does this mean that reason is to be prioritized? The obvious counter-argument, already discussed in length in this book, is that without empathy, we are lost: it is a necessary constituent in understanding that other creatures are subjects who have value in themselves. Because of this, the cultivation of moral agency should aim for further advancing our empathic ability, which is still limited and often misled or prevented by disconnected, optimizing rationality and various culturally constituted beliefs or overshadowed by other, more self-directed emotions and wants. It is likely that moral agency would become much more inclusive and nuanced if our empathy skills were developed further. Instead of sculpting such agency into a purely rational direction, we should, therefore, render it first and foremost more empathetic.

This is not to say that reason is surplus or unrequired, for it, too, is needed for a holistic take on morality, and often it does entwine with varieties of empathy. Reasoned analysis is important and can also form an integral part of empathy.[25] Rational scrutiny of our motives and of the origins and consistency of our beliefs renders morality into something extensively more fine-tuned than were we to simply follow empathy, helps to clarify the nature of empathy and is vital for such basic matters as the construction and justification of principles – it offers us nothing less than a system of moral beliefs. However, this does not render it into something that is necessary for core moral agency – after all, there are many instances of moral judgement where it is not required and, as demonstrated by psychopathy, should we seek to become primarily rational, we would lose rather than develop our moral capacity. Reason can improve moral agency towards a significantly more considered and complex direction and help to solve conflicts, but the core foundation of that agency lies on affective ability, and without the latter, the former leads to amorality.

One option is to view moral agency as a plural capacity which can take many forms, ranging from a rudimentary *core moral agency* rested on affective empathy to an *emotive form* grounded mainly in both varieties of empathy and further emotions and ultimately to a *reflective form* based on empathy, emotions and rationality, all ideally combined into an attentive epistemology.

Affective empathy would, then, form the baseline of morality, while other emotions and rational reflection can offer it more content and precision. Such a take on moral agency would combine sentimentalism and rationalism without overlooking either empathy or reason. Therefore, perhaps moral agency is a *multi-tier affair*, with one core capacity providing the foundations for agency and other capacities taking it into further, more nuanced directions.

Such a model allows for divergence in moral agency, as some individuals are chiefly emotion based and some more reason orientated: there is no prototype of "humanity", as our inclinations and traits differ to the extent that our ways of practicing moral agency can also be quite heterogenic, and the multi-tier model would acknowledge this. It would also allow for the basis of one's agency to shift, so that an individual can adopt different types of agency during her lifetime and cultivate her ability further, becoming more inclusive and capable of reflectively and attentively syncing varieties of empathy, emotive outlooks, and reasoned analyses. At the core stands the necessary feature of moral awareness: affective resonance with the experiences of others, and when cultivated with other emotive, rational abilities, this core can extend, as if advancing from an inner circle into outer rings.

Therefore, affective empathy functions as the key capacity of moral agency, enabling core moral agency. Emotions, ranging from anger to love, can bring that agency forward and give it particular content, and rationality can do the same, as can perhaps many other capacities thus far unnoted. Yet the latter do not constitute the initial spark of morality and as such fail in their respective claims to be the single, necessary requirement for moral ability. Reflective empathy is an ideal way of bringing all these dimensions together as it contains both the "inner circle" of resonation and the outer rings of emotions and reason – if moral agency is a multi-tier affair, reflective empathy is the most fertile method of cultivating it further.

Therefore, the rationalist critique fails. Both emotion and reason are required, but affective empathy is the guiding factor at the core of our moral agency. Moreover, reflective empathy offers the route to cultivation, a perspective via which to evaluate both other varieties of empathy, emotions and reason. It was suggested earlier that we need something to explain why only given forms of emotions count as "moral". This role can be filled by reflective empathy, for it enables one to locate, regulate and ignite appropriate emotive responses (Patricia Churchland argues that empathy raises moral emotions in us – see Churchland 2011 – and arguably it is precisely reflective empathy which accomplishes this task). It is the gatekeeper that can push aside those emotions merely revolving around one's self-directed gaze or unfounded cultural stereotypes and presumptions and invite in emotions and forms of empathy that accommodate the perspectives of other individuals. It can also govern and guide emotions towards morally apt paths.

Furthermore, reflective empathy rescues reason from detachment, which all too easily leads to utilitarian calculations or even callous manipulation of others. Reason can be used to justify the worst possible moral crimes, as it may offer an incentive to remove oneself from empathic consideration of others (Monin, Pizarro and Beer 2007, 19).[26] As Arthur Schopenhauer argues, reason can be harnessed to serve wholly egoistic motives and thereby easily loses grasp of morality: "It is quite possible to act in the most reasonable way, that is, according to conclusions scientifically deduced, and weighed with the nicest exactitude; and yet to follow the most selfish, unjust, and even iniquitous maxims. . . . 'Reasonable' and 'viscious' are terms that go well together; indeed great, far-reaching crimes are only possible from their union" (Schopenhauer 2005, 37–38). As such, reason can hinder rather than advance moral agency, and this is most likely to happen when empathy is missing (something that applies regrettably frequently in relation to other animals, as their instrumentalization is justified and grounded on rational, utilitarian optimization). Reflective empathy remedies the situation by combining both immediate resonance and other forms of empathy and reasoned deliberation, thereby allowing each to support one another in a manner that aids the development of moral ability. As a consequence, we become more resonative, reflectively attuned, reasoned moral creatures.

EMPATHY OR ANGER?

There is a relatively new criticism to consider, according to which empathy is not as productive a moral emotion as anger. For instance, Jesse Prinz (2011) maintains that anger can evoke both concern and effective moral action-taking more fluently than empathy. This criticism also has been discussed in relation to non-human animals, as T. J. Kasperbauer, who largely rests on Prinz's philosophy, has posited that anger is a much more fruitful ground for animal ethics than empathy. Kasperbauer goes so far as to assert that due to its various failures in producing moral concern and action, empathy is neither necessary nor central to moral agency. Instead, emotions such as anger ought to be afforded more attention, since, according to Kasperbauer, they "are more strongly engaged with producing moral concern for animals" (Kasperbauer 2014, 2). Kasperbauer rests on a plethora of empirical studies that he argues support various distinct claims, which will here be categorized as follows: (1) empathy does not lead to greater moral concern, (2) empathy is limited, biased and insufficient and (3) anger is more capable of motivating moral action than empathy. What are the merits of these claims? Is empathy really as unproductive as suggested, and should we rather favour anger as a foundation of moral agency, in animal ethics as well? (Since the second of these claims was already discussed,[27] only the first and third will be explored below.)

When it comes to empathy and moral concern, Kasperbauer argues that empathy does not make us more likely to pay moral heed to other animals. He cites a study according to which prompts can make us more prone to feel empathy and concern in regard to non-human animals (Sevillano, Aragones and Schultz 2007) but posits that since those who are not prompted also do feel some amount of moral concern, such concern does not require empathy (Kasperbauer 2014). However, the claim here is unconvincing for the simple reason that those not prompted probably do feel empathy as well – after all, empathy is a rather universal condition in human beings, and unless the test subjects were suffering from disorders such as psychopathy, they will have been capable of being guided by empathy even when not prompted to do so. In other words, although prompts may trigger us to feel more empathy, they of course are not necessary for its existence and those not prompted may also be influenced by it, which again means that also their moral concern may rest on empathy (I may feel greater resonation when shown images of war-zone children if I am nudged towards an empathic mode, but I will also resonate when not so prompted).

Kasperbauer (2014) proceeds to suggest that empathy can coincide with abuse, demonstrated by how empathic people can also be cruel towards other animals. Hence, empathy does not necessarily lead to concern and may even entwine with cruelty. This is a rather evident state of affairs: the great majority of people are capable of empathy, yet some of them also take part in abusive, violent behaviours in relation to both humans and animals. Does this demonstrate the insufficiency of empathy? The answer is simple: no. As suggested earlier, we must recognize how other factors, including culturally produced beliefs and prejudices, may weaken empathy and how such a state may even lead to desubjectification and violent behaviour. This is not a failing of empathy but rather a failing in our culture. Often such beliefs direct empathic individuals to follow their empathy only in relation to given types of individuals while ignoring or denying the subjectivity of others, which again means that people warm and kind towards, say, their relatives or those of their own ethnic background turn into abusers in the context of strangers or people of a different skin colour. This also explains cruelty towards non-human animals, for just as a racist may be capable of empathy towards her own "kind" while being disinclined to direct it towards those of dissimilar pigmentation, an anthropocentric person may be wholly empathic towards humans while being abusive towards other animals. To reiterate, the violence that follows is not a failing of empathy but instead stems from problems in our cultural doctrines which fail to support empathy in a manner that would make it more inclusive.

But if empathy can be diminished by an external impact, does this not render it a weak basis for morality? This is something that Kasperbauer argues, as he goes on to refer to the famous Milgram experiments, in which empathic people were willing to commit violent acts if triggered to follow incentives other than empathy (again, empathy coincides with violence). For Kasperbauer, this reflects poorly on empathy, since the experiment appears to suggest that empathy is capable of guiding our moral concern and actions only when the context permits it to flourish – it is a weak basis for moral agency, for it can be bypassed with ease if other incentives (such as authority, which in the Milgram experiments pushed people towards immoral acts) exist. This is particularly problematic from the viewpoint of animal ethics, since most animal use takes place in precisely the sort of settings (laboratories, hunting fields, farms, etc.) which are likely to concern incentives that overrule empathy. Following suit, Kasperbauer claims that if animal ethics is to rest on empathy, the prospects are poor: "If the failure to treat animals well in intensive animal agriculture, for instance, is a result of an empathy failure, then it would seem that empathy is too weak to rely on for any of our moral claims" (Kasperbauer 2014, 8). Indeed, since the society is anthropocentric and prone to muddle our empathy towards animals – since it is filled with incentives that sideline empathic responses – perhaps empathy indeed is an insufficient basis on which to build moral concern for other animals.

However, two things should be noted. First, following the Milgram experiment, other moral motivations – including anger, as advocated by Kasperbauer and Prinz – could be overruled if the right contextual triggers exist. Simply stated, even a person who has developed a strong sense of justice on account of her anger towards witnessing the unfair treatment of others may be lured to sideline her moral concern when faced with authority. The Milgram experiment points to the way in which moral motivations in general can be bypassed by external inputs: it does not point out that only empathy can be so overruled. Even a wholly rational person who grounds her stance on animals on reasoned, Singerian argumentation could fall under the spell of authority and thus ignore her rational ethic in a Milgram-like setting. We are vulnerable creatures, often mixed up, confused, externally influenced and easily led astray, and empathy is just one moral motivation which may be externally suspended (it is important to highlight "may", for not all individuals fail in the Milgram experiment).

Second, if external factors and cultural influences are curtailing empathy, instead of abandoning empathy, one ought to eliminate those factors and influences. Our moral motivations are always vulnerable to being impacted by further elements, for we are not, nor can we be, immune to the outside world, and when those elements are detrimental to our motivations, we ought to alter them, make them more attuned with our sense of morality (as

Schopenhauer also was careful to remind us, empathy is often overrun by egoism, convention and fear; see Schopenhauer 2005). Once more it is important to recognize that the society ought to support the cultivation of empathy, for we are fallible creatures who need such support – as pointed out, the Aristotelian task of societal institutions is to educate and strengthen our moral ability (see again Rorty 1997), and the same goes for their duty to deepen our empathic capacities. Whereas Kasperbauer declares that we ought to forget about empathy, what we really need is ever more poignant reminders of why empathy matters, broadcasted across society. Simply put, the social, political, economic and cultural realm should be rendered both more inclusive and more capable of fostering empathy.

In animal ethics, this means placing more pressure on those cultural, economic and political forces that stand as the Milgramian authority, pushing people towards animal consumption while hampering their empathy towards the objects of their consumption. Instead of forsaking empathy, the aim should be to mould societal settings, from education to marketing, so that they invite empathy towards pigs, cows and chickens as well. Such a reform would mean that there is no industrial farming, capable of producing aloofness towards non-human suffering, nor hunting, grounded on ignoring the value of animal subjectivity. If Kasperbauer takes the existence of these to signal that empathy is bound to fail, the more fruitful alternative is to restructure society in a manner that both adheres to and reaffirms empathic capacities – an undertaking that would get rid of practices of instrumentalizing animals rather than empathy.

Therefore, the first criticism fails, for it does not prove that empathy is not central to moral concern, that empathy supports cruelty or that empathy ought to be forsaken due to its vulnerability to external causes. If anything, the intriguing question is just how central and necessary empathy may be and what would happen if it was culturally, societally and politically supported to a greater extent so that individuals were more prone to cultivate it further. What sort of possibilities would such culturally promoted and individually developed empathy offer for the expansion of our moral capacities, and also in animal ethics?[28]

Finally, Kasperbauer argues that empathy may be less motivational than other moral emotions, such as anger. He refers to a study (Krueger et al. 2013) which suggests that oxytocin, a hormone related to empathy, makes us more concerned for victims of wrongdoing but not more eager to punish the wrongdoer, and he takes this to imply that empathy may lead to concern but not to moral action (Kasperbauer 2014). Therefore, the claim is that while empathy may encourage concern, it does not encourage us to behave morally. In animal ethics, this of course would be a detrimental failure: it is not enough that we care or weep for maltreated fishes and cows, for we should also act so as to better their situation. Could we go so far, following Kasperbauer's claim, as to suggest that the way in which many profess to care for or even love other animals while still consuming their body parts is linked directly back to empathy – that is, is it empathy which is causing many to both "love" and take part in institutions that cause suffering? Earlier it was argued that self-directed forms of empathy may lead to such a sorry scenario, but could other-directed empathy be similarly guilty?

Again, the answer is no. This criticism remains unconvincing simply because "moral action" needs to be separated from "retribution" – there are many instances where the latter is not the morally sound action to take. Hence, while the criticism assumes that those who did not want retribution were not taking action, such an assumption is unfounded. Indeed, perhaps in the relevant experiment, empathy enabled the test subjects to pay empathic regard to the wrongdoer as well and thereby to adopt a more inclusive moral outlook, capable of perceiving options other than retribution as the morally sound act. Therefore, it is misleading, on such ambiguous grounds and when considering all the evidence to the contrary, to argue that empathy does not motivate us to behave morally.

Now, Kasperbauer's main intention here is to demonstrate that anger plays a more foundational role in motivating action, which in his opinion "provides ethicists a reason to privilege moral anger, and not empathy" (Kasperbauer 2014, 11). Therefore, even if empathy is motivational, anger is more so, and for this reason it ought to be prioritized. This is a difficult claim to dispute, as we all know how motivational anger can be – it can spark the most intense actions with frightening speed, as we at times instantly fly into action after anger has got its moody hold of us. Moreover, as has been claimed by many philosophers, anger can also be a morally applicable emotion. According to Hume (1969), it can enable us to perceive virtue and vice, and Thomas Aquinas maintained in *Summa Theologica* that anger can enable us to perceive what is "just" and thus even stand as a virtue (see also Rota 2007).

Yet – and this is an important point – anger is also an incredibly volatile emotion, capable of spurring explosive and ill-considered deeds without a hint of moral scrutiny and reflection, and it is this which renders its moral meaningfulness suspect. As Plato already warned, anger can spark morally unjustifiable, even atrocious actions and is one of those emotions most likely to cause us, in the frenzied clutches of passion, to overrule reasoned reflection to the point where we kill others and start wars. This means that despite its moral potential, anger can also remain quite immoral. Such immorality applies when it is self-directed and unable to pay notice to the subjectivity and value of others – when it pushes us to knife unfaithful spouses, punch individuals who have slighted us or declare wars on nations, anger clearly has lost its capacity to take the perspective of others into account, and with that it has lost its moral compass. When such a self-directed state makes us explosively motivational, the consequences threaten rather than advance moral agency.

These are all also pertinent considerations in animal ethics, where anger may similarly provoke self-directed ethics. The most obvious example of this includes large predators and animals whom are considered "vermin", both of which are routinely targeted with anger, hate and deadly vengeance. Another example are animal activists, who may also become the target of anger responses to the point of being labelled as preachy "terrorists" whose moral messages ought not to be given any consideration. Although anger can illuminate what "justice" means, in regard to animal issues (feeling anger at the sight of mistreated animals is a powerful moral incentive), it can also cloud moral judgement and form a serious obstacle to moral awareness. The crucial factor here is whether such anger is self-directed (feeling anger due to having one's personal gains or desires threatened) or other-directed (feeling anger on behalf of another). Only in the latter instance is anger's motivational force morally relevant.

This leads us to a pivotal issue. Anger needs to be anchored in something that enables it to become or stay other-directed, and here empathy emerges yet again as pertinent. It is via empathy that anger can gain other-directedness and avoid the pitfalls of egoistic, morally destructive action. Here, other-directed forms of empathy lend anger its foundation, as we feel anger not due to having our egoistic projects slighted but because we note how the individual value of others is being wronged. Indeed, we can talk of "empathic anger", where empathy towards the victim transforms into anger towards the wrongdoer (Hoffman 1990, 159)[29] and which is nearly as intense as personal anger. The more empathy we feel, the greater the anger (Batson et al. 2007).[30] It is precisely such anger, rooted in empathy, which must be afforded attention. This again means that the empathy critique fails, for we do not need anger *instead of* empathy but rather anger *based on* empathy. Anger should not be naively endorsed as a potential moral motivator, for often the motivation it offers comes without moral awareness; nor should anger be placed as an alternative to empathy, for only by resting on the latter can it maintain its moral focus.

Anger also requires empathy for a related reason. Anger may lead to unwise, tantrummy and antagonistic actions on behalf of other animals, sparking aggression and hostility in both advocates and those they target rather than persuading people to change. Allowing only anger that is based on empathy to guide action ought to be the goal, and here one has empathy towards all parties concerned – not only the animals but also those who take part in mistreating them. Only such anger-induced action can be persuasive, for in order to alter the habits of a meat eater, she should not be screamed at or met with antagonistic bundles of accusations, but instead her motivations and views should be taken into account and compellingly moved towards a direction where she will not retreat (often the inevitable consequence of hostility) and will rather become capable of cultivating her own empathy towards non-human animals.

To summarize, negative emotions such as anger, even when potent and efficient in producing action, can be quite self-directed and thereby fail to fully note the subjectivity of others (Royzman, Leema and Baron 2009, 161). The sense of "justice" they provide may be misleading, and the actions they spark may be morally unwise and even catastrophic. In order for them to escape this issue and include the sort of other-directedness that morality requires, negative emotions need to be entwined with empathy. One should not first feel anger and then perceive something to be unjust (a self-directed approach) but rather first note the injustice and then feel anger, and in order for this to happen, empathy is needed, for it enables us to recognize the harms suffered by others and thereby points towards injustices.

Before concluding, it is worthwhile to explore in greater detail the criticism of empathy's motivational power, presented by Jesse Prinz. As stated, Prinz endorses anger as an emotion that ought to be prioritized instead of empathy,[31] for it succeeds in motivating moral action much more efficiently than empathy. He proceeds to claim that liberal politics, which revolve around notions of empathy, harm and vulnerability instead of autonomy, justice and punishment (factors often linked to anger), may be so demotivated against taking action that they become ineffective and lead to a passive image of human agency. Within such politics, moral agents remain kind and tolerable to such a degree that they become passive against wrongdoers and thereby via omission aid moral injustices; thus, empathic politics leads to political inactiveness and ineffectiveness against moral wrongs. Prinz claims that feminism acts as one example of such politics, as care ethics may lead to pouring empathy on all those involved and in so doing risks pacifying people from effectively standing up against injustice or even from perceiving what the injustice is. For one to achieve political change, anger and outrage are required, for they will enable one to note and locate moral failings and to act so as to prevent them from happening again. In this vein, Prinz argues that "liberation, it seems, requires outrage. . . . And outrage based morality might be more effective" (Prinz 2011, 225). The simple suggestion behind Prinz's claims appears to be this: empathy is overly understanding and thereby "soft", and as such it does not spark the type of determined, strong action required for moral and political change.[32]

Therefore, liberal politics also would gain substance from placing more attention on anger and less attention on empathy. Indeed, Prinz claims that empathy and compassion may act as poor moral guides, since they invite "compliance and complacency" (Prinz 2011, 226). The image of politics grounded on empathy is, therefore, not an appealing one, as it would pacify us to a point of "grotesque crimes of omission" (ibid.). Bringing forth anger would be a more fruitful option since it sparks notions of justice and active willingness to do something about the matter.

These concerns hold clear bearing in relation to animal politics. Empathy can, at times, coincide with passivity, demonstrated in how many of those filled with empathy passively take part in those very practices that cause suffering to other animals and equally remain passive in the face of bettering the status of those animals. Many empathize but nonetheless do nothing. The question that emerges is whether animal liberation should shift focus from empathy to anger. Would doing so render people more prone to noting the wrongness of the practices of instrumentalizing other animals and more willing to take action? Do we need more fury and fire? Could it even be that empathy is standing in the way of animal liberation? Is it making us too "soft"?

As seen, such a conclusion would be premature, for anger also requires empathy as its foundation. Therefore, even the most action-inducing anger needs empathy in order to be morally productive. Secondly, passivity and empathy may coincide, but this should not be taken to mean that the latter causes the former. Studies demonstrate that high empathy leads to a significant increase in helping behaviour (see Batson et al. 2002), and it has also been shown to give rise to various positive emotions and social awareness, which again offer motivation to act (Thompson and Hoffman 1980; Hoffman 1990; Leith and Baumeister 1998; Batson et al. 2002). Hence, empathy both leads to action in itself and sparks other emotions capable of motivating action. As suggested, anger can be one of these emotions, and as a result the activity it sparks is, when morally productive, founded on empathy. We can at times benefit from fury but only when its origins lie in empathic responses.

The passivity coinciding with empathy is, then, caused by other factors, such as a sense of being powerless in the face of institutionally supported moral crimes. Arguably, empathy fails to ignite activity when there is a sense of pessimism in regard to one's ability to effect a change (something to be discussed in the conclusion). In animal ethics, too, while empathy may support and greatly motivate action, other factors often hamper one's willingness to follow this motivation – for instance, the power of the animal industries may appear hopelessly vast, particularly when one sees support for them everywhere in the society, and this can be deeply demotivating. Individuals may also bypass action by assuming that institutional wrongs are something that politicians and other official channels ought to address, and hence the empathizer will keep consuming meat and milk while hoping that animal welfare legislation will address the relevant issues. The source of the problem does not lie in empathy but in our experiences of helplessness and our willingness to transfer responsibility. The solution is to highlight how action is always possible, even if just on the level of personal consumer choices, and to thereby invite optimism, to call on our duty to accept responsibility instead of transferring it to others and to map out and advertise more of those routes which action can take. Empathy needs the support of methodologies of optimism in the political arena.

This issue is not limited to empathy. Anger may offer potent incentives for action, but the same problem also applies to it, as arguably anger often leads to short bursts of action that are then forsaken as the vastness of the issue begins to become evident. Therefore, the animal advocate motivated by anger may be ferociously active for a few days or weeks and then become completely pacified after realizing the enormity of the problem. Again, any moral emotion can coincide with inaction, and empathy should not be singled out as the main offender. To restate, what is required is not less empathy and more anger but rather a focus on enhancing a sense of optimism in regard to one's capacity to have an effect.

Hence, empathy is not too "soft" a choice for moral agency and can offer a strong motivation for action. It does not invite compliance but rather can be affected by forces that do so, and when these forces are kept in check, empathy's motivational pull can flourish. This also applies to animal advocacy, where reflective empathy in particular is needed to steer both our sense of the need for action and other action-inducing emotions, such as anger. Outrage can be productive, but without empathy its meaning evaporates, and reflective empathy offers the platform via which to both channel anger and link empathy more firmly to action.

This leads to the final point. Reflective empathy offers the solution to the problems underscored by the supporters of anger, most importantly because it helps to detect and curtail the influence of external cultural and political factors. We can withdraw from empathic concern as a consequence of such factors, which superficially lessens empathy's moral footprint, but reflective empathy invites us to note and root out their impact and even to structure our societal settings in a manner capable of fostering empathic skilfulness and clarity. Reflective empathy also allows us to pinpoint our capacities for taking action by picking out the sort of (often culturally reinforced) pessimisms and feelings of powerlessness that erode active agency. With its metalevel attentiveness, it therefore offers hope for fighting the windmills of those societal forces which muddle the potentialities of empathy. It also acts as the perfect foundation and guide for the sort of anger that is morally wholesome rather than destructive. The question is not "anger or empathy" but rather how to ground our different varieties of empathy and anger in a way that cultivates morality ability, and here reflective empathy can act as the source of illumination.

COMPASSION FATIGUE

There is one further risk worthy of notice. High levels of empathy may be overwhelming when they lead to focusing so intensely on the other that she engulfs us; continually feeling with the emotions of another can ignite a loss of boundaries and even (when empathizing with the suffering of another) states of unbearable anguish. Here, one loses a sense of self and becomes lost in the other being: we become too empty of what is ours and too immersed in the concerns of the other. The more pain we witness in this frame of mind, the more fragile and ultimately fragmented our own psyche threatens to become, until we are consumed by the hurt of the world. As a coping mechanism, many resort to "compassion fatigue",[33] a state in which we simply refuse to empathize anymore. Empathy has felt too uncomfortable and overwhelming, leading to "empathic overarousal", and psychological defences shut it down to the point where we simply cease caring. In order to protect themselves from further harm, those undergoing compassion fatigue may avoid any triggers that could cause empathy (such as images of suffering), and they may become despondent to such triggers, even turning hostile towards the notion of empathy.

Compassion fatigue is often evident in our empathic inabilities towards other human beings, as many who become overwhelmed with noting the scale and extent of suffering both near and far withdraw from empathizing with particularly given groups of people and offer various justifications (one cannot do anything about the suffering, the sufferers have brought their suffering on themselves and so forth) for their refusal or incapacity to empathize further. It is also evident in relations with non-human animals, whose sufferings may appear so vast in number and intensity that they become intolerable to notice and empathize with and are thereby delegated away from one's awareness.

Depoliticized Others and the Blurring of Boundaries

The mechanisms of compassion fatigue are multifarious. Lilie Chouliaraki argues one source to be the notion that suffering is an unavoidable part of life, which again risks rendering it into something acceptable rather than a phenomenon with a negative normative charge. It is this lack of normativity, the absence of a moral dimension, which can cause compassion fatigue and which is made possible particularly by decontextualizing suffering, whereby it becomes "natural" rather than (often) a result of human politics. Naturalized suffering becomes both unavoidable and hopeless, a matter which we cannot do anything about, and thus we cease empathizing and caring. When suffering is naturalized, the sufferers are often depicted as creatures lacking subjectivity, the distance between "us" and "them" is emphasized and suffering, when represented in the media, is carefully edited so as to render it clinical and thereby tolerable to the audience. A typical example is the depiction of African people's suffering as somehow natural, non-political and desubjectified: "The sufferers themselves have no agency at all . . . they are passive objects, integral to the landscape" (Chouliaraki 2006, 109). Chouliaraki argues that in order to avoid compassion fatigue, naturalization has to be contested. Here, we need to concentrate on viewing the sufferers as subjects, not as a faceless "them", and as creatures whose suffering – particularly when politically caused – has moral overtones. Suffering, when mediated, ought to be contextualized, and its subjective, political and moral dimensions ought to be brought forward (Chouliaraki 2006).

Stanley Cohen, on the other hand, argues that the naturalization of suffering does not offer a sufficient explanation. Cohen's suggestion is that we ought to speak of "media fatigue", within which it is not the audiences who no longer feel empathy but rather the media, which has become incapable of depicting suffering in a manner that can communicate it effectively. He goes so far as to suggest that the notion of "compassion fatigue" is used as a means of justifying the political and cultural tendency to downgrade the importance of empathy: we are led to believe that it is inevitable that we cannot empathize and that as a result we ought to ignore suffering. Cohen summarizes, "The message is: get real, wise up and toughen up; the lesson is that nothing, nothing after all, can be done about problems like these or people like this" (Cohen 2002, 195).[34] What is more, simultaneously a sense of helplessness is evoked, as we feel that nothing can be done about the enormity of suffering. Here, we have a "sense of a situation so utterly hopeless and incomprehensible that we cannot bear to think about it" (Cohen 2002, 194). As a consequence, many withdraw from active empathy: "Much passivity results not from lacking the right feelings, but from perceiving that an ordinary person like me can do nothing about such a monstrous problem" (Cohen 2002, 219).

Therefore, compassion fatigue can be brought on by naturalization and depoliticization of suffering, as well as the cultural, political tendency to edit suffering into a bite-sized format, which distances us from the sufferers and sparks the notion that empathy is both futile and unnecessary; moreover, it can be evoked by feelings of helplessness. To add to these suggestions, Susan Moeller has posited that compassion fatigue is brought on by overexposure, wherein the media offers continually more harrowing scenes of suffering and we become numb to what is considered "lesser" suffering – to use a simple example, when hundreds are killed, the death of twenty appears insignificant.[35] Less and less appears to make an impact.[36] This ignites culture of trauma, wherein overexposure leads to shock and ensuing fatigue, or what Amy Coplan (2011a) calls "empty empathy", wherein we quickly move on and forget after witnessing suffering.

These considerations are significant in the context of animal ethics. Non-human animals are far too frequently desubjectified – they are depicted as "natural entities" rather than as subjects with their own internal emotions, thoughts and perspectives. This enables the naturalization of their suffering, and indeed such suffering is repeatedly branded as unavoidable, part of the "natural order of things" within which violence and suffering are the norm, and the lot of other animals is to serve the benefit of human beings, even when this causes them harm. The normative dimension of non-human suffering is erased, which helps even the most empathic of people to ignore their plight. Moreover, the politics behind animal suffering are often simultaneously hidden, as industrial farming is framed as somehow inevitable, again a part of the cycle of nature, and even as an essence of human existence – the subjugation of other animals into vast units of production becomes depoliticized, a natural phenomenon that cannot be avoided, as if those units were an essential part of evolution rather than something founded on specific cultural, economic and political interests and thereby a human choice, not a natural necessity. Non-human animals become a faceless "them" whom "we" are, as if teleologically, meant to exploit and whose sufferings it is thus utterly futile to empathize with.

Simultaneously, the media is often unwilling to portray non-human suffering (we do not see slaughterhouses on television), and even when this does happen, such suffering is usually taken out of context and branded as the wrongdoing of one individual or one company rather than as a consequence of our broader societal attitudes towards other animals (therefore, even if there is a media exposé on slaughterhouses, the blame is pinpointed on one malfunctioning company or sadistic individual within the industry and thus depoliticized). The media invites compassion and empathy for companion animals and wild animals in distant places (more comfortable targets because they fail to raise awkward political questions) but is guilty of compassion avoidance in relation to those animals who are utilized the most – farmed animals and fishes. When their suffering is (rarely) shown, it is of extreme nature, and the depictions avoid bringing forward the routine suffering, faced by tens of billions of animals every day and caused by living in monotonic conditions that wholly go against their species-specific traits, needs and capacities; following Moeller, only the most harrowing will do, while vast amounts of suffering go wholly unnoted.

A strange combination takes place. On the one hand, there is trauma over witnessing animal suffering. Many complain that they cannot bear to see any more images of plighted animals, and this can reveal a collective shock over what we, as a society, are doing to non-humans. The treatment and pains of animals haunt and taunt many of us. On the other hand, Coplan's "empty empathy" appears common, as many instantly forget the deep empathy they underwent for a pig or a sheep just a moment before. Empathy becomes both traumatic and (perhaps as a defence) forgettable. All this entwines with the culturally common notion that perhaps it is silly, naive or "soft" to empathize with non-humans and that perhaps one ought to simply, as Cohen put it, toughen up and not care.

Hence, avoidance of empathy takes place on many levels and is affected by how suffering is mediated, contextualized and politicized. These levels also reveal how compassion fatigue can be eradicated. What is required is highlighting the contexts and politics behind suffering and also mediating the subjectivity of the sufferers. Pigs and cows need to be given faces and to be depicted as individual beings with their own internal landscapes; also, the wider societal and political causes behind their suffering need to be made manifest, as well as the fact that they are not a generic "them" but creatures who belong to a wider community with human beings. Simultaneously, the value of empathy ought to be discussed and endorsed so that it becomes less easy to declare it as something surplus and unrequired.

Moeller also offers an important reminder: often it is positive rather than negative images that spark the greatest empathic responses, for "the public resorts to compassion fatigue as a defence mechanism against the knowledge of horror" (Moeller 1999, 226). Although depictions of suffering are vital in order for us to remember and note the fates of others (Sontag 2004), for the subjectivity of those others to fully emerge and invite empathy, positive imagery is also required. In short, when empathy also offers joy, it becomes more comfortable and the less harrowing elements more endurable; moreover, when witnessing non-human animals in positive mental states, their subjectivity opens up to a more encompassing view. Therefore, compassion fatigue may be partly eased by bringing forward realistic accounts of animal well-being and subjectivity, whether it be of playful gorillas in nature documentaries or curiously roaming, affectionate pigs in farmed-animal sanctuaries.

What is also pivotal is the accentuation of our own agency. We are not helpless and incapable but rather active agents able to have at least some effect on the political causes of suffering, and it is the sense of this ability which pushes both towards moral action and empathy. We are safe to empathize without psychological avoidance strategies because we do not feel overwhelmed as long as we channel our empathy into action (Hoffman 2014). As Susan Sontag has argued, ultimately compassion fatigue touches on our sense of agency:[37] it is when we feel defeated and passive that we cease paying notice to the suffering of others, and it is when we feel capable of taking action that we are open to reflectively, with moral care, witness such suffering. Hence, Sontag states that "it is the passivity that dulls feeling" (Sontag 2004, 91) and concludes: "Compassion is an unstable emotion. It needs to be translated into action, or it withers" (ibid., 90). Quite simply, it is easier to pay attention when doing so can entwine with active agency. Like Chouliaraki, Sontag suggests that such a sense of agency is enabled by rendering evident the political terrains behind suffering, for it is then that we notice what can and should be done (ibid.). Indeed, political awareness, the eradication of ignorance, is vital for our sense of agency and the setting aside of compassion fatigue. In order to maintain a hold on empathy, one must pay attention to the political causes behind the pains of others and thereby strengthen one's ability to act.

In regard to animal ethics, this means that animal suffering should not be depicted as something that only takes place either "naturally" or as a result of rare, sadistic individuals or instances, and instead the cultural, political and economic factors behind the ways in which trillions of non-human animals are treated each year should be brought under scrutiny and morally problematized, which again will make apparent the ways in which each of us can take some action (even if by omission, such as refraining from consuming animal products) in order to alleviate the situation. This further highlights and complicates the relation between moral agency and empathy: the latter may lead to the former, but the former will also help to cultivate the latter. When we feel capable of taking politically considered moral action, we are also much more inclined to stay clear from compassion fatigue and thereby much more persuaded to keep training and using our empathy skills. In practice, when we know the causes of the cow's misery, when we know her history and her context, we can more readily take action in order to alleviate her state, and the possibility of such activity and agency instantaneously counteracts the lethargy embedded in compassion fatigue. We do not tire of empathy because we have means with which to follow it.

However, it is not always enough to know the politics related to suffering in order to avoid becoming almost asphyxiated under the weight of empathy. This is because at times such knowledge does not appear to facilitate action – rather, we come to realize that there is strikingly little we can do. The world is filled with pain. We cannot stop most of it. The most sensitive of us become tired, wounded, withdrawn and hesitant to face any more signs of suffering and many simply choose not to care. The most obvious answer is to offer more creative ways and methods of taking action against those societal institutions that maintain the state of misery. Yet even this is not always enough, for even the most ardent activist can one day collapse under her banners and websites, feeling that she cannot have a significant enough impact and that the machineries of animal utilization are stronger. Indeed, there are those who are incredibly active in alleviating non-human suffering but who nonetheless feel overburdened and stressed with empathy to the point where they declare, like the main character from J. M. Coetzee's novel *Elizabeth Costello*, "Calm down, I tell myself, you are making a mountain out of a molehill. This is life. Everyone else comes to terms with it, why can't you? *Why can't you?*" (Coetzee 1999, 69).

The problem here may be overt concentration on all those vast numbers of animals one cannot help while failing to pay adequate attention to the way in which one's actions do offer crucial alleviation for many – the focus is misplaced away from what can be achieved to what perhaps can never be achieved. When fixing one's attention on the vastness of suffering, the criteria of what counts as "successful action" becomes wholly unrealistic, for nothing less than the eradication of all non-human suffering would suffice. The ideal is pushed far beyond reason. Instead, attention needs to be placed on smaller successes, ranging from personal consumption choices to saving stray dogs or injured wildlife or campaigning for the gradual alteration of cultural attitudes towards animals, and here action is always both beneficial and very much needed. Such a change of focus may well help render empathy into something inviting rather than exhausting. A related means of developing agency, while focusing on smaller successes, is cultivating everyday empathic concern and sympathy. When we let ourselves care for others on a practical level, compassion fatigue is less likely (Klimecki et al. 2014). In regard to animals, this suggests that it is good to assist them when needed – taking care of, say, an injured pigeon may feed one's feeling of agency in a world where ideals cannot be reached and again counteract compassion fatigue.

Next to unachievable ideals, another, more fundamental source of exhaustion may be the loss of boundaries. It is important to distinguish empathy from emotional contagion. The latter refers to a somewhat automatic partaking in the experiences of others, akin to mimicry and also called "emotional convergence" (Hatfield, Cacioppo and Rapson 1994, 5). Here, "another person's emotion is not just sensed or understood; it is, to varying degrees, caught and expressed", as we first automatically mimic the expressions of another, and that expression again sparks the related emotions (mimicking the smile of another will spur happiness in the self; Doherty 1997, 149). Emotional contagion erodes the boundaries between the experiences of the self and those of the other to the point where the origin of those experiences is lost. As a result, we may feel anxiety in the company of an anxious person without knowing why or laugh in hysterics with another without knowing the catalyst for the hysteria. Empathy, on the other hand, requires and is rested on the firm understanding of the boundaries between the experiences of oneself and those of another – in a state of empathy, we note the distinctions concerning ourselves and others and continually remember that we are empathizing with someone else. In short, we know it is the other with whose experiences we are resonating, and hence we remember where our emotive state stems from (Decety and Jackson 2006).[38] Whereas emotional contagion blurs boundaries, empathy is rested on them. This again highlights how empathy is entwined with agency, the knowing of the specificity of oneself and the other.[39] Indeed, Martha Nussbaum (2001) argues that empathy rests on two-fold attention, within which we note the experiential differences between ourselves and others – there is no empathy without some underlying awareness of how our experiences differ from those of others.

The confusion between emotional contagion and empathy may also help to explain compassion fatigue. Empathy must involve a clear differentiation between the sphere of the self as opposed to the sphere of the other, and maybe it is when the line between these two collapses that distress follows (some or many of those prone to high distress during empathy may unwittingly merge the self and the other together, thus confusing categories and boundaries). Indeed, the differentiation between self and other is necessary if we are to avoid personal distress and truly pay heed to the experiences of the other: "Agency is a crucial aspect that enables a selfless regard for the other rather than a selfish desire to escape aversive arousal" (Decety and Lamm 2006, 1154). Without the distinction between self and other, one easily falls into various distraction methods, such as denial, used to avoid overt personal distress, which again will lead to compassion fatigue. From this viewpoint, the solution to compassion fatigue is to reaffirm the distinction so as to ensure both empathy and pro-social behaviour: "The prerequisite for social communication, including the experience of empathy, is that the two agents can preserve their individuality. Social cognition relies both on similarities and differences between individuals" (ibid., 1153). As argued by Jean Decety and Claus Lamm, the consequence of empathy should not be distress in the empathizer but instead action on behalf of the distress of others, and a clear boundary between the individuals enables such action.[40]

Should an overlap take place, the result can be utterly overwhelming for the empathizer and thus is not adaptive (even in an evolutionary sense; see Jackson, Rainville and Decety 2006). If we continually catch the emotions of others without keeping a hold of the boundaries, we become overburdened – as indeed those with compassion fatigue do. This reveals the root of such fatigue, for it may often originate not from empathy but from emotional contagion. We no longer maintain boundaries between ourselves and others and instead become swallowed in the pains of the other as if they were our own. The end result can be torturous, but ironically it can also push us into egoism: when exhausted under the weight of feeling the emotions of others, we stop caring. The experiences of others become our own, and when a critical point is achieved, we ultimately cease emotive involvement in favour of a more self-absorbed outlook.

Perhaps in cultures unaccustomed to empathy emotional contagion is used as its unrefined substitute. We begin to feel with others, as infants who cry when others cry without ever quite knowing what the other is undergoing and why. This is the primitive ancestor of empathy and a state into which we are pushed on a collective level with given types of humanitarian imagery and even (perhaps particularly) marketing. We are offered images of suffering that provoke tears while we remain ignorant of where those images come from, who we are feeling with, what their contexts are and the politics from which their suffering stems. Emotions become detached from those undergoing them – the identity of the suffering subjects becomes murky, irrelevant, and unnoted. It is precisely this type of contagion, dressed as empathy, which can wound us the most, for it is unreflected and as such creates feelings of overwhelming helplessness. Suffering enters us, but because it comes with no grasp of subjectivity or awareness of the context and politics entwined with suffering, we can do nothing but suffer. In the state of emotional contagion, the suffering merely *is*, and via such sheer, raw existence, raises overarousal and fatigue.

This leads to a further issue stemming from the difference between contagion and empathy, already hinted at above. Jean Decety and Philip Jackson underscore that complete identification, often generated by emotional contagion, within which boundaries between oneself and the other disappear paradoxically leads to self-directedness and egoism. This is because it sparks emotional distress, which may lead to a painful emotional overload and ultimately to being more concerned with ending one's own distress than providing for the other individual: "Experiencing another's distress state as one's own experience could lead to empathic over-arousal, in which the focus would then become one's own feelings of stress rather than the other's need" (Decety and Jackson 2006, 57). Only by persistently noting the distinction between oneself and others can such overarousal and egoism be avoided. Confusion between the two can be detrimental, as effective care and action depend on one's ability to separate between one's own distress and that of the other: "When unsuccessful in differentiating, the observer may get overwhelmed by his/her distress and a cascade of further distress and helplessness is likely in both the observer and the significant others" (Goubert et al. 2005, 287). The greater the sense of distress, the greater the ensuing egoism.

Here, whether we are self- or other-directed plays a clear role, for the first of these options heightens personal distress and compassion fatigue. Indeed, whereas emotional contagion can remain self-absorbed, in its more fruitful forms, empathy is vehemently other-directed (Volbrecht et al. 2007; Gallagher 2012). For instance, in the context of projective empathy, "imagine the self" and "imagine the other" lead to different responses: the latter to empathic concern, and the former to personal distress. Thus, Decety and Lamm point out that "projecting oneself into an aversive situation leads to higher personal distress and lower empathic concern, while focusing on the emotional and behavioral reactions of another's plight is accompanied by higher empathic concern and lower personal distress" (Decety and Lamm 2006, 1152).[41] In the case of "imagine the self", pro-social behaviour may thereby become difficult, for instead of helping others, one wishes to save oneself from feeling distressing empathy: "If perceiving another person in an emotionally or physically painful circumstance elicits personal distress, then the observer may tend not to attend fully to the other's experience and as a result lack sympathetic behaviors" (ibid., 1152). Therefore, although those who experience heightened personal distress for others may feel that they are wholly concerned over those others, some of them may in fact place overt emphasis on projective imagination, thus thinking of how they themselves would feel in a similar situation, and it may be this that results in higher degrees of distress and ensuing fatigue. The solution is to stay firmly other-directed and to avoid focusing on the self as a reference point.

Significantly, perspective taking is important – it just has to be anchored in the other rather than the self "as another". That is, simulations should be other-directed. Studies show that if one is prompted to remain wholly detached and objective before empathizing with others, the level of empathy will remain considerably lower, while if one is urged to take part in simulative perspective taking, this will enhance emotional arousal and greatly increase empathy levels. Therefore, prompts for perspective taking are highly effective in generating empathy, together with positive attitudes towards the victim and her peers. Moreover, individuals, who have been prompted towards perspective taking will be significantly more eager to help than those individuals who have been told to remain objective (see Batson et al. 2002). The lesson here is that we are to simulate but in an other- rather than self-directed fashion.

The distinction between oneself and other[42] is also vital for empathy's normative relevance, for it is only when we acknowledge the other as a specific, distinct individual that we can have moral respect for her – and vice versa, because emotional contagion can feed egoism, and because it fails to notice the uniqueness of the other, it risks muddling moral awareness. This is something that Max Scheler pointed out in his critique of Schopenhauer. Whereas Schopenhauer (2005) felt that empathy (or "sympathy") is based on our noting similarity and ultimately sameness in another, for Scheler this was nothing more than egoism (even when – as it usually is – well intended). He maintained that should we empathize with ourselves in others and blur boundaries, we end up doing nothing more than loving ourselves – sameness reduces into egoism. In order to pay genuine moral regard to others, boundaries, distinctions and differences are to be emphasized. Scheler warns us of emotional identification within which the other is replaced by or immersed into the self or vice versa: "Identification can come about in one way through the total eclipse and absorption of another self by one's own" (Scheler 2009, 18) or, conversely, "where 'I' . . . am so overwhelmed and hypnotically bound and fettered by the other 'I' . . . that my formal status as a subject is usurped by the other's personality . . . in such a case, I live, not in 'myself', but entirely in 'him', the other person" (ibid., 19). He is critical of identification, for we will be unable to have empathy (or what he called "fellow-feeling") for others when their specificities, and thereby their very selves, are set aside. Moral agency, therefore, relies on the self-other distinction, as enabled by (to differing degrees) empathy rather than emotional contagion. Paradoxically, then, those who go through severe, crippling distress over the pain of others may not always be advancing their moral agency.

Again, this is evident also in "empathy" towards non-human animals, for arguably many become overwhelmed with empathy precisely because they use self-directed projection and think of how they themselves would feel in a similar situation. This can render their distress intolerable while disabling their moral concern, and thus in order to save themselves, they choose not to pay any more attention to the plights of non-human others and give up on efforts to help. The higher the state of distress, the more likely compassion fatigue will occur. One counterforce for compassion fatigue is, therefore, the willingness for other-directedness, which simulations strengthen and which may also develop our capacities for further forms of empathy: we are to envision what it is like for a pig to exist in a crate or for the crocodile to navigate in her lagoon, and in so doing ditch our fixation on the human perspective by "imagining the other".

Those with a developed capacity for emotional convergence are prone to fatigue, for they take on the sufferings of other animals and become haunted by images of their pains. Emotions become mixed, intensified, even chaotic as interpretations of non-human emotions flood into one's mentation and become tortuous to the point where one declares she no longer wants to know or to care. These individuals should be proud of their ability for emotional attunement, but they should also seek to align their experiences with the distinction between oneself and others, for doing so will often be enough to eradicate compassion fatigue. They should also keep in mind that productive moral regard for non-human animals requires that their specificity is acknowledged and that becoming wholly "immersed" with another may ultimately and paradoxically lead to ignoring her.

It is important to feel with, to go through distress with another (the argument here is not that we should observe suffering neutrally – far from it). Remaining entirely neutral, unattached to any personal perspective, will suffocate important empathic reactions. Maintaining the self-other distinction does not, therefore, signal that one is to become depersonified from either the other or from one's own emotions. Therefore, empathy towards other animals is not grounded in staying oddly neutral, as if one were an emotionless observer, but rather in being other-directed and considerate of the self-other distinction – it is not a matter of "objectivity" in the sense of detachment from individual specificity. Yet empathy should not become so overwhelming that it devitalizes us, and it ought always to stem from noting distinctions.

Another, more significant source of alleviation here is reflective empathy, for it offers the type of consideration required for cultivating one's ability to note boundaries and distinctions.[43] It calls for us to recognize both the experiences of others and those of our own and as such makes evident that we are indeed separate beings. It can also impact how we relate to those around us: when emotionally overaroused and distressed, reflection helps us to ease the situation by warning us about what is taking place and reminding us of the need to balance between resonation and self-soothing. In short, by constantly calling for reflective awareness of how and why we are empathizing, reflective empathy reveals and discourages compassion fatigue and ensures that we stay other-directed. Reflection helps also with self-directedness and egoism. Clinical research speaks of "executive control", which refers to one's ability to monitor and control emotive responses. In regard to compassion fatigue, we are to control our empathic responses so as to ensure they do not become fixated on the self: "Executive control may be necessary to inhibit distress experienced by the self and allow for the full, though non-egocentric and self-regulated, consideration of the other's situation" (Decety and Lamm 2006, 1153).[44] When self-directed concerns (such as personal distress) impact the situation, more executive control – for instance, in the form of self-other contemplation and perspective taking – is required (Lamm, Meltzoff and Decety 2010). Reflective empathy supports executive control and in so doing promises a route out of the self-directed, egoistic dimensions of compassion fatigue.[45]

Moreover, reflective empathy helps us to navigate through the naturalization, desubjectification and depoliticization of suffering and the sort of compassion fatigue or compassion refusal they propel into existence. When we pay attention to the causes and nature of our empathy, we are quicker to notice mistakes in it and quicker to critically evaluate both how we ourselves and the culture around us depict others and their sufferings. In a state of critical reflection, one may suddenly wonder why she focuses only on dog suffering while failing to notice fish suffering, and she may ask appropriate questions concerning the ways in which media and cultural beliefs impact one's choices. Reflective empathy can also help to ward off the culture of harshness, which downplays empathy, for again reflective attunement with how and why one empathizes may reveal larger cultural mechanisms and politically coloured beliefs impacting our psyches. Here, it is reflection over one's emotive responses to others that can expose the ways in which, say, liberalistic egoism affects one's refusal to empathize and calls for a state of blunt disregard.[46]

With reflection, action also becomes easier, and this again helps to politicize empathy and to curtail the powers of compassion fatigue. One does not become overwhelmed by resonation with the pains of cows or geese if one can move from that state of sheer resonation into more enabling metalevels. Reflective empathy helps in locating what can be done and how one's own mental processes can lead to a false sense of pessimism over the possibility of action – it lends a lens through which to notice the psychological events that impact our action-related decisions and ideally assists in igniting an optimistic willingness to practice active moral agency.

When empathizing with the plight of non-human animals, it is often the nonqualified, nonreflective empathy – empathy that stays on the first-order level – which sparks discomfort, helplessness and fatigue. A meat-eating person identifying as an "animal lover" may, in the face of images of the suffering of those she eats, become disquieted, nervous, helpless and distressed, for she is not letting her empathy reach the reflective mode of responding. She will declare that she cannot bear to know more of what is happening, that she is burdened with empathy, and this happens because she does not have a metalevel from which to scrutinize her own position as an empathizer or from which to safely explore her beliefs and emotions and direct her actions in a productive manner. The same will happen to the vegan who cannot sleep at night due to the distress she is feeling over the horrors faced by other animals and who similarly may, as a psychological defence, simply begin numbing herself. Both need the help of reflective empathy as a sort of backdrop that will allow other forms of empathy to become enabling rather than distressing phenomena.

Empathy Shutdown

But what if the plight of hens and pigs provokes no empathy at all? Studies demonstrate that empathy may be turned off, and indeed empathy is discouraged in many settings, such as war and hunting (Hollan and Throop 2011). At times, this may be because of compassion fatigue, but often such disregard takes place independently, as many simply do not empathize with given groups of animals. The anthropocentric and anthropathic cultural tenets evident all around us nurture ways of approaching other animals that are quite oppositional to empathy and which actively suggest that empathy is not the appropriate choice. We are taught to suppress empathy towards goats and geese, as next to neutral disengagement, various negative emotions, such as contempt, a sense of superiority, resentment, even disgust and hate, are often allocated more room, and as optimizing, utilitarian reason is perceived as the decisive approach to non-humans to such an extent that the existence of those negative emotions, which often motivate it (sense of superiority may offer the impetus for seeing pigs as nothing but resources to be witnessed via rational optimization), is not even acknowledged. Therefore, we often detach from empathic responses before they even take flight. If this is particularly common in animal ethics, how do we deal with it?

The solution is, again, simple, for reflective empathy helps in locating and remedying empathy failures – if we consider why we empathize in given contexts and not in others, we can learn the causes behind our deficiencies and improve our empathic ability. Metalevel positioning not only of empathy but of its failures may help to comprehend the sources from which those failures stem. When faced with images of beaten pigs yet failing to undergo the type of empathy some others are capable of, it may be worthwhile to pay attention to what other emotions and beliefs are taking place and to explore how they impact the situation. Also, the aforementioned perspective taking is helpful, as simulating the viewpoints of other animals can be a powerful trigger towards further forms of empathy.

The first task in locating these failures is awareness of anthropocentric attitudes and their impact on our empathy. Emphasizing empathy as one foundation of moral agency easily forms the impression that the causal pathway between empathy and beliefs is one-directed: empathy sparks beliefs. However, the direction can also run the other way, as beliefs of course impact who we feel empathy towards and when. This is something highlighted by David Pizarro, who maintains that "empathic responses may differ in accordance with the antecedent belief systems at work in the individual, limiting the empathic response to only those entities included in a moral code" (Pizarro 2000, 366). Preexisting attitudes and beliefs may have a strong hold on our empathic capacities, which accentuates how empathy is not a "pure" state but rather something entangled with our surroundings and other mental states. This also bears an impact on animal ethics, as anthropocentric beliefs concerning other animals may directly influence what kind of empathy and on what level, if any at all, we feel towards hens or sheep. Indeed, Pizarro also points this out: "This may be the reason animal lovers cringe at the sight of a slaughtered cow while avid carnivores don't flinch. If the beliefs differ, emotive responses are affected. . . . Hence, a moral code that includes cows as fundamentally sacred and thus morally important allows the empathic response to occur when the individual is presented with a victimized cow" (Pizarro 2000, 365). Therefore, although empathy may have a strong effect on our beliefs concerning non-human animals, those beliefs may also bear an impact on empathy.

According to Pizarro, two things can happen as a consequence: we either change our beliefs in accordance with empathy or empathy is curtailed by preexisting beliefs. In the latter case, empathic suppression is at work. Here, "moral beliefs are held so strongly that the empathic arousal is seen as intrusive and unwanted" (Pizarro 2000, 369). Suppression can have very dangerous effects, as arguably it was precisely what Nazis used in order to deal with their own mass violence. Pizarro alarmingly states that "in suppressing empathic arousal by changing attributions concerning a victim or by focusing on differences, the motivational consequences to help those suffering are also eliminated, enabling horrific acts to take place with little or no internal constraint" (ibid., 369) before concluding, "Focusing on similarities or difference, and choosing whether or not to perspective-take, individuals can select situations that will be less likely to induce empathy" (ibid., 370). Moreover, suspension of moral consideration may take place: "People manage to do things that they would initially be uncomfortable doing, by either redefining the situation to remove morality from the equation, or by justifying the violation as a small one in the service of a greater good" (Monin, Pizarro and Beer 2007, 19).[47] Therefore, as argued earlier, we become empathetically biased because our beliefs support bias, and empathy may be altogether avoided if it is deemed awkward from the viewpoint of one's beliefs; finally, even morality can be sidelined so as to erase empathy. The implications for animal ethics are evident: empathy can be wholly curtailed and blocked off if it does not match anthropocentric notions of human-animal relations, and this again can support and maintain the sort of violence towards non-human beings manifested in animal industries.[48] The difference of animals can be overemphasized, which helps to justify the lack of empathy, and in the extreme, both empathy and moral consideration can be straightforwardly supressed.

In order to render empathic attention less partial and less prone to shutdowns, anthropocentric dogma need to be exposed, analysed and eradicated: beliefs should be moulded to follow the demands of empathy, not the other way around. However, deeper undercurrents may lie behind anthropocentric beliefs. As suggested above by Cohen, the neoliberal, economy-based cultures of the contemporary era tend to celebrate harshness, while empathy is downgraded. Those without empathy for non-human beings may also be quite unempathic towards their conspecifics, and arguably various cultural elements are pulling towards both emotive and moral indifference, and even callousness. With the birth of the faceless, consumeristic, information- and market-based society governed by fragmented social spheres, an increasingly optimizing, instrumentalizing, profit-orientated approach to existence and the diminishment of embodied, attentive encounters, we are quickly detaching from the experiential lives of others. This signals loss of empathy and a naive celebration of indifference. Even emotions become brands which are used to sell us ever more products, and simultaneously the subjectivity behind those emotions (human or non-human) becomes murkier, superficial and unnoted

– perhaps both in ourselves and in others. Our approach to life becomes that of purchase, as everything (including emotions) is buyable, sellable and instrumental and as we avoid those emotions which are culturally deemed as undesirable and which cause us discomfort or demand any form of sacrifice.[49]

It could, then, be argued that the contemporary society and its various institutions are eroding empathy – or at least those forms of empathy capable of sparking other-directedness. Faceless, market-based instances eager to measure the world with price tags are affecting our psyches and making us view others via their logic. We become detached, optimizing, gratification-seeking beings prone to overlooking the subjectivity of others and even prone to thinking that such disregard is to be celebrated, a character trait worthy of pursuing. Intriguingly, and as claimed earlier, perhaps animal industries play a dual role here – that is, perhaps anthropocentrism impacts this callousness and vice versa. Those industries bring us bodies from which experiences have been ripped or in which those experiences are being denied and present this nullification of subjectivity and experience as perfectly acceptable, a "norm". It becomes "normal" and "natural" that beings capable of feeling, sensing and thinking are viewed solely as usable bodies, as products with no inherent value, destined to serve our wants and desires.

This strengthens a peculiar worldview in which humans can and ought to view others as resources and thereby also offers its blessing to the neoliberal, consumeristic logic. Anthropocentrism may thus entwine with optimizing and the following catastrophic tendency to downplay and devalue empathy, leading us back to anthropathy. Animal industries may form one building block supporting the logic of detachment and guiding capitalist consumerism towards its ultimate state – the complete loss of subjectivity, the complete loss of empathy and anthropathic neglect. Such a cultural ethos will, again, reaffirm anthropocentric beliefs, as the commodifying mindset will all too easily deny the moral value of non-human beings while posing hierarchies between species. In a society threatening to view empathy as surplus, empathy towards other animals also becomes less likely.

In order to contest such detachment and culturally produced callousness, it is important to explore and reveal the cultural mechanisms that endorse egoistic disregard. The institutions and beliefs readily enticing us towards viewing others without empathy should be pointed out and critiqued, and politics of empathy ought to be actively endorsed throughout the different layers of society. We need a culture that celebrates empathy rather than callousness, and such a culture needs to be vigorously promoted in all the societal sectors, ranging from education to law and economics. Doing so will also increase empathy towards non-human beings, but importantly, in light of the above, speaking out against anthropocentrism may, in itself, help to promote empathy on a more general level; if indeed anthropocentrism is one catalyst for egoistic disregard and the culture of callousness, then critiquing it will also help to diminish the influence of the latter.

This means that teaching empathy towards non-human animals, developing our capacity to reflectively resonate with pigs and cows, could be a radical act of defiance against a whole cultural, political logic of detachment and egoism. Cultivating empathy towards other animals would be an act of rebellion and a path towards the rearrangement and reconstruction of those utilitarian, optimizing and instrumentalizing societal ramifications and institutions that currently spread compassion fatigue and empathy refusal.[50] Therefore, we are faced with a dual task aimed at breaking the vicious cycle between anthropocentrism and the culture of callousness: we must seek to abolish both and their tendency to downplay empathy by critiquing the ways in which they do the latter and by offering more empathic ways for the society to move forward, starting from its treatment of non-human animals.

NOTES

1. For further examples on hiding one's mental states, see Throop 2011, and on misusing information gained from mind reading, see Hollan 2011.

2. Cultural examples demonstrate that empathy can facilitate conservative ends, as it may serve "individual solace, rather than social or political action" (Hollan and Throop 2008, 390). This is particularly when empathy is perceived as "mind reading" and thereby both a potential source of manipulation and an intrusion on one's privacy – suspicion of it leads to downplaying its significance, which again manifests as a societal tendency to sideline empathy while accentuating "each to their own" thinking.

3. Worryingly, prioritizing cognition or reason may prevent affective empathy and push also empathic creatures to commit the most horrific acts (de Waal 2008, 291).

4. Perhaps good will and a sense of duty towards others are important as well. René Descartes, despite of his hostile attitudes towards non-human animals, offered important reminders concerning these factors. According to him, if we are to avoid akrasia, a state wherein we go against our moral judgement, we must embrace what he called "generosity" – a state of existing for others as well, within which we not only rationally and autonomously reflect on our moral choices but also maintain a sense of duty towards others, accompanied by good will, the desire to do good (*Philosophical Writings*, vol. 3, V, no. 83). As will be seen later, moral agency is complex and heterogenic, and various emotive and reflective abilities can render it stronger – including generosity.

5. An opposite example are companion dogs, who come to be called humans' "best friends" and who are even defined as furry human beings. As discussed in relation to projective empathy, although the intentions can be sincere, here empathy can grow crooked, expect the wrongs things from non-human animals, see humanity

where none exists and become ignorant of the specificity of dogs in ways that digress into their mistreatment.

6. Hoffman emphasizes that rationality must not sideline empathic responses. The latter are given priority, as they enable one to have lived experiences of morality: one can begin to fathom abstract moral principles only via an affective response towards them. Hence, reason is to aid empathy, but the latter continually holds primacy (Hoffman 1990).

7. For both, it is intersubjectivity that gives flight to morality: individuals come to form norms via joint development.

8. This form of empathy is, according to Hoffman (1990), particularly important for coming to understand different dimensions of justice since it paves the way for concern for whole groups of people, with their specific historical and social positions.

9. This is an important critique. For instance, affective empathy runs the risk of not offering adequate regard for the contextual, political milieus of our experiential lives – when all energy is placed on resonation in the present moment, both past and future considerations (why we suffer, what would prevent us from suffering in the future) can become murky. However, empathy should not be judged too harshly. No moral emotion, or indeed any single facet of moral psychology, can be expected to account for all that is morally and politically relevant as if offering us a full and total view to morality. Affective empathy may serve a pivotal function in revealing to us the intricacies of experience, and this is all that can be asked of it – for political, cultural and historical specificities, we have to turn elsewhere. Grasp of the wider settings of experience are vital for alleviating harms suffered by others and for enhancing the capacity for balanced, reflected, contented and gentle lives – in short, it is necessary for politically, causally aware moral action. Yet it may not be, in any deeper, wider sense, necessary for arousal of the one simple thought which forms the very key to morality: "The experiences of another matter to me". With all the contextual, political awareness in the world, with all possible reasoned acknowledgement of the causalities underlying our experiences, without affective empathy this sentence will not arise and hold us captive. Therefore, both "pure empathy" and contextual awareness are required and serve different functions.

10. Moreover, while allowing us to locate our own embeddedness, this also facilitates identifying the contextual ramifications of the other.

11. As is now commonly pointed out among Wittgenstein scholars, Wittgenstein did not, as is usually thought, suggest that knowledge of other animals is impossible, only that we tend to be so immersed in our human biases that we do not even strive towards it.

12. Moreover, we can empathize with experiences we have not had. As Scheler posits: "We can have a lively and immediate participation in joy and sorrow, can share with others their appreciation of value, and can even enter into another person's commiseration for a third party, without ever having sampled that particular quality of experience before. A person who has never felt mortal terror can still understand and envisage it, just as he can also share in it" (2009, 47). This is also an important factor in empathy towards non-human animals, as differences in experience do not necessarily exclude empathy.

13. Moreover, as McGreer (2008) points out, there are limits to the autism example, for it may tell us about autistic moral agency in particular rather than moral agency on a more general level (for instance, rationality may be a compensatory factor in autism while having less relevance in typical moral agency).

14. These claims are also significant in relation to non-human animals. As argued, perhaps the contemporary anthropocentric culture is fostering collective psychopathy in human attitudes towards other animals, as they are increasingly instrumentalized and manipulated, with little or no affective resonance with their experiences. Moreover, perhaps overt affective empathy, when combined with little support from other forms of mind reading, may render one prone towards removing oneself from emotive contact with other animals and into withdrawing from sources of affective empathy. Here, resonation becomes too painful, too uncomfortable, and the individual wishes not to feel it and disengages from those situations where it might be sparked; thereby, heightened states of affective empathy with little cognitive support lead to compassion fatigue. It may be this that enables someone with deeply felt resonation with other animals to become oddly and wilfully removed from their plight, as she may even resort to detached reasoned analyses in order to find argumentative justification for her sudden emotive disconnection. However, her moral agency is still partly founded on her affective empathy, even if she removes herself from it in given contexts, and thus she remains in an uncomfortable state, perhaps feeling ambiguous guilt over her choices.

15. The narcissistic element of psychopathy is related to high cognitive functioning, whereas callousness is linked to low cognition. Thus, psychopathy may fall into different subtypes, separated from each other by their intellectual ability (Fontaine et al. 2008). Significantly, moral ability can be severely impaired even when cognitive ability is perfectly normal (Oliveira-Souza, Hare and Bramati 2008).

16. The above highlights the way in which accentuating rationality at the expense of emotional involvement may lead to catastrophic consequences. Whereas occasional cruelty towards other animals may be at times explained via something akin to antisocial impulsivity, where the person in question lashes out unthinkingly, the sort of systemic violence towards other animals evident in most cultures is supported by removing emotive engagement from the equation and giving all prominence to rational optimization, which again is motivated by hedonistic gain. When considering moral agency in relation to other animals, it is difficult to see how irrationality could explain the worst acts of moral neglect; instead, these acts appear to be evoked and maintained by detached, calculating reason, such as that exemplified in animal industries and the economies of animal consumption, which quite rationally aim for the most efficient use and marketing of pigs and hens. Hence, when it comes to the evaluation and treatment of other animals, perhaps what is required is less rationalizing and more affective attunement. Arguably, human-non-human relations would benefit from considerably more abundant emotive engagement, capable of arousing moral regard towards non-human creatures. In short, when it comes to animal ethics, more emotion is required; with less coolly calculative hints of anthropathy and more emotively aware traits of the Williams syndrome, humane ways of treating other animals would perhaps be quite different and more in line with the ideals of moral agency.

17. There is one category of morality within which norm contents can be clearly detached from empathy, and this is morality concerning non-individuals, one example being environmental ethics. Yet even here affective empathy may play a part on the metalevel, for it enables us to perceive value outside of ourselves – the fact that we resonate with humans and pigs removes our self-directed viewpoint, and the following capacity to note value in the external world may enable us to value also those things and entities with which we cannot empathize.

18. It is also important to draw a distinction between the content of norms and the content of moral agency: even if the former do not always manifest empathy on any obvious level, the latter may require it. That is, the foundation of our morality depends on affective empathy, even when specific norm contents do not seem to rest on it. Relatedly, the seeming absence of emotion in a given moral judgement does not show that emotions are not the basis of moral agency. This is because *apparent* and *foundational* levels of moral agency are to be distinguished from each other: the latter defines the grounds of our moral ability (forming our "core moral agency"), while the former concerns the immediately evident form of that ability and can take many shapes. Quite simply, we first become creatures capable of noting value and then carry on to make ever more specific evaluations, often partly guided by something quite different from the original source that "sparked" our moral agency into existence. To use the simple metaphor of a tree, the foundational basis of moral agency is the trunk, which enables differently shaped branches to form and grow in their own varying directions.

19. The claim is that "human capacity for selective moralization cannot be entirely at the mercy of our natural emotional proclivities (and may realize much of its potential even when the aforesaid proclivities are in serious disrepair)" (Royzman, Leema and Baron 2009, 171).

20. Moreover, those cases, in which no emotions arise tend to concern "convention transgression" rather than "moral transgression". Tax avoidance demonstrates this well: for many, paying taxes has become a matter of convention (a legal obligation), and therefore no strong sentiments are stirred by the existence of tax dodgers. The relevance of emotion can be discovered by testing whether adding emotion to the mixture transforms a convention transgression into a moral transgression or whether a morally charged depiction of a convention sparks emotive responses. This appears to be the case. For instance, if we are shown tax avoidance in a moral light – for instance, through an explanation of how welfare support systems would collapse without taxes or by exemplifying how it is unjust that one should escape her duty while others have to pay – emotions (even if only mild ones) arguably become quickly apparent (and conversely, if we invite resonation towards those who are harmed by tax evasion, the moral dimension begins to appear). Therefore, it is possible that emotions are absent only when we do not fathom the moral dimension of a given situation and instead approach it as a matter of convention. Indeed, even burning flags and other similar events are often linked to harm and empathy (Gray and Wegner 2011).

21. Therefore, reason can postulate that others are "ends in themselves", and emotions such as love can imbue others with value, but they may also serve to instrumentalize others for one's egoistic gain. It is only affective empathy that anchors these

evaluations in those *others* rather than in our potentially self-directed emotions or aloof theorizations.

22. This comes close to Harry Frankfurt's "higher order volition", where we do not only want something but want to want it.

23. Understanding or judging is not always something grounded on intellectual analysis but can, following the philosophy of Wittgenstein, also consist of meaningfully behaving in certain ways in relation to our surroundings, thus taking part in *doing* rather than *thinking* (Gustafsson 2014, 89).

24. It also should be noted that reason often fails to guide away from conflict: in fact, as already implied, it is because of reason's failings that conflicts prevail. People can readily admit that they cannot defeat their opponent's logic and that, rationally speaking, they ought to alter their moral judgements but still quite consciously adhere to their views simply because the emotions or cultural dogma underlying those views have such a strong hold. This again demonstrates how much tighter the grip of emotions can be in comparison to reason and how, even in cases of conflict, it is important to first undergo emotive, empathic alteration – precisely the sort that reflective empathy enables.

25. Separating emotion and reason into closed off, antagonistic categories is unfruitful: they impact each other and are often entwined to the point where it is impossible to speak of wholly irrational empathy or rational argumentation void of any emotion. As Monin, Pizarro and Beer point out, "The truth is much more complex than a simple emotion/reason dichotomy" (Monin, Pizarro and Beer 2007, 6). (This is something brought forward in animal ethics as well by Mary Midgley; see Midgley 1983.)

26. We often approach the immoralities of others with emotions but our own immoralities with reason, seeking to find justification for them (Monin, Pizarro and Beer 2007).

27. As seen earlier, there are good reasons for this criticism, as differences between species, not to mention unfamiliarity with numerous animals, evidently constitute a reason for many of the failures in empathy towards non-human creatures. However, as also seen earlier, biases are often related to cultural beliefs and prejudices rather than empathy, and therefore Kasperbauer is mistaken in pointing the blaming finger at empathy. It must be emphasized here that the same bias holds true for other moral motivations as well, and therefore anger is equally prone towards bias, as we may feel the most anger on behalf of those who are closest to us. To pinpoint empathy as the cause of bias and to assume anger to be free from it is, thereby, quite misleading.

28. Kasperbauer also argues that if empathy were a sufficient ground for animal ethics, then surely those people who spend much time with other animals (farmers, etc.) would be highly empathic – since they are not, interaction with other animals cannot suffice for empathy and moral concern. However, the crucial thing to note is that interaction per se does not constitute the type of intersubjectivity required for empathy; on the contrary, it can be wholly self-directed, wherein one simply manipulates another as an instrument while remaining wholly ignorant of her subjectivity. As seen throughout this book, it is not *that* we spend time with others that evokes empathic concern but rather *how* we spend that time.

29. Other negative emotions also can serve a moral function. As McGreer (2008) points out, negative emotions are part of morality and may, for instance, appoint blame where blame is deserved and maintain social orders deemed valuable on the affective level.

30. According to Batson and colleagues (2007), moral outrage needs to be separated from personal anger (which promotes self-interest) and empathic anger (which results from anger on behalf of someone else's interests). For them, the latter two are not moral outrage because they are not "provoked by a violation of a moral standard" (Batson et al. 2007, 1273), which involves the notion of justice. However, it remains wholly unclear why empathy would not involve precisely such a standard (see also Deigh 2011).

31. Prinz rests his stance partly on Haidt's argument (Haidt & Graham 2007), which suggests that negative emotions enrich our emotive landscapes and thereby also may widen our moral ability.

32. Of course, one could probe for gender politics behind this suggestion: Why are emotions typically classified as "female" considered "soft" and emotions such as anger, typically linked to men, considered "strong" and "active"?

33. One could also talk of "empathy fatigue", but since the term "compassion fatigue" is common in literature, it will be deployed here.

34. Cohen does acknowledge that we may become overwhelmed by empathy but argues this to be "compassion avoidance" (denial) rather than fatigue – a term with which he refers to a "sense of a situation so utterly hopeless and incomprehensible that we cannot bear to think about it" (Cohen 2002, 194).

35. Cohen has discussed the standard view, according to which compassion fatigue follows from information overload, wherein we are bombarded with too many representations of suffering on an overly intense scale, and as a result our responses begin to fade. He maintains that this thesis is unwarranted simply because many still do empathize regardless of witnessing much suffering (Cohen 2002). However, this criticism is not convincing, for even if there are those who care regardless of overexposure, arguably some cease caring, as witnessing images of suffering on a daily basis risks normalizing it. Information overload is a limited explanation but may still have some validity.

36. Like Chouliaraki, Moeller (1999) also highlights the importance of political ignorance, as we do not know why suffering is taking place and hence become incapable of empathizing with full accord.

37. Moeller (1999) also argues that compassion fatigue is sparked by the feeling that one's actions have little bearing on the suffering of others and that empathy is thus futile.

38. Affective empathy and emotional contagion are interlinked in the sense that the more we have of the latter, the more prone we are to embrace the former (Doherty 1997) – yet only the former maintains a sense of boundary.

39. This was also emphasized by Stein (1989), according to whom Theodore Lipps made a false correlation between empathy and emotional contagion with his notion of "*Einfühlung*".

40. Other emotions may also affect compassion fatigue. Interestingly, studies manifest that guilt-proneness is linked to empathy, whereas shame-proneness is

not, and that guilt entwines with the cognitive elements of empathy, such as perspective taking, while shame entwines with affective elements, such as emotional concern. Since shame is also linked to empathic distress, self-obsession and disregard for the perspective of the other, one suggestion is that affective aspects of empathy may be counterproductive (Leith and Baumeister 1998). In other words, perhaps it is precisely feeling with another which causes distress and compassion fatigue. However, the point here is that it equally could be the loss of the self-other distinction which spurs shame – the ashamed begins to merge with the viewpoint of the other, and is even swallowed by it, thus becoming detached from her own self-understanding.

41. Decety and Lamm clarify that "participants' behavioural and neural responses are more self-centered when they adopt a first-person perspective. On the other hand, attending to the other in a more detached way results in an amplification of other-orientated responses" (Decety and Lamm 2006, 1157).

42. It should be noted that this distinction does not imply atomism: in the latter, individuals are seen to be beyond each other's reach, whereas in the former, such reach is quite possible, even though it takes place from distinct viewpoints.

43. Chouliaraki (2006) also calls for "reflexive identification", wherein we take some distance in order to develop a holistic, politically informed view of what is happening.

44. Here, also, control of emotions is important. Those, who can better regulate their emotions are also better at empathy and pro-social behaviours. Without this ability, one quickly succumbs to personal distress (Decety and Lamm 2006).

45. Here, self-awareness stands as pivotal. In order to practice the sort of control that enables other-directedness, one needs a sound understanding of one's own responses. Self-awareness is critical for fruitful, successful social relations and is particularly important for understanding the mental states of others (Decety and Lamm 2006).

46. The case for reflective empathy is made stronger when we note that even if we are aware of the boundaries between oneself and others, we can become exhausted under the weight of others' suffering (contagion is not always the root cause). This happens when empathy remains a terrain unmapped and unexplored and in its unfamiliarity, beyond any control, a source of helplessness and discomfort. We feel but do not know exactly what we feel and what we ought to do with that feeling. Reflection helps to escape from such a state of exhausting confusion by cultivating our ability to focus emotions in a way that is productive both for others and for ourselves.

47. It is precisely moral disengagement that "leads to some of the worst horrors perpetrated by humankind" (Monin, Pizarro and Beer 2007, 225), and this entwines with empathy withdrawal – a situation quite manifest in regard to the treatment of other animals.

48. Next to beliefs, personal costs also impact the willingness to empathize. In studies, individuals will avoid empathy-inducing material if they know that they are invited to offer help (thus minimizing their chances of actually feeling motivation to help; see Pizarro 2000, 370).

49. It is perhaps because of this that narcissism – the personality disorder noted for its lack of empathy – has demonstrably become more common (Konrath, O'Brien and

Hsing 2011) and has even been argued to form a side product of the contemporary capitalist, consumeristic society, with its concentration on individualistic, hedonistic and egoistic gain (Fromm 1955; for another sociological analysis on the relation between Western American culture and narcissism, see Lachs 1979).

50. It could even help to pave the way towards rethinking education, finance, social welfare and legal policy in ways that are grounded on empathic awareness, for cultivating empathy towards utterly different and distant creatures in the non-human world will surely cultivate such ability towards other humans as well.

Conclusion

Projective, simulative, cognitive, affective and embodied varieties of empathy all have something to offer to our capacity to understand others, and yet they all also come with their own difficulties and limitations. Ideally, we would use particularly the latter four in combination, whereby they could support each other in their various failings, thus laying out a more holistic view into what it is to be another creature. The sixth candidate, reflective empathy, includes precisely such a combination of the other alternatives, set against an attentive, second-order frame of mind, that allows us to continuously seek to remain attuned to how, why and with whom we are empathizing and how we could cultivate our ability to both know and experience others. Because of its heterogenic richness and its capacity to support attentive cultivation, out of the six varieties, reflective empathy is the most promising one.

From the outlook of morality, affective empathy is the most vital ingredient due to the way in which it enables the immediate, experiential other-directedness necessary for noting the other's individuality and well-being as significant in their own right. It is a normatively charged condition, capable of manifesting the other as a valuable being, and without which any moral ability will remain partial and hollow. However, instead of favouring only one capacity, a multi-tier approach to morality offers the most comprehensive way of understanding what it is to value and act as a moral agent. In such an approach, affective empathy forms the core around which other capacities begin to mount, rendering our moral ability more refined. Other varieties of empathy, other emotions and rationality form further circles around the core, and at the outer ring stands reflective empathy as the combination of both empathic ability and reflection and as a guide to developing moral agency into further, ever more regardful directions.

These considerations apply to animal ethics as well – that is, to how we understand, value and treat other animals. Due to cultural causes and strong anthropocentric tenets in many contemporary societies, empathy towards hens and cows has often been inadequate and even seen as a form of overt gentleness. However, as this book has aimed to argue, emotions and empathy are necessary for both mentally understanding and morally recognizing others, and without them, any animal ethic will remain drastically insufficient, with potentially catastrophic results. In the contemporary world, such results are heinously wide-scale and particularly evident in animal industries, which value and treat non-human animals as material bodies meant for utilization rather than as specific, experiencing subjects of value. The results are also present in anthropathy, the collectively maintained attitude towards other animals that focuses on egoism, hedonistic gain and utilization of others while overlooking both empathy and moral concern. In order to remedy the situation, what we need is more empathy and more attention on what type of empathy we are undergoing, in relation to what type of beings and why. In particular, we are in need of reflective empathy, with its ability to evoke both affective resonation with geese and pikes, and attentive cultivation of our wider empathic, moral ability. It is here that we find the solution to desubjectification, mentioned in the introduction: others will appear as valuable subjects as long as we develop a reflectively empathic standpoint to them.

But what of those who simply cannot empathize with other animals on any significant, experiential level? Arthur Schopenhauer maintains that empathy is extremely difficult to teach: "It is far easier to change lead into gold than to accomplish such a task" (Schopenhauer 2005, 126). However, this is a vast overstatement, and in fact teaching empathy is quite possible via a multiplicity of options.

Empathy is related to our sense of selfhood: Do we exist as separate, independent units enclosed in our own private spheres, or can we also interweave with others in an intersubjective sense, letting them co-constitute what it is to be "me"? Teaching empathy, or empathic pedagogy, should begin with highlighting the latter option (Schertz 2007). The liberalistic, individualistic cultures surrounding us tend to emphasize the idea that we are our own encapsulated, autonomous creatures, and it is easy to follow this line of thinking, thereby becoming less likely to engage in empathy. We learn both empathy and avoidance of empathy from our surroundings, and when those surroundings endorse atomistic, private individualism, empathy can become challenging, and in particular when such individualism is combined with authoritarian or even abusive models for behaviour, repeated by our parents, social institutions or other influences, the situation is dire (ibid.). Empathy is partially societally constructed and involves not only how those closest to us – our families, friends, teachers, neighbours – relate to others but how the societal infrastructures and institutions relate to what it is to be an "individual" and how they themselves treat those individuals. In a consumeristic world, propelled by the desire to concentrate on one's own wants and interests, it is easy to become desubjectifying, as others begin to appear as objects that can give us something rather than as subjects to whom we ought to give something of ourselves.

What is required, then, is forsaking the atomistic model and replacing it with intersubjectivity, the idea that we constantly evolve in relation to others, are impacted by and open to those others and due to this dynamic, also capable of understanding them. As Anita von Poser, in her anthropological research on empathy, has noted: "The idea of an autonomous and unfettered self, developed during the eighteenth century, came to dominate the modern Western image of the self", while "empathy is more likely to flourish on the grounds of a relational model of sociality than an individualist one" (von Poser 2011, 187). It is our grasp of what it is to exist as a "self" among other selves that impacts empathy, and for too long this "self" has been not only an anthropocentric but also an individualistic one. What is needed is a more relational attitude towards other animals – human or non-human – wherein we seek to attune ourselves to their needs and to define ourselves via our ability to do so. Therefore, those who feel unable to empathize with rats and cats can reflect on how they approach animal life: Is it something external and far removed from the human "self" or something that we can relate to, evolve with and to some extent access? Moreover, in order for all of us to take part in empathy pedagogy, the social presumptions and institutions which repeat overt individualism ought to be critically reviewed and modified so as to become more intersubjective and relational in regard to pigs and hens as well.

Yet another tool of evoking empathy is simulation. Via intentionally imagining the perspectives of others, it is more effortless to empathize with them on a resonative level. Here, the challenge is to envision what it is like for the rat, cat or bat to dwell in this world. Taking into account their physiologies, capacities and circumstances, what may life be like for them? Literature, drama, films and our own imagination are the key, as we are to simulate non-human experience. Even though no definitive answers can be found, these sorts of exercises can be highly productive and can amply advance other varieties of empathy as well (see, for instance, Goldstein and Winner 2012).

Next to becoming more intersubjective and simulating the viewpoints of other animals, concentrating on individual tigers or kangaroos will also help, for empathy towards an individual can awaken empathy towards her group. This is particularly evident in the case of stigmatized individuals and the collectives they form: when empathy towards individuals is induced, empathy for the relevant stigmatized group, and hence other individual members, grows (Batson et al. 2002). This is significant in human-non-human relations. Empathy spurs from responding to individual beings rather than abstract, faceless categories – we cannot feel empathy towards a generic "pig" or a "human", but instead our responses are founded on meeting specific, unique creatures – that or this specific pig or human. As a consequence, when trying to encourage empathy towards other animals, individual perspectives need to be focused on, and as a result specific animal stories are to be centralized. The person feeling unempathic towards "pigs" in general may well alter her mind when faced with one particular pig.

There are further ways to invite empathic processes. In empathy, play with the rigidity of identity is relevant. Just as presuming that we are atomistic creatures isolated from others is dangerous, so is the belief in fixed, prototypic, predetermined and generic "selves", such as "humanity". We are not destined to be compressed into some mythical and preset "human" psychology but are also animals able to broaden our terrains to non-human existence. Alternating between and inventively experimenting with different ways of being an animal invite an attitude of gentle disruption to and recomposition of what we are used to and a sense of ferality and even wildness as we contest our human presumptions and habits. We are to play, to become unruly in the face of fixed categories and identities, to vivaciously deconstruct boundaries and (imaginatively or concretely) fly with seagulls, smell the grass with cows, wrestle with dogs on their terms, sniff the air with foxes, stand still with herons or run around with pigs, thereby liberating ourselves from some of the norms concerning "human identity" and getting closer to animal life-worlds. Empathy, then, is not always a stern, serious undertaking but one that requires both lightness of touch and the readiness to jumble notions of "human" and "animal".

This flexibility also offers one answer to the risk of the "humanizing gaze", within which empathy becomes a form of assimilation. At its best, empathy knows no rigid barriers or unyielding identity categories – rather, it exists in a state of constant alteration and flux, as our mental states vary, move and change. To come to meet the specificity of another is to flow with her outside of any categories that could indicate assimilation. In short, there is nothing to assimilate to, no broader class or genus into which one can drown others as long as we do not insist, as the humanizing gaze does, on the rigidity of the categories "human" and "animal". When moving with another, empathy becomes a meeting point, not a place of immersion. Here, Gilles Deleuze's notion of "becomings" is pertinent, the main claim being this: life and mental states exist as movement and change, wherein unbending categories and identities make little sense. One is to take "lines of flight" between different modes of animal existence and to seek to grasp something of what it is like to exist as another, and all this is made possible by both the absence of strict categories and the constant, processlike alteration of our mindedness (Deleuze and Guattari 1988). It is this that empathy can, at best, facilitate, as it invites us to know and move with others, without seeking to submerge those others into identity classifications of our own invention.

Next to play, humility is also required for empathy to flourish. It consists of noting how contexts, beliefs and emotions affect us; how our personal preferences often cloud our judgement; and how little we still know of non-human ways of being. Most of all, we need humility in the face of the animal other so that her opacity, difference, similarity and specificity can finally surface and form the reference point of inquiry. In other words, it is paramount to avoid the presumption that humans are the pinnacle of evolution, perfect in their knowledge and the standard for all comparisons. Instead, we are one, vulnerable animal among many, fallible and limited in our ways of knowing and in need of taking others seriously.

One last important criticism remains. Does not a focus on empathy imply an individualistic ethic, one that is incapable of doing justice to non-individuals, such as forests, art and the oceans? In the era of the sixth mass extinction and global warming, this question is more pertinent than ever. It has been partly the liberalistic, individual-centred ethos of the Western world which has paved the way for the sort of market economies and overaccentuation of use-value underlying industrialization, consumerism and ultimately environmental destruction. It has been the "I" which has eagerly demanded her presupposed individual rights to use and consume. Should we not, instead of once more prioritizing only the individual, speak of moral agency and ethics also capable of noting the non-subjects, like natural habitats, species and ecologies? The answer is simple: yes. There is more to moral ability than recognizing the value of subjects. Empathy may stand at the root of morality, but the latter also extends to more than individuals. In this epoch of climate challenges and species annihilation, a radical alteration of our moral grasp of non-individuals is desperately required. What is needed is an urgent push towards experiences of moral awe in the context of natural entities and wholes, be they places of wilderness, local ecologies or global biospheres.

Yet this does not downplay the importance of empathy. Moral considerability cannot be reduced to individual subjects, and more holistic matters deserve recognition and respect, but the subject (and thus empathy) can still hold principal relevance and support the appreciation of non-individual things. Indeed, in the ideal situation, concern for the individual being helps to guide us towards concern for environmental entities, for the former can only fair well when the latter flourish. Calling for the radical alteration of our environmental attitudes can therefore coincide with and be aided by empathic concern for individuals. Particularly when taking into account the perspectives of almost countless other beings – non-human animals spread out across the earth in the most varied physiologies and forms – one has hope of also noting value in the existence of species, ecologies, environments and finally life. As has also been noted in empathy studies, even if individuals should never be seen as mere faceless representatives of groups, they are nonetheless always parts of some collective, which partly defines their well-being (Oceja et al. 2014). If we truly notice the lived viewpoints of other animals, we will also begin to recognize value in the wider settings and entities which allow them to exist. In the midst of the current crisis, empathy is therefore essential, even if other emotions, such as elevation, awe and melancholy, not to mention reasoned analysis, also can coax us towards noting inherent value in nature. More importantly, it is precisely empathy towards non-human animals which can spark radically new environmental concern and politics.

Cultivating empathic abilities will enable a new world to emerge in how we perceive and treat others. Max Scheler describes how after an increase in empathy, it is "as if a light were suddenly shone, or a window opened, in a darkened room" (Scheler 2009, 50). Being restricted to one's own well-being, or the well-being of those closest to one, limits our grasp of reality and suffocates it into one tiny dot, where it indeed is dark, confined and desolate and where anthropathy all too easily prevails. Opening that dot and letting empathy flow towards novel orientations allows for new spaces to materialize and illuminates reality and fellow creatures inhabiting it afresh. This enriches and deepens our own flourishing, but most of all, it assists the flourishing of all those our actions concern. In the process, others become nothing less than real. Scheler posits how "the dissipation of this [egoistic] illusion follows, necessarily and uniquely, from the effect of fellow-feeling in enabling us to grasp how a man, or living creature, as such is our equal in worth. . . . This equality of worth once established, the other person also becomes equally real to us, thereby losing its merely shadowy and dependent status. . . . He exists as really and truly as yourself" (ibid., 60). The other creature is no longer a distant, faceless thing, something that lives in the shadows of our own self-regarding wants as if not quite existent in her own right, but surfaces as her very own being, as real as ourselves and as worthy as we are. This is something perhaps most beautifully captured by Iris Murdoch's description of love (as synonymous to attentiveness): "Love is the extremely difficult realisation that something other than oneself is real" (Murdoch 1959, 51).

These observations stand as the fundamental reason for advocating the use and cultivation of empathy. Without empathy, we sink into dots, while others are all too easily lost into the fogs of our self-directed interests, aloof rationalizations or cultural prejudices. Reflective empathy in particular can eradicate the dots and fogs and thereby transform this bleak scene into a landscape of other-regarding lucidity. Via reflective empathy, we come to witness other animals – be they humans, fishes, vipers, bees, bears or antelopes – as concrete creatures with their own experiences, wants and traits and therefore their own realities, equally as valid and valuable as those of our own. The animal is no longer a distant object of anthropocentric dreams but a breathing, feeling, thinking subject.

References

Aaltola, Elisa. 2013a. "Empathy, Intersubjectivity and Animal Ethics". *Journal of Environmental Philosophy* 10 (2): 20–35.
Aaltola, Elisa. 2013b. "Skepticism, Empathy and Animal Suffering". *Journal of Bioethical Inquiry* 10 (4): 457–67.
Aaltola, Elisa. 2014a. "Affective Empathy as Core Moral Agency: Psychopathy, Autism and Reason Revisited". *Philosophical Explorations* 17 (1): 76–92.
Aaltola, Elisa. 2014b. "Animal Suffering: Representations and the Act of Looking". *Anthrozoös* 27 (1): 19–31.
Aaltola, Elisa. 2014c. "Varieties of Empathy and Moral Agency". *Topoi – an International Review of Philosophy* 33 (1): 1–11.
Aaltola, Elisa. 2015. "Wilderness Experiences as Ethics: From Elevation to Attentiveness". *Ethics, Policy & Environment* 18 (3): 283–300.
Acampora, Ralph. 2006. *Corporal Compassion: Animal Ethics and Philosophy of Body*. Pittsburgh, PA: University of Pittsburgh Press.
Agamben, Giorgio. 2003. *The Open: Man and Animal*. Stanford, CA: Stanford University Press.
Ahmed, Sarah. 2004. *The Cultural Politics of Emotion*. Edinburgh: Edinburgh University Press.
Ali, Farah, Sousa Amorim, Ines, and Chamorro-Premuzic, Tomas. 2009. "Empathy Deficits and Trait Emotional Intelligence in Psychopathy and Machiavellianism". *Personality and Individual Differences* 47: 758–62.
Ashley, P. 2007. "Toward an Understanding and Definition of Wilderness Spirituality". *Australian Geographer* 38 (1): 53–69.
Bailey, Cathryn. 2007. "On the Backs of Animals: The Valorization of Reason in Contemporary Animal Ethics". In *The Feminist Care Tradition in Animal Ethics*, edited by Josephine Donovan and Carol Adams. New York: Columbia University Press.
Baker, Steve. 1993. *Picturing the Beast: Animals, Identity and Representation*. Manchester: Manchester University Press.
Baron-Cohen, Simon. 2011. *Zero Degrees of Empathy: A New Theory of Human Cruelty*. London: Penguin Books.

Baron-Cohen, Simon, and Chakrabarti, Bhismadev. 2008. "Social Neuroscience". In *Child Neuropsychology*, edited by Jonathan Reed and Jody Warner-Rogers. London: Wiley-Blackwell.

Baron-Cohen, Simon, and Wheelwright, Sally. 2004. "The Empathy Quotient: An Investigation of Adults with Asperger Syndrome or High Functioning Autism and Normal Sex Differences". *Journal of Autism and Developmental Disorders* 34 (2): 163–75.

Barrett, Lisa Feldman. 2017. *How Emotions Are Made: The Secret Life of the Brain*. London: MacMillan.

Batson, Daniel, Chang, Johee, Orr, Ryan, and Rowland, Jennifer. 2002. "Empathy, Attitudes, and Action: Can Feeling for a Member of a Stigmatised Group Motivate One to Help the Group?" *Personality and Social Psychology Bulletin* 28 (12): 1656–66.

Batson, Daniel, Kennedy, Christopher, Nord, Lesley-Anne, Stocks, E., Fleming, D'Yani et al. 2007. "Anger at Unfairness: Is It Moral Outrage?" *European Journal of Social Psychology* 37: 1272–85.

Bergson, Henri. 2005. *Laughter: An Essay on the Meaning of the Comic*. London: Dover.

Blair, R. J. 1995. "A Cognitive Developmental Approach to Morality: Investigating the Psychopath". *Cognition* 57: 1–29.

Blair, R. J. 1999. "Psychophysiological Responsiveness to the Distress of Others in Children with Autism". *Personality and Individual Differences* 26: 477–85.

Blair, R. J. 2005. "Responding to the Emotions of Others: Dissociating Forms of Empathy through the Study of Typical and Psychiatric Populations". *Consciousness and Cognition* 14: 698–718.

Blair, R. J. 2008. "Fine Cuts of Empathy and Amygdala: Dissociable Deficits in Psychopathy and Autism". *Quarterly Journal of Experimental Psychology* 61 (1): 157–70.

Blair, R. J., and Blair, K. 2009. "Empathy, Morality and Social Convention: Evidence from the Study of Psychopathy and Other Psychiatric Disorders". In *The Social Neuroscience of Empathy*, edited by Jean Decety and William Ickes. Cambridge, MA: MIT Press.

Bloom, Paul. 2016. *Against Empathy*. New York: Ecco.

Blum, Lawrence. 1988. "Gilligan and Kohlberg: Implications for Moral Theory". *Ethics* 98 (3): 472–91.

Boler, Megan. 2006. "The Risks of Empathy: Interrogating Multiculturalism's Gaze". *Cultural Studies* 11 (2): 253–73.

Book, Angela, Quinsey, Vernon, and Langford, Dale. 2007. "Psychopathy and the Perception of Affect and Vulnerability". *Criminal Justice and Behaviour* 34 (4): 531–44.

Brown, K. W., and Ryan, R. M. 2003. "The Benefits of Being Present: Mindfulness and Its Role in Psychological Well-Being". *Journal of Personality and Social Psychology* 84 (4): 822–48.

Brown, Todd, Sautter, John, Littvay, Levente, Sautter, Alberta, and Bearnes, Brennen. 2010. "Ethics and Personality: Empathy and Narcissism as Moderators of

Ethical Decision Making in Business Students". *Journal of Education for Business* 85 (4): 203–8.

Cain, Nicole, Pincus, Aaron, and Ansell, Emily. 2008. "Narcissism at the Crossroads: Phenotypic Description of Pathological Narcissism across Clinical Theory, Social/Personality Psychology, and Psychiatric Diagnosis". *Clinical Psychology Review* 28: 638–56.

Chouliaraki, Lilie. 2006. *The Spectatorship of Suffering*. London: Sage.

Churchland, Patricia. 2011. *Brainstorm*. Princeton, NJ: Princeton University Press.

Coetzee, J. M. 1999. *The Lives of Animals*. Princeton, NJ: Princeton University Press.

Coffey, K. A., Hartman, M., and Fredrickson, B. L. 2010. "Deconstructing Mindfulness and Constructing Mental Health: Understanding Mindfulness and Its Mechanisms of Action". *Mindfulness* 1 (4): 235–53.

Cohen, Stanley. 2002. *States of Denial: Knowing about Atrocities and Suffering*. Cambridge: Polity Press.

Cole, Jonathan. 2001. "Empathy Needs a Face". In *Between Ourselves: Second-Person Issues in the Study of Consciousness*, edited by Evan Thompson. Thorverton, UK: Imprint Academic.

Coplan, Amy. 2004. "Empathic Engagement with Narrative Fictions". *Journal of Aesthetics and Art Criticism* 62 (2): 141–52.

Coplan, Amy. 2011a. "Empathy and Trauma Culture: Imaging Catastrophe". In *Empathy: Philosophical and Psychological Perspectives*, edited by Amy Coplan and Peter Goldie. Oxford: Oxford University Press.

Coplan, Amy. 2011b. "Will the Real Empathy Please Stand Up? A Case for a Narrow Conceptualization". *Southern Journal of Philosophy* 49 (1): 40–65.

Corona, Rosalie, Dissanayake, Cheryl, Shoshana, Arbelle, Wellington, Peter, and Sigman, Marian. 2008. "Is Affect Aversive to Young Children with Autism? Behavioral and Cardiac Responses to Experimenter Distress". *Child Development* 69 (6): 1494–1502.

Crary, Alice. 2009. *Beyond Moral Judgment*. Cambridge, MA: Harvard University Press.

Crist, Eileen. 1999. *Images of Animals: Anthropocentrism and Animal Mind*. Philadelphia, PA: Temple University Press.

Cummins, Ariane, Piek, Jan, and Dyck, Murray. 2007. "Motor Coordination, Empathy, and Social Behaviour in School-Aged Children". *Developmental Medicine and Child Neurology* 47 (7): 437–42.

Dadds, Mark, Hawes, David, Frost, Aaron, Vassallo, Shane, Bunn, Paul et al. 2009. "Learning to 'Talk the Talk': The Relationship of Psychopathic Traits to Deficits in Empathy across Childhood". *Journal of Child Psychology and Psychiatry* 50 (5): 599–606.

Davis, Mark. 1996. *Empathy: A Social Psychological Approach*. Boulder, CO: Westview Press.

Day, Andrew, Casey, Sharon, and Gerace, Alan. 2010. "Interventions to Improve Empathy Awareness in Sexual and Violent Offenders: Conceptual, Empirical, and Clinical Issues". *Aggression and Violent Behavior* 15 (3): 201–8.

Decety, Jean, and Ickes, William, eds. 2009. *The Social Neuroscience of Empathy*. Cambridge, MA: MIT Press.
Decety, Jean, and Jackson, Philip. 2006. "A Social-Neuroscience Perspective on Empathy". *Current Directions in Psychological Science* 15 (54): 54–58.
Decety, Jean, and Lamm, Claus. 2006. "Human Empathy through the Lens of Social Neuroscience". *Scientific World Journal* 6: 1146–63.
Decety, Jean, and Moriguchi, Yoshiya. 2007. "The Empathic Brain and Its Dysfunction in Psychiatric Populations: Implications for Intervention across Different Clinical Conditions". *Biopsychosocial Medicine* 1 (22): 20–31.
Deigh, John. 2011. "Empathy, Justice and Jurisprudence". *Southern Journal of Philosophy* 49 (1): 73–90.
Deleuze, Gilles, and Guattari, Félix. 1988. *A Thousand Plateaus: Capitalism and Schizophrenia*. Translated by Brian Massuoni. London: Athlone.
Dennett, Daniel. 1999. "Animal Consciousness: What Matters and Why". In *Humans and Other Animals*, edited by A. Mack. Columbus: Ohio State University Press.
de Waal, Frans. 2008. "Putting the Altruism Back into Altruism: The Evolution of Empathy". *Annual Review of Psychology* 59: 279–300.
de Waal, Frans. 2009. *The Age of Empathy*. New York: Random House.
Diamond, Cora. 2004. "Eating Meat and Eating People". In *Animal Rights: Current Debates and New Directions*, edited by Cass Sunstein and Martha Nussbaum. London: Routledge.
Doherty, Willian. 1997. "The Emotional Contagion Scale: A Measure of Individual Differences". *Journal of Nonverbal Behaviour* 21 (2): 131–54.
Donovan, Josephine. 2007. "Attention to Suffering: Sympathy as a Basis for Ethical Treatment of Animals". In *The Feminist Care Tradition in Animal Ethics*, edited by Josephine Donovan and Carol Adams. New York: Columbia University Press.
Dziobek, Isabel, Rogers, Kimberley, Fleck, Stefan, Bahnemann, Markus, Heekeren, Hauke, et al. 2008. "Dissociation of Cognitive and Emotional Empathy in Adults with Asperger Syndrome Using the Multifaceted Empathy Test (MET)". *Journal of Autism and Developmental Disorders* 38 (3): 464–73.
Eisenberg-Berg, Nancy, and Mussen, Paul. 1978. "Empathy and Moral Development in Adolescence". *Developmental Psychology* 14 (2): 185–86.
Fischer, Robert. 2015. "Disgust and the Collection of Bovine Foetal Blood". In *Animal Ethics and Philosophy: Questioning the Orthodoxy*, edited by Elisa Aaltola and John Hadley. London: Rowman & Littlefield International.
Flanagan, Owen. 2013. *The Bodhisattva's Brain: Buddhism Naturalized*. Cambridge, MA: MIT Press.
Fontaine, Nathalie, Barker, Edward, Salekin, Randall, and Viding, Essi. 2008. "Dimensions of Psychopathy and Their Relationships to Cognitive Functioning in Children". *Journal of Clinical Child & Adolescent Psychology* 37 (3): 690–96.
Fromm, Erich. 1955. *The Sane Society*. London: Routledge.
Furnham, Adrian, McManus, Chris, and Scott, David. 2003. "Personality, Empathy and Attitudes to Animal Welfare". *Anthrozoös* 16 (2): 135–46.
Gaita, Raimond. 2002. *The Philosopher's Dog*. London: Routledge.

Gallagher, Shaun. 2012. "Empathy, Simulation and Narrative". *Science in Context* 25 (3): 355–81.
Gilligan, Carol. 1993. *In a Different Voice: Psychological Theory and Women's Development*. Cambridge, MA: Harvard University Press.
Glenn, Andrea, Kurzban, Robert, and Raine, Adrian. 2011. "Evolutionary Theory and Psychopathy". *Aggression and Violent Behaviour* 16: 371–80.
Glover, Jonathan. 2014. *Alien Landscapes? Interpreting Disordered Minds*. Cambridge, MA: The Belknap Press of Harvard University Press.
Goldie, Peter. 2000. *The Emotions: A Philosophical Exploration*. Oxford: Clarendon Press.
Goldman, Alvin. 2009. "Mirroring, Simulation and Mindreading". *Mind and Language* 24 (2): 235–52.
Goldstein, Thalia R., and Winner, Ellen. 2012. "Enhancing Empathy and Theory of Mind". *Journal of Cognition and Development* 13 (1): 19–37.
Gordon, Robert. 1995. "Sympathy, Simulation, and the Impartial Spectator". *Ethics* 105 (4): 727–42.
Goubert, L., Craig, K., Vervoort, T., Morley, S., Sullivan, M., et al. 2005. "Facing Others in Pain: The Effects of Empathy". *Pain* 118: 285–88.
Gray, Kurt, and Wegner, Daniel. 2011. "Dimensions of Moral Emotions". *Emotion Review* 3: 258.
Greene, Joshua, and Haidt, Jonathan. 2002. "How (and Where) Does Moral Judgment Work?" *Trends in Cognitive Sciences* 6 (12): 517–23.
Groark, Kevin. 2008. "Social Opacity and the Dynamics of Empathic In-Sight among the Tzotzil Maya of Chiapas, Mexico". *Journal of the Society for Psychological Anthropology* 36 (4): 427–48.
Gruen, Lori. 2007. "Empathy and Vegetarian Commitments". In *The Feminist Care Tradition in Animal Ethics*, edited by Carol Adams and Josephine Donovan. New York: Columbia University Press.
Gruen, Lori. 2015. *Entangled Empathy: An Alternative Ethic for Our Relationships with Animals*. New York: Lantern Books.
Gustafsson, Ylva. 2014. "Three Perspectives on Altruism". In *Language, Ethics and Animal Life: Wittgenstein and Beyond*, edited by Niklas Forsberg, Mikel Burley and Nora Hämäläinen. London: Bloomsbury.
Haidt, Jonathan. 2001. "The Emotional Dog and Its Rational Tail: A Social Intuitionist Approach to Moral Judgment". *Psychological Review* 108: 814–34.
Haidt, Jonathan. 2003a. "Elevation and the Positive Psychology of Morality". In *Flourishing: Positive Psychology and the Life Well-Lived*, edited by C. L. M. Keyes and J. Haidt. Washington, DC: American Psychological Association.
Haidt, Jonathan. 2003b. "The Moral Emotions". In *Handbook of Affective Sciences*, edited by R. J. Davidson, K. Scherer and H. Goldsmith. Oxford: Oxford University Press.
Haidt, Jonathan. 2007. "The New Synthesis in Moral Psychology". *Science* 18: 998–1002.
Haidt, Jonathan, and Björklund, Fredrik. 2008. "Social Intuitionists Answer Six Questions about Morality". In *Moral Psychology*, vol. 3, *The Neuroscience of Morality*, edited by W. Sinnott-Armstrong. Cambridge, MA: MIT Press.

Haidt, Jonathan, and Graham, Jesse. 2007. "When Morality Opposes Justice: Conservatives Have Moral Intuitions That Liberals May Not Recognize". *Social Justice Research* 20 (1): 98–116.

Haidt, Jonathan, Rozin, Paul, Lowery, Laura, and Imada, Sumio. 1999. "The CAD Triad Hypothesis: A Mapping between Three Moral Emotions (Contempt, Anger, Disgust) and Three Moral Codes (Community, Autonomy, Divinity)". *Journal of Personality and Social Psychology* 76 (4): 574–86.

Haraway, Donna. 2003. *The Companion Species Manifesto*. Cambridge: Prickly Paradigm Press.

Haraway, Donna. 2007. *When Species Meet*. Minneapolis: University of Minnesota Press.

Harding, Sarah. 1991. *Whose Science? Whose Knowledge?* Ithaca, NY: Cornell University Press.

Harrison, Mary-Catherine. 2008. "The Paradox of Fiction and the Ethics of Empathy: Reconceiving Dickens's Realism". *Narrative* 16 (3): 256–78.

Hatfield, E., Cacioppo, J., and Rapson, R. 1994. *Emotional Contagion*. Cambridge: Cambridge University Press.

Hicks, B., Markon, K., Patrick, C., Krueger, R., and Newman, J. 2004. "Identifying Psychopathy Subtypes on the Basis of Personality Structure". *Psychological Assessment* 16: 276–88.

Hinds, J. 2011. "Exploring the Psychological Rewards of a Wilderness Experience: An Interpretive Phenomenological Analysis". *Humanistic Psychologist* 39 (3): 189–205.

Hoffman, Martin. 1990. "Empathy and Justice Motivation". *Motivation and Emotion* 14 (2): 151–72.

Hoffman, Martin. 2001. *Empathy and Moral Development*. Cambridge: Cambridge University Press.

Hoffman, Martin. 2014. "Empathy, Justice and Social Change". In *Empathy and Morality*, edited by Heidi Maibom. Oxford: Oxford University Press.

Hogeveen, Jeremy, Inzlicht, Michael, and Obhi, Sukhvinder S. 2014. "Power Changes How the Brain Responds to Others". *Journal of Experimental Psychology* 143 (2): 755–62.

Hojat, Mohammadreza, Mangione, Salvatore, Nasca, Thomas J., Rattner, Susan, Erdmann, James B., et al. 2004. "An Empirical Study of Decline in Empathy in Medical School". *Medical Education* 38: 934–41.

Hollan, Douglas. 2011. "Vicissitudes of 'Empathy' in a Rural Toraja Village". In *The Anthropology of Empathy*, edited by Douglas Hollan and Jason Throop. New York: Berghahn Books.

Hollan, Douglas, and Throop, Jason. 2008. "Whatever Happened to Empathy?" *Ethos* 36 (4): 385–401.

Hollan, Douglas, and Throop, Jason. 2011. Introduction to *The Anthropology of Empathy*, edited by Doug Hollan and Jason Throop. New York: Berghahn Books.

Holton, Richard, and Langton, Rae. 1998. "Empathy and Animal Ethics". In *Singer and His Critics*, edited by Dale Jamieson. Oxford: Oxford University Press.

Hourdequin, Marion. 2012. "Empathy, Shared Intentionality, and Motivation by Moral Reasons". *Ethical Theory and Moral Practice* 15: 403–19.

Huebner, Bryce, Dwyer, Susan, and Hauser, Marc. 2008. "The Role of Emotion in Moral Psychology". *Trends in Cognitive Sciences* 13 (1): 1–6.
Hume, David. 1969. *A Treatise of Human Nature*. Edited by Ernest C. Mossner. London: Penguin Books.
Hume, David. 2007. *An Enquiry Concerning Human Understanding*. Edited by Peter Millican. Oxford World's Classics. Oxford: Oxford University Press.
Husserl, E. 1970. *The Crisis of European Sciences and Transcendental Philosophy*. Translated by David Carr. Evanston, IL: Northwestern University Press.
Husserl, E. 1989. *Ideas: Pertaining to a Pure Phenomenology and to a Phenomenological Philosophy*. Translated by R. Rojcewicz. Dordrecht, Netherlands: Springer.
Ishikawa, Sharon, Raine, Adrian, Lencz, Todd, Bihrle, Susan, and Lacasse, Lori. 2001. "Autonomic Stress Reactivity and Executive Functions in Successful and Unsuccessful Criminal Psychopaths from the Community". *Journal of Abnormal Psychology* 110 (3): 423–32.
Jackson, Philip, Meltzoff, Andrew, and Decety, Jean. 2005. "How Do We Perceive the Pain of Others? A Window into the Neural Processes Involved in Empathy". *NeuroImage* 24: 771–79.
Jackson, Philip, Rainville, Pierre, and Decety, Jean. 2006. "To What Extent Do We Share the Pain of Others? Insight from the Neural Bases of Pain Empathy". *Pain* 125: 5–9.
Jamieson, Dale. 2002. "Science, Knowledge, and Animal Minds". In *Morality's Progress: Essays on Humans, Other Animals, and the Rest of Nature*, edited by Dale Jamieson. Oxford: Oxford University Press.
Järvinen, Anna, Korenberg, Julie, and Bellugi, Ursula. 2013. "The Social Phenotype of Williams Syndrome". *Current Opinion in Neurobiology* 23 (3): 414–22.
Johansson, Eva. 2007. "Empathy or Intersubjectivity? Understanding the Origins of Morality in Young Children". *Studies in Philosophy and Education* 27: 33–47.
Jones, Alice, Happe, Francesca, Gilbert, Francesca, Burnett, Stephanie, and Viding, Essi. 2010. "Feeling, Caring, Knowing: Different Types of Empathy Deficit in Boys with Psychopathic Tendencies and Autism Spectrum Disorder". *Journal of Child Psychology and Psychiatry* 51 (11): 1188–97.
Jones, Karen. 2006. "Metaethics and Emotions Research: A Response to Prinz". *Philosophical Explorations* 9 (1): 45–53.
Kalliopuska, Mirja. 1983. "Relationship between Moral Judgment and Empathy". *Psychological Reports* 53: 575–78.
Kant, Immanuel. 1964. *Groundwork of the Metaphysic of Morals*. Translated by H. J. Paton. New York: Harper and Row.
Kasperbauer, T. J. 2014. "Rejecting Empathy for Animal Ethics". *Ethical Theory and Moral Practice* 18 (4): 817–33.
Kaukiainen, Ari, Björkqvist, Kaj, and Lagerspetz, Kirsti. 1999. "The Relationships between Social Intelligence, Empathy, and Three Types of Aggression". *Aggressive Behaviour* 25: 81–89.
Kean, Hilda. 1998. *Animal Rights: Political and Social Change in Britain since 1800*. London: Reaktion Books.
Kennett, Jeannette. 2002. "Autism, Empathy and Moral Agency". *Philosophical Quarterly* 52 (208): 340–357.

Kennett, Jeanette. 2006. "Do Psychopaths Really Threaten Moral Rationalism?" *Philosophical Explorations* 9 (1): 69–82.

Kennett, Jeanette. 2008. "Reasons, Reverence and Value". In *Moral Psychology*, vol. 3, edited by Walter Sinnott Armstrong. Cambridge, MA: MIT Press.

Kennett, Jeannette, and Fine, Cordelia. 2009. "Will the Real Moral Judgment Please Stand Up?" *Ethical Theory and Moral Practice* 12: 77–96.

Kiehl, Kent. 2006. "A Cognitive Neuroscience Perspective on Psychopathy: Evidence for Paralimbic System Dysfunction". *Psychiatry Research* 15 (142): 107–28.

Kielland, C., Skjerve, E., Østerås, O., and Zanella, A. J. 2010. "Dairy Farmer Attitudes and Empathy toward Animals Are Associated with Animal Welfare Indicators". *Journal of Dairy Science* 93 (7): 2998–3006.

Klimecki, Olga M., Leiberg, Susanne, Ricard, Matthieu, and Singer, Tania. 2014. "Differential Pattern of Functional Brain Plasticity after Compassion and Empathy Training". *Social Cognitive and Affective Neuroscience* 9 (6): 873–79.

Konrath, S. H., O'Brien, E. H., and Hsing, C. 2011. "Changes in Dispositional Empathy in American College Students over Time: A Meta-Analysis". *Personality and Social Psychology Review* 15: 180–98.

Krueger, F., Parasuraman, R., Moody, L., Twieg, P., de Visser, E., et al. 2013. "Oxytocin Selectively Increases Perceptions of Harm for Victims but Not the Desire to Punish Offenders of Criminal Offenses". *Social Cognitive and Affective Neuroscience (SCAN)* 8: 494–98.

Lachs, Christopher. 1979. *The Culture of Narcissism*. New York: Norton.

Lamm, Claus, Batson, Daniel, and Decety, Jean. 2007. "The Neural Substrate of Human Empathy: Effects of Perspective-Taking and Cognitive Appraisal". *Cognitive Neuroscience* 19 (1): 42–58.

Lamm, Claus, Meltzoff, Andrew N., and Decety, Jean. 2010. "How Do We Empathize with Someone Who Is Not Like Us? A Functional Magnetic Resonance Imaging Study". *Journal of Cognitive Neuroscience* 22: 362–76.

Langer, Ellen, and Modoveanu, Mihnea. 2000. "The Construct of Mindfulness". *Journal of Social Issues* 56 (1): 1–9.

Leith, Karen, and Baumeister, Roy. 1998. "Empathy, Shame, Guilt and Narratives of Interpersonal Conflict: Guilt-Prone People Are Better at Perspective Taking". *Journal of Personality* 66 (1): 1–37.

Levinas, Emmanuel. 1961. *Totality and Infinity*. Translated by Alphonso Lingis. Pittsburgh, PA: Duquesne University Press.

Lloyd, Genevieve. 1993. *The Man of Reason: "Male" and "Female" in Western Philosophy*. Minneapolis: University of Minnesota Press.

Loughnan, Steve, Bastian, Brock, and Haslam, Nick. 2014. "The Psychology of Eating Animals". *Current Directions in Psychological Science* 23: 104–8.

MacIntyre, Alasdair. 1984. *After Virtue: A Study in Moral Theory*. Notre Dame, IN: University of Notre Dame Press.

Mahmut, M., Homewood, Judi, and Stevenson, R. 2008. "The Characteristics of Non-criminals with High Psychopathy Traits: Are They Similar to Criminal Psychopaths?" *Journal of Research in Personality* 42 (3): 679–92.

Maibom, Heidi. 2005. "Moral Unreason: The Case of Psychopathy". *Mind & Language* 20 (2): 237–57.
Maibom, Heidi. 2009. "Feeling for Others: Empathy, Sympathy, and Morality". *Inquiry: An Interdisciplinary Journal of Philosophy* 52 (5): 483–99.
Mathura, Vani, Cheon, Bobby, Harada, Tokiko, Scimeca, Jason, and Chiao, Joan. 2016. "Overlapping Neural Response to the Pain or Harm of People, Animals, and Nature". *Neuropsychologia* 81: 265–73.
Maxwell, K., Donnellan, B., Hopwood, C., and Ackerman, R. 2011. "The Two Faces of Narcissus? An Empirical Comparison of the Narcissistic Personality Inventory and the Pathological Narcissism Inventory". *Personality and Individual Differences* 50: 577–82.
McDonald, M., Wearing, S., and Ponting, J. 2009. "The Nature of Peak Experience in Wilderness". *Humanistic Psychologist* 37: 370–85.
McGreer, Victoria. 2008. "Varieties of Moral Agency: Lessons from Autism (and Psychopathy)". In *Moral Psychology*, vol. 3, *The Neuroscience of Morality*, edited by W. Sinnott-Armstrong. Cambridge, MA: MIT Press.
Meale, L. 1995. "The Sociobiology of Sociopathy: An Integrated Evolutionary Model". *Behavioral and Brain Sciences* 18: 523–40.
Merleau-Ponty, Maurice. 1964. *Sense and Non-sense*. Translated by Rubert Dreyfus and Patricia Dreyfus. Evanston, IL: Northwestern University Press.
Merleau-Ponty, Maurice. 1968. *The Visible and the Invisible*. Translated by Alphonso Lingis. Evanston, IL: Northwestern University Press.
Mervis, Carolyn, and Becerra, Angela. 2007. "Language and Communicative Development in Williams Syndrome". *Mental Retardation and Developmental Disabilities Research Reviews* 13: 3–15.
Mervis, Carolyn, and John, Angela. 2011. "Cognitive and Behavioral Characteristics of Children with Williams Syndrome: Implications for Intervention Approaches". *American Journal of Medical Genetics Part C: Seminars in Medical Genetics* 154 (2): 229–48.
Mervis, Carolyn, and Klein-Tasman, Bonita. 2000. "Williams Syndrome: Cognition, Personality, and Adaptive Behavior". *Mental Retardation and Developmental Disabilities Research* 6 (2): 148–58.
Midgley, Mary. 1983. *Animals and Why They Matter*. Athens: University of Georgia Press.
Minio-Paluello, Ilaria, Baron-Cohen, Simon, Avenanti, Alessio, Walsh, Vincent, and Aglioti, Salvatore. 2009. "Absence of Embodied Empathy during Pain Observation in Asperger Syndrome". *Biological Psychiatry* 65: 55–62.
Moeller, Susan. 1999. *Compassion Fatigue*. London: Routledge.
Monin, Benoit, Pizarro, David, and Beer, Jennifer. 2007. "Reason and Emotion in Moral Judgment: Different Prototypes Lead to Different Theories". In *Do Emotions Help or Hurt Decision Making? A Hedgefoxian Perspective*, edited by K. D. Vohs, R. F. Baumeister and G. Lowenstein. New York: Russell Sage Foundation.
Morgan, Alex, and Lilienfeld, Scott. 2000. "A Meta-Analytic Review of the Relation between Antisocial Behavior and Neuropsychological Measures of Executive Function". *Clinical Psychology Review* 20 (1): 113–36.

Mullins-Nelson, J., Randall, T., Salekin, T. and Leistico, A. M. 2006. "Psychopathy, Empathy, and Perspective-Taking Ability in a Community Sample: Implications for the Successful Psychopathy Concept". *International Journal of Forensic Mental Health* 5 (2): 133–49.
Murdoch, Iris. 1959. "The Sublime and the Good". *Chicago Review*, Autumn 1959.
Murdoch, Iris. 1971. *The Sovereignty of Good*. London: Routledge.
Murdoch, Iris. 2003. *Metaphysics as a Guide to Morals*. London: Vintage.
Nagel, Thomas. 1974. "What Is It Like to Be a Bat?" *Philosophical Review* 83: 435–50.
Nichols, Shaun. 2002. "How Psychopaths Threaten Moral Rationalism: Is It Irrational to Be Amoral?" *Monist*, 85 (2): 285–303.
Nilsson, Peter. 2003. "Empathy and Emotions: On the Notion of Empathy as Emotional Sharing". Umeå Studies in Philosophy 7. PhD diss., Umeå University, Sweden.
Nussbaum, Martha. 1990. *Love's Knowledge*. New York: Oxford University Press.
Nussbaum, Martha. 2001. *The Upheavals of Thought: The Intelligence of Emotions*. Cambridge: Cambridge University Press.
Oceja, L. V., Heerdink, M. W., Stocks, E. L., Ambrona, T., López-Pérez, B. et al. 2014. "Empathy, Awareness of Others, and Action: How Feeling Empathy for One-among-Others Motivates Helping the Others". *Basic and Applied Social Psychology* 36 (2): 111–24.
Oliveira-Souza, Ricardo, Hare, Robert, and Bramati, Ivanei. 2008. "Psychopathy as a Disorder of the Moral Brain: Fonto-Temporo-Limbic Grey Matter Reductions Demonstrated by Voxel-Based Morphometry". *NeuroImage* 40: 1202–13.
Palmer, Clare. 2001. "Taming the Wild Profusion of Existing Things? A Study of Foucault, Power and Animals". *Environmental Ethics* 23 (4): 339–58.
Pandya, Rashmika. 2012. "Suffering in Silence: Emmanuel Levinas and Jean-Luc Marion on Suffering, Understanding and Language". In *On Suffering: An Interdisciplinary Dialogue on Narrative and Meaning of Suffering*, edited by Nate Hinerman and Mathew Lewis Sutton. Oxford: Interdisciplinary Press.
Patrick, Christopher, Fowles, Don, and Krueger, Robert. 2009. "Triarchic Conceptualization of Psychopathy: Developmental Origins of Disinhibition, Boldness, and Meanness". *Development and Psychopathology* 21 (3): 913–38.
Patterson, Charles. 2003. *Eternal Treblinka: Our Treatment of Animals and the Holocaust*. New York: Lantern.
Pedersen, Reidar. 2008. "Empathy: A Wolf in Sheep's Clothing?" *Medicine, Health Care and Philosophy* 11: 325–35.
Piazza, Jared, and Loughnan, Steve. 2016. "When Meat Gets Personal, Animals' Minds Matter Less: Motivated Use of Intelligence Information in Judgments of Moral Standing". *Social Psychological and Personality Science* 7: 867–74.
Pizarro, David. 2000. "Nothing More than Feelings? The Role of Emotions in Moral Judgment". *Journal for the Theory of Social Behaviour* 30 (4): 355–75.
Preston, S. D., and de Waal, F. 2002. "Empathy: Its Ultimate and Proximate Bases". *Behavioral and Brain Sciences* 25 (1): 1–20.

Prinz, Jesse. 2006. "The Emotional Basis of Moral Judgments". *Philosophical Explorations* 9 (1): 29–43.
Prinz, Jesse. 2011. "Is Empathy Necessary for Morality?" In *Empathy: Philosophical and Psychological Perspectives*, edited by Amy Coplan and Peter Goldie. Oxford: Oxford University Press.
Regan, Tom. 1983. *The Case for Animal Rights*. Berkeley: University of California Press.
Rick, Jon. 2007. "Hume's and Smith's Partial Sympathies and Impartial Stances". *Journal of Scottish Philosophy* 5 (2): 135–58.
Rifkin, Jeremy. 2010. *The Empathic Civilisation*. New York: Tarcher.
Ritter, Kathrin, and Dziobek, Isabel. 2011. "Lack of Empathy in Patients with Narcissistic Personality Disorder". *Psychiatry Research* 187: 241–47.
Ritvo, Harriet. 1997. *The Platypus and Mermaid and Other Figments of the Classifying Imagination*. Cambridge, MA: Harvard University Press.
Robbins, Joel, and Rumsey, Alan. 2008. "Cultural and Linguistic Anthropology and the Opacity of Other Minds". *Anthropological Quarterly* 81 (2): 407–20.
Roberts, William, and Strayer, Janet. 2008. "Empathy, Emotional Expressiveness, and Prosocial Behavior". *Child Development* 67 (2): 449–70.
Roe, K. 1980. "Early Empathy Development in Children and the Subsequent Internalization of Moral Values". *Journal of Social Psychology* 110 (1): 147–48.
Roeser, Sabine. 2006. "The Role of Emotions in Judging the Moral Acceptability of Risks". *Safety Science* 44 (8): 689–700.
Rogers, Kimberley, Dziobek, Isabel, Hassenstab, Jason, Wolf, Oliver, and Convit, Antonio. 2007. "Who Cares? Revisiting Empathy in Asperger Syndrome". *Journal of Autism Development Disorder* 37: 709–15.
Romaioli, Diego, Faccio, Elena, and Salvini, Alessandro. 2008. "On Acting against One's Best Judgment: A Social Constructionist Interpretation for the Akrasia Problem". *Journal for the Theory of Social Behaviour* 38: 179–92.
Rorty, Amelie. 1997. "The Social and Political Sources of Akrasia". *Ethics* 107: 644–57.
Rota, Michael. 2007. "The Moral Status of Anger: Thomas Aquinas and John Cassian". *American Catholic Philosophical Quarterly* 81 (3): 395–418.
Royzman, Edward, Leema, Robert, and Baron, Jonathan. 2009. "Unsentimental Ethics: Towards a Content-Specific Account of the Moral-Conventional Distinction". *Cognition* 112: 159–74.
Ruonakoski, Erika. 2011. *The Familiarity and Foreignness of Animals: A Reinterpretation of the Phenomenological Theory of Empathy and Its Application to Our Experience of Non-human Animals*. Helsinki: University of Helsinki.
Rushkoff, Douglas. 2014. *Present Shock: When Everything Happens Now*. London: Penguin.
Salekin, Randall, Neumann, Craig, Leistico, Anne-Marie, and Zalot, Alecia. 2004. "Psychopathy in Youth and Intelligence: An Investigation of Cleckley's Hypothesis". *Journal of Clinical Child & Adolescent Psychology* 33 (4): 731–32.
Scheler, Max. 2009. *The Nature of Sympathy*. Translated by Peter Heath. London: Routledge and Kegan Paul.

Schertz, Matthew. 2007. "Avoiding 'Passive Empathy' with Philosophy for Children". *Journal of Moral Education* 36 (2): 185–98.
Schopenhauer, Arthur. 2005. *The Basis of Morality*. Translated by Arthur Broderick Bullock. New York: Dover.
Segerdahl, Pär. 2012. "Humanizing Nonhumans: Ape Language Research as Critique of Metaphysics". In *Language, Ethics, and Animal Life: Wittgenstein and Beyond*, edited by Niklas Forsberg, Mikel Burley and Nora Hämäläinen. London: Bloomsbury Academic.
Semple, R. J. 2010. "Does Mindfulness Meditation Enhance Attention? A Randomized Controlled Trial". *Mindfulness* 1 (2): 121–30.
Sevillano, Veronica, Aragones, Juan, and Schultz, Wesley. 2007. "Perspective Taking, Environmental Concern, and the Moderating Role of Dispositional Empathy". *Environment and Behaviour* 39 (5): 685–705.
Shapiro, Johanna, Morrison, Elizabeth, and Boker, John. 2004. "Teaching Empathy to First Year Medical Students: Evaluation of an Elective Literature and Medicine Course". *Education for Health* 17 (1): 73–84.
Signal, Tania, and Taylor, Nicola. 2005. "Empathy and Attitudes to Animals". *Anthrozoös* 18 (1): 18–27.
Signal, Tania, and Taylor, Nicola. 2007. "Attitudes to Animals and Empathy: Comparing Animal Protection and General Community Samples". *Anthrozoös* 20 (2): 125–30.
Singer, Jonathan. 2015. "'The Flesh of My Flesh': Animality, Difference and 'Radical Community' in Merleau-Ponty's Philosophy". In *Animal Ethics and Philosophy: Questioning the Orthodoxy*, edited by Elisa Aaltola and John Hadley. London: Rowman & Littlefield International.
Singer, Peter. 1975. *Animal Liberation: A New Ethics for Our Treatment of Animals*. New York: Avon Books.
Skeem, Jennifer, Johansson, Peter, Andershed, Henrik, Kerr, Margaret, and Louden, Jennifer. 2007. "Two Subtypes of Psychopathic Violent Offenders That Parallel Primary and Secondary Variants". *Journal of Abnormal Psychology* 116 (2): 395–409.
Slote, Michael. 2007. *The Ethics of Care and Empathy*. London: Routledge.
Smith, Adam J. 2006. "Cognitive Empathy and Emotional Empathy in Human Behaviour and Evolution". *Psychological Record* 56: 3–21.
Smith, Adam J. 2009. "The Empathy Imbalance Hypothesis of Autism: A Theoretical Approach to Cognitive and Emotional Empathy in Autistic Development". *Psychological Record* 59: 489–510.
Smith, Adam. 2009. *The Theory of Moral Sentiments*. Edited by Ryan Patrick Hanley. London: Penguin Books.
Spinrad, Tracy, and Eisenberg, Nancy. 2014. "Empathy and Morality – a Developmental Psychology Perspective". In *Empathy and Morality*, edited by Heidi Maibom. Oxford: Oxford University Press.
Sprinkle, Julie E. 2008. "Animals, Empathy, and Violence: Can Animals Be Used to Convey Principles of Prosocial Behavior to Children?" *Youth Violence and Juvenile Justice January* 6: 47–58.

Söderström, Henrik. 2003. "Psychopathy as a Disorder of Empathy". *European Child & Adolescent Psychiatry* 12: 249–52.
Soenens, Bart, Duriez, Bart, Vansteenkiste, Maarten, and Goossens, Luc. 2007. "The Intergenerational Transmission of Empathy-Related Responding in Adolescence: The Role of Maternal Support". *Personality and Social Psychology Bulletin* 33 (3): 299–311.
Sontag, Susan. 2004. *Regarding the Pain of Others*. London: Penguin.
Stein, Edith. 1989. *On the Problem of Empathy*. Translated by Watraut Stein. Washington, DC: ISC.
Stueber, Karsten. 2006. *Rediscovering Empathy: Agency, Folk Psychology, and the Human Sciences*. Cambridge, MA: MIT Press.
Swann, A., Lijffijt, M., Lane, S., Steinberg, J., and Moeller, F. 2009. "Trait Impulsivity and Response Inhibition in Antisocial Personality Disorder". *Journal of Psychiatric Research* 43 (12): 1057–63.
Tangney, J., Stuewig, J., and Mashek, D. 2007. "Moral Emotions and Moral Behaviour". *Annual Review of Psychology* 58: 345–72.
Teasdale, John. 1999. "Metacognition, Mindfulness and the Modification of Mood Disorders". *Clinical Psychology and Psychotherapy* 6: 146–55.
Thomas, Keith. 1983. *Man and the Natural World: Changing Attitudes in England, 1500–1800*. London: Penguin Books.
Thompson, Evan. 2001. "Empathy and Consciousness". In *Between Ourselves: Second-Person Issues in the Study of Consciousness*, edited by Evan Thompson. Thorverton, UK: Imprint Academic.
Thompson, Ross A., and Hoffman, Martin L. 1980. "Empathy and the Development of Guilt in Children". *Developmental Psychology* 16 (2): 155–56.
Throop, Jason. 2011. "Suffering, Empathy, and Ethical Modalities of Being in Yap (Waqap), Federated States of Micronesia". In *The Anthropology of Empathy*, edited by Douglas Hollan and Jason Throop. Oxford: Berghahn Books.
Toadvine, Ted. 2007. "'Strange Kinship': Merleau-Ponty on the Human-Animal Relation". In *Phenomenology of Life from the Animal Soul to the Human Mind*, edited by A. T. Tymieniecka. Analecta Husserliana (The Yearbook of Phenomenological Research) 93. Dordrecht, Netherlands: Springer.
Turner, James. 1980. *Reckoning with the Beast: Animals, Pain, and Humanity in the Victorian Mind*. Baltimore, MD: Johns Hopkins University Press.
Twenge, Jean, and Campbell, Keith. 2003. "Isn't It Fun to Get the Respect That We're Going to Deserve? Narcissism, Social Rejection, and Aggression". *Personality and Social Psychology Bulletin* 29: 261.
Twine, Richard. 2010. *Animals as Biotechnology*. London: Earthscan.
Van Kleef, G. A., Oveis, C., Van Der Löwe, I., LuoKogan, A., Goetz, J., et al. 2008. "Power, Distress, and Compassion: Turning a Blind Eye to the Suffering of Others". *Psychological Science* 19 (12): 1315–22.
Vargas, Manuel, and Nichols, Shaun. 2007. "Psychopaths and Moral Knowledge". *Philosophy, Psychiatry, & Psychology* 14 (2): 157–62.
Verducci, Susan. 1998. "Moral Empathy: The Necessity of Intersubjectivity and Diologic Confirmation". *Philosophy of Education*: 335–41.

Verducci, Susan. 2000. "A Moral Method? Thoughts on Cultivating Empathy through Method Acting". *Journal of Moral Education* 29 (1): 87–99.

Vignemont, Frederique, and Frith, Uta. 2008. "Autism, Morality and Empathy". In *Moral Psychology*, vol. 3, *The Neuroscience of Morality*, edited by W. Sinnott-Armstrong. Cambridge, MA: MIT Press.

Volbrecht, Michele, Lemery-Chalfant, Kathryn, Aksan, Nazan, Zahn-Waxler, Caroly, and Goldsmith, Hill. 2007. "Examining the Familial Link Between Positive Affect and Empathy Development in the Second Year". *Journal of Genetic Psychology* 168 (2): 105–29.

von Poser, Anita. 2011. "Bosmun Foodways: Emotional Reasoning in a Papua New Guinea Lifeworld". In *The Anthropology of Empathy*, edited by Douglas Hollan and Jason Throop. Oxford: Berghahn Books.

Wai, Michael, and Tiliopoulos, Niko. 2012. "The Affective and Cognitive Empathic Nature of the Dark Triad of Personality". *Personality and Individual Differences* 52: 794–99.

Wallace, Alan. 2001. "Intersubjectivity in Indo-Tibetan Buddhism". In *Between Ourselves: Second-Person Issues in the Study of Consciousness*, edited by Evan Thompson. Thorverton, UK: Imprint Academic.

Weil, Kari. 2012. *Thinking Animals: Why Animal Studies Now?* New York: Columbia University Press.

Weil, Simone. 1973. *Waiting for God*. Translated by Emma Craufurd. London: HarperCollins.

Weil, Simone. 2002. *Gravity and Grace*. Translated by Emma Crawford and Marion von der Ruhr. London: Routledge.

Wittgenstein, Ludwig. 1969. *On Certainty*. Edited by G. E. M. Anscombe and G. H. von Wright. Translated by Denis Paul and G. E. M. Anscombe. Oxford: Blackwell.

Wittgenstein, Ludwig. 1983. *Remarks on the Philosophy of Psychology*, vol. 2. Translated by G. E. M. Anscombe. London: Wiley Blackwell.

Wittgenstein, Ludwig. 1992. *Zettel*. Edited and translated by G. E. M. Anscombe. Oakland: University of California Press.

Zahavi, Dan. 2001. "Beyond Empathy: Phenomenological Approaches to Intersubjectivity". In *Between Ourselves: Second-Person Issues in the Study of Consciousness*, edited by Evan Thompson. Thorverton, UK: Imprint Academic.

Zahavi, Dan. 2007. "Expression and Empathy". In *Folk Psychology Re-assessed*, edited by D. Hutto and M. Ratcliffe. Dordrecht, Netherlands: Springer.

Zahavi, Dan. 2008. "Simulation, Projection and Empathy". *Consciousness and Cognition* 17: 514–22.

Index

Aaltola, Elisa, 17, 20, 25, 44, 63, 69, 149, 170
Acampora, Ralph, 14, 20, 112, 113, 118, 120, 127nn4, 10
affective empathy the baseline of morality, 184;
 key capacity of moral agency, 184
affective moral agency, 93
Agamben, Giorgio, 72
Ahmed, Sarah, 157
Ali, Farah, 64, 79n6
alterity, 122, 123, 130.
 See also difference
anger, 5, 16n5, 58, 61, 86, 91, 93, 105, 134, 155, 163, 178, 179, 182, 184, 185, 187–93, 213n27, 214nn30, 32;
 requires empathy, 190
animal advocacy, 11, 12, 31, 38, 97, 193
animal mentation, 32, 50, 51
animal philosophy, 13, 20, 24, 112, 134
animals, non-human/other. *See* alterity; difference, specificity
Ansell, Emily, 67, 68
anthropathy, 69, 74–78, 97, 149, 208, 211n16, 218, 222
Anthropocene era, 73
anthropocentrism, 16n10, 21, 49, 50, 51, 56, 69, 70, 72, 73, 75, 76, 77, 96, 112, 118, 154, 169, 208, 209
anthropomorphism, 31, 32, 33, 35, 39, 51, 53nn3, 7, 133, 135
Aquinas, Thomas, 189;
 Summa Theologica, 189
Aragones, Juan, 186
Aristotle, 76, 121, 176
Ashley, P., 149
attentiveness, 7, 14, 72, 119, 137, 139, 141–50, 151n4, 160, 161, 162, 193, 222
autism, 170–73, 211n13

Babe, 32, 43
Bailey, Cathryn, 16n10
Bambi, 31, 32
Baron, Jonathan, 178, 191, 212n19
Baron-Cohen, Simon, 21, 58, 79n3, 82, 172
Barrett, Lisa Feldman, 9, 58, 89
Bastian, Brock, 24
Batson, Daniel, 18, 30, 38, 46, 190, 192, 202, 214n30, 219
Baumeister, Roy, 192, 215n40
Becerra, Angela, 87, 175
Beer, Jennifer, 179, 185, 207, 213nn25, 26, 215n47
Bellugi, Ursula, 87

Björklund, Fredrik, 6
Björkqvist, Kaj, 18
Blair, James, 18, 19, 57, 58, 64, 65, 170, 173
Bloom, Paul, 156;
    Against Empathy, 156
Blum, Lawrence, 47
Boker, John, 30, 38
Boler, Megan, 40, 41, 54n8
Book, Angela, 57, 64, 65, 66, 170
Bramati, Ivanei, 211n15
Brown, K. W., 139

Cacioppo, J., 199
Cain, Nicole, 67, 68
care theory, 13.
    See also feminism
Cartesian dualism, 72, 113
Casey, Sharon, 153
Chakrabarti, Bhismadev, 79n3
Chamorro-Premuzic, Tomas, 18
Chouliaraki, Lilie, 194, 195, 198, 214n36, 215n43
Churchland, Patricia, 3, 184
Coetzee, J. M., 198, 199;
    Elizabeth Costello, 198
Coffey, K. A., 139, 141
cognitive empathy:
    a reason-based state, 58.
    See also manipulation; psychopathy
Cohen, Stanley, 1, 195, 197, 207, 214nn34, 35
Cole, Jonathan, 25
compassion fatigue, 44, 103, 104, 105, 109, 155, 194, 195, 197–201, 211n14, 214nn33, 35, 37, 40, 215n40
conservative ethics, 176
Coplan, Amy, 29, 38, 195, 196;
    empty empathy, 195, 196
Corona, Rosalie, 173
Crary, Alice, 3, 15n2
Crist, Eileen, 21, 33
cultural diversions, 157
cultural preconceptions, 39, 158

cultural stereotypes, 6, 10, 158, 161, 184
cultural tenets, 205
culture, role in emotion, 13
Cummins, Ariane, 19

Dadds, Mark, 19
Damasio, Anthony, 4
Davis, Mark, 18
Day, Andrew, 153
Decety, Jean, 8, 19, 23, 30, 82, 83, 84, 90, 100nn1, 2, 153, 156, 160, 199, 200, 201, 202, 204, 215nn41, 44, 45
Deigh, John, 18, 19, 214n30
Deleuze, Gilles, 119, 220
Dennett, Daniel, 168
Descartes, René, 117, 209n4.
    See also scepticism
de Waal, Frans, 18, 23, 25n2, 65, 83, 154, 155, 156, 157, 209n3
Diamond, Cora, 13, 38
Dickens, Charles, 38, 39, 41, 53n4
difference, 9, 10, 11, 17, 22, 24, 37, 45, 46, 48, 51, 52, 54nn7, 8, 63, 88, 94, 95, 98, 99, 103, 109, 110, 111, 121–24, 127n3, 128n16, 130, 136, 150n1, 156, 200, 202, 207, 210n12, 213n27, 221.
    See also alterity
Disney, 12, 22, 31, 42, 43, 53n3
Doherty, William, 199, 214n38
Donovan, Josephine, 13
Dwyer, Susan, 178
Dyck, Murray, 19
Dziobek, Isabel, 67, 69, 172, 173

egoism, 8, 29, 45, 50, 51, 52, 54n8, 64, 65, 68, 69, 70, 74, 98, 145, 149, 151n9, 162, 163, 188, 200, 201, 202, 204, 205, 209, 218
Eisenberg-Berg, Nancy, 19
embodied empathy:
    corporeal compassion, 14
    helps in understanding mindedness, 105.

See also Acampora, Ralph
emotional contagion, 82, 83, 100n1, 110, 111, 199–203, 214nn38, 39
empathic anger, 190, 214n30
empathy towards other animals an act of rebellion, 209
empathy versus reason, 169–70
empathy withdrawal, 215n47
environmental ethics, 212n17

Faccio, Elena, 76
farmed animals, 32, 42, 44, 73, 119, 130, 143, 157, 161, 196
farmers, 60, 119, 213n28
feminism, 13, 191
feminists, 20, 30, 33
Fine, Cordelia, 170, 171, 173, 179, 181, 182
Fischer, Robert, 134
Flanagan, Owen, 141
Fontaine, Nathalie, 173, 211n15
Fowles, Don, 79n4
Frankfurt, Harry, 213n22
Fredrickson, B. L., 139, 141
Frith, Uta, 172
Fromm, Erich, 216n49
Furnham, Adrian, 20

Gadamer, Hans-Georg, 164
Gaita, Raimond, 107
Gallagher, Shaun, 38, 35, 37, 47, 49, 89, 90–93, 126n1
Geertz, Clifford, 30
Geracy, 153
Gilligan, Carol, 13
Glenn, Andrea, 78, 174
Goldie, Peter, 29
Goldman, Alvin, 29
Goldstein, Thalia R., 38, 219
Gordon, Robert, 29, 114
Goubert, L., 82, 83, 156, 201
Graham, Jesse, 175, 214n31
Gray, Kurt, 212n20
Greene, Joshua, 7, 16n8, 182
Groark, Kevin, 22, 154

Gruen, Lori, 13, 14, 16n11, 20, 32, 136, 137, 151n9;
entangled empathy, 136, 137
Guattari, Félix, 220
Gustafsson, Ylva, 213n23

Haidt, Jonathan, 6, 7, 16nn7, 8, 18, 53n2, 134, 151n3, 175, 179, 180, 182, 214n31
Haraway, Donna, 116, 120
Harding, Sarah, 165
Hare, Robert, 211n15
Harrison, Mary-Catherine, 38, 41, 53nn4, 5
Hartman, M., 139, 141
Haslam, Nick, 24
Hatfield, E., 199
Hauser, Marc, 178
Heidegger, Martin, 127n10, 164
heterogenic openness, 9, 24, 45, 48
Hicks, B., 174
Hinds, J., 149
Hoffman, Martin, 8, 17, 18, 19, 82, 160, 163, 164, 183, 190, 192, 197, 210nn6, 8
Hogeveen, Jeremy, 159
Hojat, Mohammadreza, 76
Hollan, Douglas, 22, 30, 105, 153, 205, 209nn1, 2
hot cognition, 19
Holton, Richard, 156, 167
Homewood, Judi, 174
Hourdequin, Marion, 17, 82
Hsing, C., 216n49
Huebner, Bryce, 178
Hume, David, 2, 3, 5, 6, 8, 25, 26n3, 27, 55, 56, 57, 64, 81–85, 95, 100n1, 127n9, 130, 155, 156, 160, 161, 162, 165, 171, 189;
Treatise on Human Nature, 2, 25
Husserl, Edmund, 1, 19, 110, 116, 117, 120–23, 125, 127n4

Ickes, William, 23
impartiality, 156, 160, 161, 163, 164, 182

intersectionality, 13
intersubjectivity, 52, 68, 113, 115–20, 122, 123, 126, 127nn7, 8, 128n14, 129, 134, 166, 210n7, 213n28, 219
Inzlicht, Michael, 159
Ishikawa, Sharon, 174

Jackson, Philip, 8, 23, 82, 83, 100nn1, 2, 199, 200, 201
James, William, 41, 43
Jamieson, Dale, 107
Järvinen, Anna, 87
Johansson, Eva, 128n14, 164
Jones, Karen, 64, 172, 181

Kalliopuska, Mirja, 19
Kant, Immanuel, 1, 2, 3, 5, 15n1, 55, 78n1, 79n2, 171, 180, 182; autonomy and reason, 2
Kasperbauer, T. J., 156, 185–89, 213nn27, 28
Kaukiainen, Ari, 18
Kean, Hilda, 11
Kennett, Jeanette, 170–74, 178–82
Kiehl, Kent, 65, 170, 174
Kielland, C., 20
Klein-Tasman, Bonita, 87, 175
Klimecki, Olga M., 199
Konrath, S. H., 215n49
Korenberg, Julie, 87
Krueger, F., 188
Krueger, Robert, 79n4
Kursban, Robert, 174

Lachs, Christopher, 216n49
Lagerspetz, Kirsti, 18
Lamm, Claus, 30, 84, 90, 153, 156, 160, 200, 201, 202, 204, 215nn41, 44, 45
Langer, Ellen, 139, 140, 141
Langford, Dale, 57, 64, 65, 66, 170
Langton, Rae, 156, 167
Leema, Robert, 178, 191, 212n19
Leith, Karen, 192, 215n40

Levinas, Emmanuel, 99, 158
liberalistic ethics, 176
liberal politics, 191
Lilienfeld, Scott, 174
Lipps, Theodore, 214n39
Lloyd, Genevieve, 13
logic of domination, 13; binaries, 13
Loughnan, Steve, 24

McDonald, M., 149
McDonald's, 32, 43
McGreer, Victoria, 3, 169, 171, 211n13, 214n29
Machiavellianism, 63, 72, 79n6, 85, 172
MacIntyre, Alasdair, 142
McManus, Chris, 20
Mahmut, M., 174
Maibom, Haidi, 174, 175, 176, 178, 181; painless, unexpected killing, 176
manipulation, 22, 24, 60, 63, 64, 65, 68, 69, 72, 73, 74, 79n6, 98, 133, 135, 153, 154, 174, 185, 209n2
Mashek, D., 93
Mathura, Vani, 84
Maxwell, K., 67, 68
Meale, L., 174
Meltzoff, Andrew, 8, 82, 84, 100n2, 160, 204
Merleau-Ponty, Maurice, 21, 104, 105, 112, 115, 117, 119, 127n4, 168
Mervis, Carolyn, 87, 175
Midgley, Mary, 12, 13, 20, 75, 213n25
Milgram experiments, 187, 188
mindfulness, 138, 139, 140, 141, 142, 144
Minio-Paluello, Ilaria, 8, 18
Moeller, Susan, 195, 196, 197, 214nn36, 37
Moldoveanu, Mihnea, 139, 140, 141
Monin, Benoit, 179, 185, 207, 213nn25, 26, 215n47
moral agency, 2, 4, 6–11, 13–17, 20, 23, 24, 41, 45, 46, 48, 51, 63–66,

68, 69, 70, 74, 78, 93–96, 98, 99,
  120, 121, 123, 124,125, 128n14,
  129, 135, 143, 144, 148, 150, 157,
  162, 169–85, 187, 190, 193, 198,
  203, 205, 206, 209n4, 211nn13,
  14, 16, 212n18, 217, 221;
  embodied moral agency, 120;
  a plural capacity, 183;
  rests on other-directedness, 9
Morgan, Alex, 174
Moriguchi, Yoshiya, 19, 83
Morrison, Elizabeth, 30, 38
Mullins-Nelson, J., 64, 65, 66, 170
Murdoch, Iris, 34, 137, 144–50, 151nn4,
  6, 222
Mussen, Paul, 19

Nagel, Thomas, 128n15, 167
narcissism, 20, 22, 67, 68, 69, 74–78,
  86, 153, 215n49, 216n49
narratives, 24, 30, 35, 36, 37, 39, 41–46,
  48, 49, 59, 66, 89–93, 95, 166
neoliberal, economy-based cultures, 207
Nichols, Shaun, 79n5, 171
Nietzsche, Friedrich, 64, 127n2
Nilsson, Peter, 25
Noddings, Nel, 25n1
Nussbaum, Martha, 4, 12, 13, 37, 40,
  41, 83, 88, 200

O'Brien, E. H., 215n49
Obhi, Sukhvinder S., 159
Oceja, L. V., 222
Old Testament, 176
Oliveira-Souza, Ricardo, 211n15
other-directedness, 9, 16n9, 17, 24, 25,
  29, 30, 33, 35, 45, 48, 60, 63, 65–
  68, 70, 74, 75, 94, 96, 99, 101n6,
  121, 123, 124, 125, 130, 135, 148,
  170, 190, 203, 208, 215n4

Palmer, Clare, 73
Patrick, Christopher, 79
Patterson, Charles, 78
Pedersen, Reidar, 164, 165, 167

personhood, 2, 36, 75, 176
phenomenologists, 19, 46, 47, 50, 53n6,
  103, 104, 110, 112, 115, 127n7,
  164
Piek, Jan, 19
Pincus, Aaron, 67, 68
Pizarro, David, 96, 179, 182, 185, 206,
  207, 213, 215nn47, 48
Plato, 59, 144, 146, 147, 158
politics behind animal suffering, 43, 196
politics of empathy, 208
power, 63–69, 72, 73, 74, 77, 79n8, 99,
  157, 159, 165, 192;
  antagonistic towards empathy, 159;
  central to anthropocentrism, 72
Prinz, Jesse, 3, 4, 5, 15nn3, 4, 16nn4, 5,
  156, 157, 162, 176, 182, 185, 187,
  191, 192, 214n31
projection, 22, 27–35, 40, 43–47, 49,
  51, 52, 53n3, 85, 91, 105, 111,
  126n2, 128n16, 129, 130, 135,
  156, 203
projective empathy self-directed, 28.
  See also simulative empathy
prosocial behaviour and empathy, 18, 19
psychopathy, 64, 65, 67, 68, 69, 74, 75,
  77, 78, 79nn4, 7, 86, 94, 95, 153,
  170, 171, 173, 174, 180, 183, 186,
  211nn14, 15

Quinsey, Vernon, 57, 64, 65, 66, 170

Raine, Adrian, 78, 174
Rainville, Pierre, 82, 200
Rapson, R., 199
rationalism, 1, 2, 16n10, 169, 171, 173,
  184
rationality, 1, 3, 6, 11, 12, 13, 16, 19,
  138, 141, 142, 143, 155, 160,
  170, 171, 174, 178, 179, 181–84,
  210n6, 211nn13, 16, 217;
  necessary constituent of moral
  decision-making, 179
Rawls, John, 19
reflexive empathy, 128n12

242 Index

reflective empathy the morally most viable option, 135
resonation, 46, 56, 65, 66, 73, 74, 75, 81–94, 97, 98, 99, 100nn1, 5, 108, 109, 111, 114, 115, 126n1, 128n16, 129, 130, 132, 134, 135, 136, 154, 165, 175, 177, 178, 184, 186, 204, 205, 210n9, 211n14, 212n20, 218
Rick, John, 29, 53n1, 161
Rifkin, Jeremy, 18
Ritter, Harriet, 70
Robbins, Joel, 22, 154
Roberts, William, 19
Roe, K., 19
Rogers, Kimberley, 172, 173
Romaioli, Diego, 76
Rorty, Amelie, 76, 188
Rota, Michael, 189
Royzman, Edward, 178, 191, 212n19
Rumsey, Alan, 22, 154
Ruonakoski, Erika, 120, 128n11
Rushkoff, Douglas, 142
Ryan, R. M., 139

Salvini, Alessandro, 76
scepticism, 21, 50, 62, 63, 67, 69, 71, 100n3, 103, 107, 117, 134;
  doubt about existence of other minds, 62;
  opacity of other minds, 105
Schadenfreude, 154, 156, 157
Scheler, Max, 25, 50, 103, 104, 105, 108, 111, 112, 113, 115, 121, 122, 123, 126n2, 127nn2, 3, 202, 203, 210n12, 222;
  The Nature of Sympathy, 25
Schertz, Matthew, 40, 54n8, 127n8, 218
Schopenhauer, Arthur, 2, 3, 11, 15n1, 25, 79n2, 81, 82, 83, 100n5, 151n5, 185, 188, 202, 218;
  The Basis of Morality, 25
Schultz, Wesley, 186
Scott, David, 20
second-order reflection, 132, 138, 141, 143

self-identity and empathy, 19, 20, 152n9
Semple, R. J., 139
sentimentalism, 2–8, 11, 12, 13, 16n5, 27, 53n4, 184
Sevillano, Veronica, 186
Shapiro, Johanna, 30, 38
Signal, Tania, 78
simulation-theory, 23, 58
simulative empathy other-directed, 28. *See also* projective empathy
Singer, Peter, 11, 12, 16n10, 120, 187
six varieties of empathy, 25, 217
Skeem, Jennifer, 174
Slote, Michael, 8, 17, 18
Smith, A. J., 60, 63, 86, 172
Smith, Adam, 25, 27–30, 33, 34;
  The Theory of Moral Sentiments, 25
Soenens, Bart, 18
Sontag, Susan, 41, 43, 91, 197, 198
Sousa Amorim, Ines, 18
specificity, 20, 24, 33, 41, 45, 46, 51, 88, 90, 97, 99, 109, 110, 115, 122, 139, 141, 143, 200, 203, 204, 210n5, 220, 221
Spinoza, Baruch, 2, 141, 142;
  Ethics, 2
Spinrad, Tracy, 19
Sprinkle, Julie E., 20
Stein, Edith, 20, 21, 25, 103, 110, 111, 113–17, 120, 121, 123–26, 127n5, 128n12, 131, 214n39
Stevenson, R., 174
Strayer, Janet, 19
Stueber, Karsten, 23, 29, 34, 167
Stuewig, J., 93
survival and empathy, 18, 120
sympathy, 1, 8, 22, 25, 27, 34, 52n1, 55, 78n1, 79n2, 93, 100n5, 182, 199, 202

Tangney, J., 93
Taylor, Nicola, 78
Teasdale, John, 138, 139
theory of mind, 23, 53n6, 58, 64, 83, 86, 106
Thomas, Keith, 70

Thompson, Evan, 127n8
Thompson, Ross A., 19, 192
Throop, Jason, 22, 30, 105, 153, 205, 209nn1, 2
Toadvine, Ted, 120, 127n4, 168
truth value, 16n5
Turner, James, 2, 11

Van Kleef, G. A., 159
Vargas, Manuel, 79n5
veganism, 12
vegetarianism, 12
Verducci, Susan, 25n1, 38, 117
Vignemont, Frederique, 172

Wai, Michael, 64

Wallace, Alan, 176
Wearing, S., 149
Wegner, Daniel, 212n20
Weil, Kari, 99
Weil, Simone, 22, 99, 137, 144, 146–50, 151n8, 152n10
Wheelwright, Sally, 58, 82
wilderness experiences, 149
Williams syndrome, 86, 87, 89, 94, 95, 175, 180, 211n16
Winner, Ellen, 38, 219
Wittgenstein, Ludwig, 13, 21, 47, 106, 167, 168, 210n11, 213n23

Zahavi, Dan, 47, 71, 104–9, 121, 122, 127n7, 128n13

About the Author

Elisa Aaltola, PhD, is a Finnish philosopher who has specialized in animal philosophy, environmental ethics and moral psychology. She has published around thirty-five peer-reviewed papers on these topics, together with books such as *Animal Suffering: Philosophy and Culture* (2012) and *Animal Ethics and Philosophy: Questioning the Orthodoxy* (2014, co-edited with John Hadley). Aaltola works as a senior research fellow at the University of Eastern Finland.

She lives in rural Finland with her canine companions, all rescues from Romania, with whom she ventures into the woods as often as she can. Her favourite things include books, frozen lakes, old spruces, wolves, elks, strange anthropods, dusk and light.